The Political History
of Modern Iran

The Political History of Modern Iran

From Tribalism to Theocracy

Mehran Kamrava

PRAEGER

Westport, Connecticut
London

Library of Congress Cataloging-in-Publication Data

Kamrava, Mehran.
    The political history of modern Iran : from tribalism to theocracy
/ Mehran Kamrava.
        p. cm.
    Includes bibliographical references and index.
    ISBN 0-275-94445-X (alk. paper)
    1. Iran—Politics and government.   2. Iran—Politics and
government—20th century.   I. Title.
    DS298.K36 1992
    955'.04—dc20   92-23068

British Library Cataloguing in Publication Data is available.

Library of Congress Catalog Card Number: 92-23068
ISBN: 0-275-94445-X

First published in 1992

Praeger Publishers, 88 Post Road West, Westport, CT 06881
An imprint of Greenwood Publishing Group, Inc.

Printed in the United States of America

The paper used in this book complies with the
Permanent Paper Standard issued by the National
Information Standards Organization (Z39.48-1984).

10 9 8 7 6 5 4 3 2 1

73272

Contents

Preface

This book analyzes the political history of Iran from the establishment of the Qajar dynasty in 1785 until the present. It examines three dominant features that have, over the centuries, come to characterize Iranian politics and history: the underlying dynamics that have historically resulted in recurrent instances of political autocracy, the intervention of outside forces, and revolutions in Iranian political history. In this pursuit, the book portends neither to present a strictly historical narrative of Iran in recent centuries, nor does it necessarily offer new and previously undiscovered data (with the exception of chapter four, which discusses the evolution of the Iranian state under the Islamic Republic). What the book does present is a new analytical framework for the study of political institutions and the broader process of state-building in Iran in particular and in other developing countries in general. Using Iran as a case study, the book examines the dynamics involved in the different stages of a developing country's political evolution. More specifically, it explore the underlying reasons that have caused Iranian politics to acquire its dominant features.

I cannot help but to feel grateful to John Dunn who first brought this question to my attention by asking, what was it about Iranian politics that made Iran so readily receptive to dictatorial systems? While his question at first seemed self-explanatory, I soon realized that neither I nor any of the available literature on Iran had adequately raised and answered his important point. My answer, though late by a few years, is in chapters four and five. The bulk of the research for the section on "factionalism" in chapter four was conducted when I was a resident consultant at the Rand Corporation. I worked under the supervision of Nikola Schahgaldian and greatly benefited from his insight and analytical acumen. I am also grateful to Peter Avery, my former academic supervisor at King's College, Cambridge, for teaching me much of what I know about Iran. His deep understanding of Iranian history and culture, coupled with his unrelenting and tough critiques of my earlier writings, have left an indelible mark on my understanding and appreciation of Iran. Michael Garrett of Rhodes College Computer Center rendered invaluable assistance in preparing the final version of the manuscript. The book's mistakes and shortcomings, of course, are my own responsibility.

The Political History
of Modern Iran

1

Introduction

Iran's modern political history has consistently embodied three prominent characteristics. Rarely have political autocracy, foreign intervention, and revolutions not been inseparable parts of Iran's politics and history. All three features of Iranian political history were particularly evident during the Qajar and the Pahlavi eras, and so far under the Islamic Republic there has been an intensification in the exercise of autocracy. Why did these and not other characteristics develop in Iran's political history? Why did other political forms not dominate the history of modern Iran? The answers to these questions lie in political developments indigenous to Iran as well as the country's role and position within the international community. Internally, Iran's geography, its geopolitical location, and the absence of real social and political reforms have historically facilitated the establishment of not only autocratic central rule, but also the exertion of influence over Iranian politicians by more powerful foreign parties and the development of sudden mass revolutionary movements. At the same time, emerging international circumstances, notably superpower rivalry (at first between Britain and Russia and later between the Soviet Union and the United States), has led to foreign intervention in Iran's internal affairs and a reinforcement of political autocracy, muting the institution of meaningful and lasting political reforms.

The history of modern Iran is essentially the history of a nation in search of an identity, an identity tainted by internal upheavals and by the economic and diplomatic conquests of European powers. Since the seventeenth century, Iranian history has been marked by a ceaseless struggle to attain a sovereign and viable state. Though nominally always the norm in Iran, sovereignty and independence have long remained elusive goals for Iranian politicians, intellectuals, and nationalists alike. It was only relatively recently in Iranian history, around the turn of the century, that the Iranian polity acquired a viable and a seemingly sovereign state which exercised some degree of control

over Iranian society. However, as the predominance of revolutionary
episodes so far in the present century indicates, the various political
establishments that have emerged in Iran have yet to prove their
longevity beyond the span of a few decades.

The Qajar era represents one of the earliest phases in Iran's
emergence as a viable, modern state. In this period, the country began to
be governed more uniformly and local tribes and disparate populations
were increasingly brought under the control of the central government.
Additionally, what was at first a highly decentralized and amorphous
administrative apparatus turned steadily, though not completely, into
an organized bureaucratic network. This evolution appeared to have
reached its height at the dawn of the Constitutional Revolution, as a
result of which political institutions were ostensibly made more
efficient and their control was wrested from outside powers.

Later on, under the Pahlavis, the political evolution of state
structures were given some doctrinal cohesion, especially during the
reign of Reza Khan, the man who later founded the Pahlavi dynasty.
Statism and a chauvinistic nationalist ideology bordering on fascism
became the most readily apparent features of the reign of the Pahlavis.
Reza Shah's son and successor, Mohammad Reza, also tried to promote
the virtues of the state under the auspices of what he called "positive
nationalism," albeit in a far less zealous manner than his father had
done. The fledgling sense of popular nationalism that was generated
during the Constitutional era reached new heights in the second half of
the twentieth century. It was this very nationalism, though not the
official nationalism of the King, that eventually resulted in the
monarch's fall and led to the abolition of monarchy in Iran. The
Islamic Republic, despite its uncompromisingly religious nature, has
also succeeded in legitimising its existence and its policies by appealing
largely to nationalist sentiments, as was made evident by its ability to
mobilize countless numbers of soldiers for a long and costly war with
Iraq.

It would be misleading or at best simplistic to consider the history
of modern Iran as one driven solely by the forces of nationalism and
state-building. The importance of dynamics other than nationalism and
the attainment of political sovereignty cannot be over looked.
Technological and industrial advancement, social and cultural
modernization, and more recently the apparent quest for Islamization
have all contributed in significant ways to the evolution of modern Iran.
Nevertheless, from a political perspective, all such developments
have occurred within the framework and under the auspices of the
state. From the Qajars and the Pahlavis to the Islamic Republic, it has
been the state that has promoted and dictated social and cultural norms
and has controlled economic and industrial growth. Thus, to understand

the history of modern Iran it is imperative to acquire an appreciation for the evolution of the Iranian state, its political structures and actors, and the traumatic encounters between Iran and foreign powers.

From a Weberian perspective, Iran's pre-1979 regimes were "Sultanistic" *par excellence*.[1] Political institutionalization was muted at the hands of over-bearing personalities who dominated the country's political life and dictated the very manner in which ideologies, orientations, and structures evolved. The monarch was not merely a king, he was the King of Kings, the very embodiment of Iranian nationhood and the personification of whatever the country stood for. He ruled by decree and directly, frequently by whim, and was restrained by no organization or body of laws except limits of his personal abilities. In quintessentially patrimonial fashion, the country was governed as if it were a family domain, with the king's brothers, cousins, and nephews in charge of important cities and regions or, as was the case during the more modern Pahlavis, in control of strategic resources and industries. Yet throughout, patrimonialism was the guiding principle of the political drama. The Qajars were, after all, like so many dynasties before them, tribal warriors who ascended to dynastic rule after defeating other tribes and peoples, who had their own distinctive identities and allegiances. In order to expand their reign across vast expanses of the country, Qajar kings relied on nothing less than outright kinship and tribal loyalties. In the process, they took the very networks that bound together their tribe and used them to rule over other parts of the country, territories they securely held onto until their eventual demise.

Under the Pahlavis, the style of rulership changed but not its substance. Unlike the Qajars, the Pahlavis were not warriors bent on hegemonizing the country by subduing other tribes. Reza Pahlavi, the new dynasty's founder, was instead a military man, a soldier who acquired power by compelling the shah to abdicate, and who later occupied that same position himself. His was a military conquest, not a tribal one, as the Qajars's had been. But the manner in which the new monarchy stayed in power differed only marginally from that of the Qajars. Patrimonialism continued to dominate the political system, providing perhaps the only state-society nexus through which Pahlavi rule was preserved. The nakedly patriarchical nature of Qajar patrimonialism also changed, with tribal and kinship networks and loyalties gradually giving way to more subtle nuances involving royal patronage and the incorporation of elites.

Despite its growing sophistication, and in parallel, its coercive efficacy, the Pahlavi state remained inherently brittle. The state's continued reliance on the person of the shah and on his wishes and

desires only accentuated the skewed and incomplete evolution of
political structures and institutions. The King of Kings remained central
to political life, and the constellation of politicians and ranking
administrators revolving around him never encompassed more than an
unrepresentative faction of the elite's elite. In the end, the exclusionary
Pahlavis crumbled at the hands of a mass movement more ferocious
than the one that had engulfed the Qajars at the turn of the century.
Out of the turmoil grew a republic, an Islamic Republic, a state which
not only broke with the monarchical heritage of the past but which has
so far held onto power through populism and not patrimonialism. The
political drama has indeed been revolutionized, unsettled, and made
uncertain as it still continues to be more than a decade after the latest
revolution.

Admittedly, a complete understanding of the evolution of the
Iranian state cannot be achieved in isolation from the country's cultural
context. Factors inherent in Iran's political culture have invariably
shaped and influenced the character and the conduct of the Iranian
state. In particular, those features most readily apparent in Iran's
political culture--feudalism, tribalism, personality cult, religion, and
the like--have in one way or another reinforced the three dominant
characteristics of the Iranian polity, namely autocracy, foreign
intervention, and revolution. Moreover, the attitudes and principles
that prevail among Iran's various social classes have also helped
shape the character and the conduct of Iranian politics. While the
political structure may not necessarily reflect or espouse values popular
in society, it does rely on certain social norms and seeks to legitimize
itself through appealing to particular groups and classes. From the
Qajars to the Islamic Republic, each regime has relied on particular
social classes for its political longevity and for popular support. The
attitudes and aspirations of these groups have in turn reinforced
features already existent in the political system. The foreign
domination of Iran's economy under the Qajars and to a lesser extent
under the Pahlavis reflected not merely international and political
developments but the desire of domestic elites to see greater European
involvement in Iranian affairs. As chapters two and three will
demonstrate, Qajar courtiers and Pahlavi technocrats and
policy-makers equated modernization with the promulgation of
economic ties with Europe and the adoption of Western social values.
The same elites who called for greater European involvement later
began demanding political privileges similar to those enjoyed by
citizens of the Western countries, thus leading to revolutionary crises
with which numerous Iranian governments were confronted.

The following chapters examine the evolution of the Iranian state
through successive phases. The political systems and processes of the

Qajar, the Pahlavi, and the Islamic Republican regimes are examined in chapters two, three, and four respectively. Chapter five analyzes Iran's political culture, exploring the dynamics that have underwritten the peculiar character of the country's politics and history. Chapter six, the conclusion, offers a general assessment of Iran's present and possible future prospects.

Note

1. Max Weber, *The Theory of Social and Economic Organization* (New York: Free Press, 1947), p 347.

2

The Qajar Dynasty

The evolution of dynastic rule in Iran in recent centuries assumed particular significance under the Qajars, whose reign stretched from 1785 to 1925. In several important respects, the Qajar era marked a significant watershed in Iran's political history. First, Iran, or Persia as it was then known to the outside world, was transformed from a predominantly tribal territory in the seventeenth and eighteenth centuries into a nation-state ruled by a central monarch. Before the Qajars' ascension to power, Iran had not been completely unified since its dismemberment by Alexander the Great and his generals at the height of the Hellenic era. Imperial rule was replaced in the interim with the rule of numerous tribes and central royal authority gave way to small, competing kingdoms. Through the centuries, numerous dynastic rulers and ventursome tribal leaders tried in vain to unify the country under their own leadership, and although some like Shah Ismail Safavi and Karim Khan Zand achieved impressive feats, none was successful in imposing his reign over all regions of the Persian plateau. It was not until the eventual victory of the Qajars, themselves one the many tribes vowing for greater dominance and hegemony, that the country was finally united under central leadership. Although the Qajars lost sizeable portions of Iranian territory to foreign powers in the process, they were, none the less, successful in turning a medieval Islamic society into one which by the end of the eighteenth century had a semblance of a representatiional government.[1]

Another equally significant feature of the Qajar era was the absence of a meaningful evolution in the structure and the behavior of the political system. Throughout the period, political institutions were meaningless and the state remained a mere reflection of the royal household, governed by imperial fiat and decree. Moreover, the era was marked by a striking paucity of meaningful social and political reforms, and what reforms did occur were mostly abandoned or were reversed soon afterward. Yet Qajar polity changed and evolved up until the 1870s, albeit haltingly and at a reluctant pace, but became highly static and in fact steadily regressed soon thereafter. This absence of political vitality and the maintenance of a backward and unresponsive regime in turn fostered the development of Iran's first nationwide revolutionary movement.

A third significant development which occurred during the Qajar era was the intense and somewhat unsavory encounter between Iran and the Great Powers. The growing contacts between Iran and the two superpowers of the time, Britain and Russia, developed not only out of diplomatic interests but also from emerging global economic and military dynamics. Within the context of the Industrial Revolution and rapid colonial expansion, and driven by their own commercial and political needs, European powers found Iran to be an increasingly important factor in the emerging international equation. European colonial expansion met with the unsuspecting enthusiasm of a few reform-minded Qajar politicians who believed that the country's progress could be expedited through increasing its economic and diplomatic ties with Europe. Also conducive to foreign penetration was the avarice of the shahs, who mindlessly secured foreign loans in order to finance their European journeys and palace escapades. These and other factors combined to turn Iran into a playground for international rivalry and competition. Beginning in the early nineteenth century, the country fell victim to a series of international developments over which it had little or no control. While the Qajars succeeded in transforming Iran from a tribal domain into a dynastic kingdom, they could never acquire for it genuine respect in the international community, economic and diplomatic independence, or true national sovereignty.

Growing awareness and resentment of political despotism and foreign domination culminated in the appearance of a number of political uprisings. The protests over the Reuter and Tobacco Concessions, in 1872 and 1891-92 respectively, grew out of the development of nationalist sentiments embedded in xenophobia. By the time of the Constitutional Revolution of 1905-11, liberal and democratic ideals had become prevalent enough to compel members of the intellectual elite and even many commoners to embark on a movement of revolutionary proportions to curtail the shah's unlimited powers. Ann Lambton, a noted authority on the history of the Qajars, has questioned the degree to which the Constitutional Revolution was a political "revolution," arguing that the leaders of the movement never intended to overthrow the political establishment and did not even view themselves as revolutionaries.[2] Lambton's point is well founded, especially considering that the phrase Constitutional Revolution (*Enghelab-e Mashruteh*) was popularized only long after the event itself took place.

However, when considered within the context of the time and the political setting in which it took place, the revolutionary nature of the constitutional movement becomes indisputable. The movement did in fact revolutionize the manner in which politics was practiced under the Qajars, turning the unreproachable and absolutist king into a coequal if not a subordinate of a newly-instituted parliament. Even if the resilience of the Constitutional order was compromised by numerous attacks from within the country and from abroad, its lasting revolutionary significance resonated in Iranian politics for decades to come. At the time, demands for the establishment of a parliament in a despotic and primitive political system were aimed at achieving nothing less than a revolutionary transformation of the prevailing order. Parliamentarianism as a political experience might not have been a historically lasting success, but the very establishment and functioning of a parliament within the Qajar polity was indeed a revolutionary feat.

AUTOCRACY

Although despotism had hardly been absent from Iran's political history before the Qajars, its inaliability to Qajar rule acquired added significance. Two reasons underlie this. First, because the Qajars were able to extend their control over almost all of Iran (except some contested areas near the Russian and Afghan borders), Qajar autocracy was exercised not only in the new imperial capital, Tehran, but also throughout the provinces via royally-appointed provincial governors. Governors, often surpassing the shah in greed and in their treacherous treatment of the local population, were made up mainly of Qajar princes or local tribal leaders who had pledged allegiance to the imperial court.[3] While Tehran became the center of the country's political life soon after the Qajars' ascension to power, all of the provincial towns were also subjected to the same royal authority. Prior to the Qajars, the existence of competing tribal dynasties enabled the peoples of different regions to throw their support behind one of the many regional kings when disenchanted with the local ruler. This opportunity ceased to exist under the Qajars' centralized rule, although rebellions against local governors continued to occur in certain provinces with relative frequency. It was this extension of royal authority throughout the kingdom that later led to the occurrence of Iran's first nationwide revolution. In previous historical instances, rebellions against the person of the ruler had almost always been limited to a particular region or a tribe. The establishment of Qajar autocracy and its extension throughout the kingdom through the provincial administrative system eventually resulted in the development of Iran's first national revolution, one which was ignited in the capital but soon spread throughout the country.

A second feature of Qajar autocracy was its relative but highly limited modernization of the country's political system, and to a lesser extent the modernization of Iranian society as a whole, especially during the long reign of Naser al-Din Shah. Naser al-Din Shah made repeated efforts to change the elementary and highly informal political apparatus through which he ruled Iran. By the end of his reign, he had created something of an institutionalized government machinery. The strictly partiarchical nature of Qajar rule gradually changed to one of patrimony as the Shah began to share some of his political centrality with a few lieutenants and advisors. While the monarch still remained the personal embodiment of imperial rule, he began routinely appointing ministers and administrators, and, early in his reign at least, actively encouraged the implementation of social and political reforms. Although he became increasingly indifferent toward reforms and the affairs of state near the end, by the time of Naser al-Din Shah's death social change had gathered enough momentum to set in motion dynamics which decades later eventually resulted in the Qajars' downfall.

Agha Mohammad Khan: The Qajar Era Established

The influence of tribal customs and characteristics were most pervasive over the Qajar dynasty during the reign of its first monarch, Agha Mohammad Khan (1785-1797), and to a lesser extent under Agha Mohammad's successor, Fath Ali Shah (1797-1834). Being the leaders of the Qajar tribe, Agha Mohammad Khan and his father had been imprisoned by the competing Zand tribe, who had reached dynastic splendor under Karim Khan. Upon Karim Khan's death, Agha Mohammad Khan escaped from the Zand capital of Shiraz and with the help of tribesmen in the northern Qajar stronghold of Mazandaran attacked the cities and provinces that were under the control of other tribal and local leaders. By 1785, he had defeated most other competing tribes and had established his supremacy over most of northern Iran. In 1786 he declared Tehran, a small town with no notable history or monuments, as his kingdom's capital and, once securely in power, crowned himself in 1796.

With Agha Mohammad Khan's reign began the indispensable Qajar practice of royal despotism. Although Qajar rule underwent significant changes from its initial establishment until its final collapse in 1925, political despotism never ceased to be a Qajar characteristic. Among the Qajar rulers, nevertheless, Agha Mohammad

Khan was the most brutal and cruel, with his absorbing passions being only power, revenge, and avarice.[4] Although generally treated well during captivity, he had been made a eunuch at the Zand court and thus could not indulge in many of the courtly pleasures which later became the trademark of his successors. This partly accounted for his chronic depression and for his love of religious passion plays depicting the martyrdom of Imam Hussien.[5]

The same reason also explained his willingness to spend much time away from his main palace and from the capital city. He personally led most major battles, the more notable ones being the campaigns against the northern provinces and against Afghanistan, and was uncharacteristically attentive to religious ethics and to the financial affairs of his court and the kingdom.[6] As the transformer of a tribe into a dynasty, "his whole life was devoted to one all-engrossing object -- the establishment of his family upon the throne of Persia. To that one end everything else was made subordinate."[7] Life in his court was highly informal and unspirited, free of the pomp and the extravagance of the Zands and of succeeding Qajar monarchs. He paid little attention to the arts and culture and was instead preoccupied with military affairs and with the expansion of his power. He trusted no one, including his closest relatives and servants, and his ruthlessness had won him the fear and the hatred of all of his subjects. In the end, in 1797, he was murdered by three servants whom he had sentenced to death during one of his campaigns against the Georgian provinces in the north.

Despite the apparent strength of Agha Mohammad Khan and the new dynasty that he had created, the foundations of his reign were far from solid. The new king gave considerable leverage to other members of the royal household and often paid close attention to the opinions and wishes of Qajar tribal elders.[8] The new king expressed respect toward his senior tribesmen more out of fear of intrigue than out of genuine respect. At the beginning of his enthronement, he faced challenges not only from other tribes but also from those closest to him in his own tribe, including his cousins and brothers. In the latter part of his reign, when he had eliminated most of his enemies within and outside of the Qajar tribe, he saw no need to seek counsel from his tribesmen and did not hesitate to have some of his closest kin assassinated.

Outside of the periphery of the capital and of the Qajar stronghold of Mazandaran, however, the influence of the royal tribe remained tenuous at best. Central and provincial authorities exerted little control over tribal areas, and local lords and tribal leaders often became powerful enough to challenge the shah's rule over their dominion. Tribal leaders often refused to provide the central government with troops or to pay taxes, and domestic military expeditions aimed at reinforcing central authority were commonplace.[9] The central government itself was highly informal, completely lacking administrative or bureaucratic centralization. The Shah had only three officers--an army officer, a finance officer, and an "advisor"--who fulfilled functions similar to those of ministers, with the king personally handling all other matters himself.[10]

Apart from a decentralized administration, the legacy of Agha Mohammad Khan's rule left unresolved the problem of succession, which later plagued the reigns of successive Qajar Shahs. As a tribe and later a ruling dynasty, the Qajars were unable to reach a complete and lasting internal cohesion, nor did they ever achieve family solidarity in any sense.[11] As a result, the question of succession was never fully and adequately settled, and the death of each Shah was followed by intense internal squabbling among different pretenders to the throne. Although the tribal nature of the Qajars changed considerably, virtually all Qajar Shahs had to overcome contenders to their reign before assuming the throne. Insecurity, both personal and political, never ceased to be a part of the Qajar era.

Fath Ali Shah: The Dynasty Nationalized

Qajar despotism changed little under the reign of its second Shah, Fath Ali, who ruled from 1797 to 1834. Fath Ali Shah was at first faced with serious challenges from Zand tribal chiefs and from other Qajar notables seeking to capture the throne.[12] Although he eventually succeeded in overcoming these challenges, he faced disturbances again when forced to give massive territorial concessions to Russia under the Gulistan and the Turkomanchai treaties in 1813 and 1828 respectively.[13]

Despite these challenges, however, he was no less of a despot than his predecessor. A nephew of the late Agha Mohammad Khan, Fath Ali had served as the governor of a number of cities and provinces before assuming the throne and had gained valuable political experience as a result. Having thus become a seasoned politician, he dealt as severely with those suspected of intrigue as his uncle had done, regardless of their position within the royal court or their services to the country. However, the new shah differed markedly from his uncle in demeanor and mood, as the younger Qajar loved to surround himself with splendor and worldly pleasures.[14] In contrast to Agha Mohammad, who had sufficed to the title of "Khan" (Lord), the new king adopted the historic and grandiose title of *Shah-an-Shah* (King of Kings). He also patronized the arts and encouraged learned men to take up residence in the court.

Fath Ali Shah's reign saw the nationalization of the Qajar dynasty, a period in which Agha Mohammad Khan's zeal and intensity were replaced by the more routinized reign of his nephew. It was also a time in which the Qajars began building a rudimentary administrative apparatus. The relative absence of regional revolts by tribal leaders and provincial governors also signified a general entrenchment of Qajar rule. While Agha Mohammad Khan had practically hauled Zand bureaucrats and administrators to his new capital to run the kingdom's administration, a somewhat more indigenous cadre of administrators, called *mirzas*, emerged during the reign of Fath Ali Shah. In order to weaken the powers of the different tribes, the shah fostered dissension among them and kept many of their leaders captive in his court in order to ensure their loyalty to the central government.[15] Tribal unity within the Qajars themselves and between the Qajars and other tribes was also strengthened, mostly through marriage alliances. The *ulama's* support was also courted and the Shah began relying on Islam more heavily in order to augment the ideological legitimacy of his reign.

Benefiting from a general absence of internal and international threats to the kingdom, the Shah also expanded both the royal household and the bureaucracy, creating a limited number of ministries and appointing a prime minister. The conduct of foreign affairs was entrusted to the capable heir apparent, Abbas Mirza, who was also the governor of the important northern city of Tabriz. As a result, foreign dignitaries resided in Tabriz instead of in Tehran, a practice abandoned after Abbas's death (before he ascended to the throne).[16]

The abuse of provincial inhabitants by the governors and by other officials such as *mirzas* and tax collectors became acute in the last years of Fath Ali Shah's reign, during which the monarch's concern for adequate management gradually gave way to his growing interests in worldly pleasures.[17] For their part, the shah's ministers dispensed with their official duties with utmost informality and without the slightest pretence to observing bureaucratic procedures and guidelines.[18] Both the shah and his ministers were unable, and to some extent unwilling, to develop a strong administrative system that would effectively enforce central control over the provinces. In the process, they neglected to devise institutional means and methods through which the country could be run. Tax collection and financial administration also continued to be chronic problems. These and other shortcomings, whose rectification was central to the governing and administration of the kingdom, were to persist through the rest of the Qajar dynasty and entangled all succeeding Qajar rulers and administrators.

Fath Ali Shah died in 1834 after having reigned for some

thirty-seven years. His rightful heir-apparent, Mohammad, was challenged for the kingship by two Qajar contenders and had to be escorted from Tabriz to Tehran by a combined force of British and Russian troops in order to assume the throne. This episode signalled the incipient growth of foreign influence in Iran as well as the persistent weakness of Qajar institutions. Challenges to the Qajar king by members of his own family demonstrated that the new dynasty was still predominantly tribal. Instead of adherence to due procedures and obedience to the designated heir to the throne, Qajar tribal leaders challenged the new shah's claim to rule. It was only after the intervention of foreign powers and through the rule of force that the designated heir-apparent could ascend to kingship.

Besides the circumstances which surrounded his ascension to the throne, the conduct of Mohammad Shah once in power (1834-1848) highlighted the fundamentally tribal nature of early Qajar rule. He imprisoned several Qajar princes in order to minimize their potential threat to his tenure. His reign also witnessed the expansion of foreign influence in Iranian affairs. Throughout his reign, the Shah remained a creature of the Russian empire. Besieged with ill health since early childhood, he was not as actively involved in the detailed running of the kingdom as were his predecessors. In fact, the Shah relegated almost all of his responsibilities to a vain and ignorant prime minister named Hajji Mirza Aghasi after four years.

Naser al-Din Shah: The Qajars at the Height of Power

Mohammad Shah died on 4 September 1848 and was succeeded by his sixteen-year-old son, Naser al-Din. The new king, who in tradition of others before him had held the governorship of Tabriz before ascending to the throne, did not encounter serious challenges in assuming the kingship. This absence of pretenders to the throne signalled the gradual transformation of the Qajars from a ruling tribal clan to a national dynasty, a transformation that was completed during the new shah's long reign. From the beginning of Naser al-Din Shah's reign until his death in 1896, the Qajars reached the height of dynastic splendor. An administrative network evolved and significant though temporary strides were made toward social and political modernization. It was also during this period that Iran was "discovered," much more exploited than respected, by European powers and became a treasure chest for foreign governments and entrepreneurs. Equally significant were the evolution of revolutionary dynamics during Naser al-Din Shah's reign, resulting in the near collapse of the Qajar dynasty.

Naser al-Din Shah's long reign marked a watershed not only for the Qajar dynasty but also for the country as a whole. Domestically, the deepest imprint was left by the tenures in office of two of Iran's most celebrated political figures, Amir Kabir (1848-51) and Mirza Hussein Khan Sepahsalar (1870-80), both of whom served as the shah's prime minister. Amir Kabir tried to centralize Qajar rule by strengthening the country's administration and by expanding the authority of the central government. For his part, Mirza Hussein Khan tried to reform what by the time of his premiership had become a cumbrous and uncoordinated collection of political institutions. The activities of the two prime ministers also resulted in the exertion of considerable economic and diplomatic influence over Iran by European powers. Socially, a period of intense intellectual flurry occurred near the end of Naser al-Din Shah's reign, when educated commoners and courtiers alike pursued intellectual activity with zeal and unprecedented intensity. It was also during the same period when the populist Babi movement, out of which later grew the Bahai faith, was launched.

In contrast to his predecessors, Naser al-Din Shah had a clearer perception of Iran's military and economic weaknesses, especially *vis-a-vis* the Great Powers.[19] He thus demonstrated a desire for reforms and progress in Iran uncommon among Qajar rulers. Soon after his enthronement, the new king appointed a reform-minded official named Mirza Taqi Khan as his prime minister, giving him the title of *Amir Kabir* (The Great Chief). Taqi Khan, the son of a palace worker, had educated himself and had become one of Naser al-Din Shah's trusted courtiers during the latter's governorship of Tabriz.[20] The new premier soon moved to consolidate his own position within the court and steadily increased his powers by dismissing most of these who opposed the implementation of even minor changes to the status quo.[21]

Having assumed considerable powers, Amir Kabir implemented a vast array of reforms, ranging from encouraging the establishment of new industries to reforming the tax system. Far-reaching financial and monetary changes were also initiated in order to maximise the positive results of a recently inaugurated tax reform. The premier sent students to France to study the French tax system, established six tax collecting centers throughout the country, and assumed personal control over the national revenue.[22] Using the revenues generated by the adequate management of taxes, Amir Kabir built armament factories and encouraged other industries, sent artisans to Russia to receive higher training in manufacturing and industry, employed foreign instructors for the army and the customs bureau, and established the secular Dar al-Funun high school. He also reformed the judiciary by trying to prevent the miscarriage of justice and the widespread use of torture. The military was patterned after European armies, and attempts were made to reduce the overwhelming influence and powers of the *ulama*.[23]

Having assumed onerous powers in order to carry out his reforms and his plans for centralizing the country's administrative machinery, Amir Kabir gradually aroused the resentment of most other courtiers and, inevitably, the suspicions of Naser al-Din Shah. Courtiers resented his financial reforms because it jeopardized their monetary privileges, while bureaucrats opposed his centralizing efforts since it undermined their positions and reduced their relatively free access to the shah.[24] Within three years after his appointment, in 1851, the Shah stripped the premier of all of his powers and placed him under house arrest. He was then exiled to the city of Kashan, where shortly after arrival he was stabbed to death on 9 January 1852.

Amir Kabir's death slowed down the centralisation and reform of the Qajar state, although the Shah himself retained a measure of interest in administrative and political reforms. A second premier was appointed but soon dismissed as the Shah decided to run the country without the help of a prime minister. In 1859, a six-man cabinet was formed and presided over by the shah, composed of the ministers of finance, foreign affairs, war, justice, interior, and pensions and endowments.[25] To ensure that the monarch was aware of the people's conditions, Justice Boxes were installed throughout the country in 1865, enabling citizens to directly voice their complaints and concerns to the shah.

But the Shah's efforts to personally keep abreast of the latest developments proved ineffective and unworkable and in 1870 he appointed another reformer, Mirza Hussein Khan, as his prime minister. The new premier, who had previously served as ambassador to the Ottoman empire, was granted the title *Moshir al-Dowleh* (Government Counselor). The young and energetic premier quickly initiated a series of reforms, managing within a short period to stir up as much controversy and uproar as Amir Kabir had done before him. These uproars over the prime minister came to a head in 1873, when news of the Reuter Concession was made public. The shah reluctantly dismissed Mirza Hussein Khan but brought him back into his inner circle and appointed him to head the foreign ministry within six months. Having taken on considerable powers, the minister was then able to remain close to the Shah and remained in office for some ten years, being finally dismissed in September 1880.

Similar to Amir Kabir's, Mirza Hussein Khan's efforts were aimed at augmenting rather than curtailing the powers of the monarch and centralizing government administration. To this end, he carried out substantial judicial, military, financial, and even political reforms during his tenure. He tried to curb the judicial duality of Iranian law into the *urf* (civil law) and the *shari'a* (religious law) by establishing independent tribunals and a unified code of law for the entire kingdom.[26] In reforming the military, Moshir al-Dowleh experimented with various plans and eventually succeeded in regulating the army's budget, developing for it a new organizational model and systematizing the conscription process. He also hired European instructors for the training of officers, put more emphasis on the education of soldiers, and increased the number of arms and ammunition factories.[27] A few months before his final dismissal, he also instituted the first Iranian police force.[28]

Equally important were Mirza Hussein Khan's political and economic reforms, most of which were directed at furthering the goals initially set by Amir Kabir. Having persuaded the Shah to grant him considerable powers, the prime minister established a cabinet system, formed a consultative assembly to advise the shah, and curbed the considerable, and all too often arbitrary, powers enjoyed by the provincial governors. In 1873, he instituted the first formal cabinet and introduced a series of regulations regarding its conduct.[29] Even the unofficial uniform that cabinet ministers and other high-ranking bureaucrats wore were changed and made more similar to the attire worn in Europe.[30] Meanwhile, his economic and financial reforms included attempts, albeit unsuccessful, to establish Iran's first national bank and eliminate bribery among government officials and administrators. He also encouraged the exploitation of mines and other natural resources, reduced the exorbitant salaries of many royal princes and other courtiers, and tried to increase the number of roads and bridges in the capital and in other cities.[31]

Despite his ceaseless efforts aimed at implementing far-reaching and fundamental reforms, by the time of his departure from office in 1880 Mirza Hussein Khan's efforts had borne little fruit. In the process of implementing his reforms, the prime minister had infringed on the privileges and the unchecked powers of highly influential courtiers and Qajar leaders, and had made a number of powerful enemies. He had never fully succeeded in establishing his authority over other high-ranking bureaucrats.[32] The provincial governors, the royal princes and other prominent courtiers, and perhaps most importantly, the *ulama* all opposed the premier since his reforms forced them to relinquish much of their previously limitless powers. The prime minister's judicial reforms met with stiff opposition from the ulama, who had traditionally been in charge of implementing *shari'a* laws and were unwilling to surrender their judicial prerogatives to the central government.[33] Additionally, the *ulama* opposed the prime minister's reforms because such reforms, which at least in the premier's view required the adoption of European technology and ways, were perceived by many to be part of a cynical plot to "Christianize" Iran.

Mirza Hussein Khan did, in fact, equate progress with

Europeanization and thought that Iran's salvation lay in the emulation of European ways and means.[34] Along with the few other "reformists" of his era, he favored the granting of large scale and all-encompassing concessions to few, or even one, foreign company in the hope of expediting the country's progress and industrial development.[35] Apart from its apparent industrial advantages, the reformists also believed that through strengthening Iran's economic ties with the predominant European power of the time, Britain, they would reduce the ominous threat of Russian expansionism. To this end, the prime minister granted lucrative concessions to British entrepreneurs and promulgated European customs and habits.

Mirza Hussein Khan's concessions to British individuals and companies aroused the anger of not only the *ulama* and the courtiers but also that of the Russians. The Russian government was so enraged by the Iranian prime minister's economic policies toward Britain that it allegedly helped Iranian politicians conspire his ouster.[36] Because of this opposition, and also because of the inarticulate and ill-conceived nature of his policies, the prime minister's reforms were to a great extent unsuccessful and were mostly abrogated soon after he left office. His propagation of European ways had aroused the opposition of the *ulama* and the skepticism of the general public. Near the end of his tenure, he had also lost his enthusiasm for reforms and instead increasingly concentrated on securing his own power base. After his second and final dismissal, Moshir al-Dowleh held a number of important governorships. However, since he had become a liability rather than an asset for the shah, he was soon retired from active political life.[37]

Naser al-Din Shah was assassinated in 1896 by a petitioner who had been granted a royal audience. (While the Shah's practice of accepting petitions suggests that he was genuinely concerned for the welfare of his subjects, in the last years of his reign his primary concern was to enjoy the pleasures of his court's harem.) After Mirza Hussein Khan's removal from office, the shah had again tried to run the country without a premier, though his second attempt achieved no more success than had his first trial. After trying in earnest to implement far-reaching political and financial reforms, often at considerable risk to his own power and prestige, the Shah became increasingly apathetic and indifferent toward the affairs of his kingdom. One observer has noted that Naser al-Din Shah "lacked application and tenacity of purpose where reform, social justice, and good government were concerned. His absorbing passions were eating, drinking, hunting, riding and money."[38] His avarice grew with age, and at one point there were some two hundred women in his harem.[39] He loved to compose and to recite poetry, whether in praise of religion or one of his favorite wives.[40] The treasury he left behind was practically empty. After 1892, a deficit of 300,000 tumon became a regular feature of the state budget.[41] The bureaucracy once again reverted into an instrument for accumulating wealth and harassing the population. The country, meanwhile, sank deeper into disorder, and anti-government riots occurred in numerous cities.[42]

Nevertheless, Naser al-Din Shah's reign was historically significant because of its overall contribution to Iran's political evolution. By its, due largely to the efforts of his two notable prime ministers, the kingdom's governing apparatus was much more centralized than it had ever been under the three previous shahs. Life in the kingdom was also much improved, although living conditions were still far from satisfactory. A few roads were built, postal services had begun, the government published an almanac containing basic data about Iran, and the number of secular schools increased considerably. Despite a devastating famine from 1869 to 1872, the population of Tehran and other cities generally grew. At the same time, while domestic conditions improved, foreign competition over Iran intensified. Naser al-Din Shah's reign in fact marked the beginning of open rivalries between Russia and Britain over controlling Iran's economy and influencing its political life.

Muzzafar al-Din Shah: The Beginnings of Revolution

Naser al-Din Shah was succeeded by his heir-apparent, Muzzafar al-Din Shah (1896-1907). Like others before him, the new shah had previously held the governorship of Tabriz. He began his reign by promising to reform the political system and to improve the general living conditions of the kingdom, appointing a progressive and popular politician named Amin al-Dowleh as his prime minister. But both the prime minister and the shah were faced with severe constraints from the beginning. Although Naser al-Din Shah was thought to have amassed great wealth while in power, Muzzafar al-Din Shah found the royal treasury empty and had to borrow money in order to finance his tour of Europe.[43] The shah was also stricken by poor health and, as he had proven during his governorship of Tabriz, was incompetent in management and administration.[44]

Amin al-Dowleh was equally unsuccessful in implementing reforms. The prime minister was genuinely interested in reforming the royal court and in bringing a degree of order into the country's dismal economy. Like others before him, however, he encountered opposition from both within as well as outside the royal court by those who perceived his efforts to be inimical to their interests. He reformed the administration of revenues, customs, mint, and taxes, and curbed some of the perennial extravagance of the royal court.[45] In his efforts, he encountered the wrath of those courtiers whose unchecked privileges he was trying to limit. Furthermore, since he used foreign loans to finance his reforms, he also faced the resentment of clerics and merchants, both of whom were emerging as the leaders of an incipient nationalist movement.[46] Additionally, his reformist tendencies also prompted the Russian government to view the premier as yet another creature of Great Britain and to press for his removal from office.[47] He was eventually removed in 1898 and his post was given to a noted reactionary politician named Amin al-Sultan, a figure well known for his pro-Russian sentiments.

Muzzafar al-Din Shah's initial promises of reforms and progress had temporarily halted the growth of revolutionary sentiments throughout the country. However, when it became evident that these promises were empty and merely designed to contain popular disquiet, a movement that aimed at establishing a system of constitutional monarchy soon developed. Faced with widespread opposition and on his deathbed because of ill health, Muzzafar al-Din Shah finally acceded to the demands of the revolutionaries and signed a declaration on 5 August 1906 conceding to the establishment of a parliament, to be called the Majles. The shah died on 4 January 1907, by which time his granting of the constitution had won him much popularity among his subjects.

Mohammad Ali Shah: Struggles with Majles

Muzzafar al-Din Shah was succeeded by Mohammad Ali on 19 January 1907. It was at this time that Qajar despotism reached its height, with the Shah trying to do whatever he could to overthrow the newly established and fragile constitutional order. The shah was, in the words of one observer, an "oriental despot of the worst type, unprincipled, untrustworthy, and avaricious."[48] He had expressed overt hostility toward the constitutional movement during his governorship of Tabriz and had deliberately withheld news of his father's signing of the Constitutional Decree from the city's residents.[49] Mindful of his intentions, Majles deputies had repeatedly forced him to pledge allegiance to the new order and to swear to uphold the parliament before allowing him to be coronated. But once on the throne, with much encouragement and assistance from Russia, the shah did everything possible to suppress the Majles and to regain for himself the unchecked powers that previous Qajar monarchs had enjoyed. In his two-year reign, he twice tried to topple the constitutional assembly, and although eventually overthrown himself, he invaded the country afterward and attempted to regain power through military means.

Mohammad Ali Shah's first unsuccessful coup against the Majles occurred in December 1907, when he summoned the cabinet to the palace and chained and imprisoned the prime minister. He also called on the Cossack troops stationed in Tehran, his household servants, and bands of thugs known as *lutis* to agitate against the Majles.[50] An outburst of sentiments in support of the Majles was soon expressed throughout the country, with many civilians and commoners vowing to take up arms to defend the new order against the shah's efforts. In February the shah was the target of an unsuccessful assassination attempt, when a bomb was thrown at his car.[51] He finally abandoned this venture, but only after he was persuaded to do so by the French and Ottoman ambassadors.[52]

Undeterred by this humiliation, he tried once more to quell the Majles in June 1908, this time successfully. Early in June he moved to the Baghishah palace, located in the outskirts of Tehran, and declared martial law in the capital. Martial law was enforced by the Cossack brigade, whose commander was the Russian Colonel Likhoff. On 23 June, the Cossacks encircled the building where the Majles met and opened fire, killing a number of nationalist leaders and Majles members.[53] The remaining constitutionalists were dispersed and most fled to Tabriz, which had been the scene of much revolutionary activity by newly established political associations called *Anjomans*.[54] In return for his services, Liakhoff was made the military commander of Tehran, where he practically ruled until Mohammad Ali Shah's abdication on 16 July 1909.[55]

The bombardment of the Majles building did not result in the suppression of the constitutional order as Mohammad Ali Shah had hoped. In fact, proponents of the new order undertook a vigorous and determined campaign to once again restore the parliamentary system. Amid much excitement and consternation, an army of revolutionary troops marched into Tehran and replaced the Shah with his twelve-year-old son, Ahmad. The deposed shah took refuge in the Russian city of Odessa. The interim period during which the Shah had temporarily suppressed the Majles became popularly known as the "Lesser Despotism" (*Istibdad-e Saghir*), and ended with the inauguration of the Second Majles in November 1909.

On 18 July 1911, the deposed shah made one last effort to regain the monarchy through a military invasion of Iran but was once again defeated and forced to return to his Russian exile. The younger Qajar ruled first under the regency of a tribal elder, named Azud al-Mulk, and later after Azud al-Mulk's death under the regency of another notable figure chosen by the Majles. In the meanwhile, the country was only nominally independent and had virtually become a colony of Great Britain and Russia. The initial unity of the nationalist revolutionaries had broken down and had given way to internal discord, chaos, and mismanagement. Due to a combination of these and other developments, the Qajar dynasty decayed and disintegrated in the 1910s as steadily as it had solidified itself in the 1780s.

Factors Inhibiting Political Development Under the Qajars

Up until the outbreak of the Constitutional Revolution, a number of factors obstructed the evolution of Qajar political institutions in a systemic and cohesive manner. One of the most important of these factors was the intense rivalry of the two superpowers and their ceaseless efforts to block whatever technical and economic assistance that the other might have rendered Iran. Yet blaming all of Iran's political ills during the Qajar era on outside powers, as is prevalent among Iranian historiographers, is reductionist at best. Several factors indigenous to the Qajars accentuated the political backwardness of their rule and those of the institutions through which they governed. An obvious factor was the avarice and rapaciousness of literally all Qajar officials and bureaucrats, from the shah down to the provincial tax collectors and beyond. The strict patrimonial ties that bound the system together only helped to strengthen a status quo built on the exploitation of the masses and the corruption of lethargic elites.

There were also the entrenched interests of groups such as the *ulama* and influential courtiers who did not wish to see extensive changes in the status quo. Those few politicians who were able to overcome the shah's suspicions and had acquired his support for reforming the system invariably fell victim to court intrigue or the condemnation of the *ulama*. Falling from the shah's favor was a risk few were willing to take. A minister's fall from office put an end not only to his innumerable political and financial privileges but was often also accompanied by the confiscation of all of his property by the shah.[56] Meanwhile, since positions and appointments could be bought and were considered as means of furthering one's wealth, they fostered greed and voracity among most officials.[57] Thus to a large extent, features that engendered corruption, avarice, sluggishness, and timidity were built into the political system itself.

Furthermore, tribalism was never very far from Qajar rule, both in respect to the Qajars themselves and in their relationship with other tribes. Internally, the Qajars remained an essentially tribal dynasty well into the reign of Naser al-Din Shah, and even, it can be argued, until the very end, when a Qajar tribal elder assumed the regency after Mohammad Ali Shah was deposed. Moreover, the Qajars were never able effectively to overcome the powers of all of the disparate tribes and were chronically threatened by tribal uprisings. Even during the reign of Naser al-Din Shah, when a concerted effort was made to increase the powers of the central government, the Bakhtiari tribe enjoyed considerable freedom and autonomy.[58] Consequently, a significant portion of the government's energies were directed toward securing the submission of the different tribes, which in the case of the Bakhtiaris was never fully achieved.

FOREIGN INTERVENTION

Patrimonial and personalist politics, elite social and political conservatism, and disruptive tribal cleavages all combined to retard any meaningful evolution of political institutions under the Qajars. The unabated intervention of foreign powers, and their relentless competition to gain a stronger hold over Iran through economic and diplomatic means, was yet another significant factor in slowing down the evolution of the Qajar political system. Furthermore, foreign intervention in Iranian affairs during the Qajar era represented the conduct and the complexities of Superpower diplomacy in general and specifically, their domination of less powerful countries.

Several consequences resulted from Qajar Iran's relations with the superpowers. To begin with, Qajar rulers from Naser al-Din Shah onward became acutely aware of Iran's disadvantageous position and its lack of military parity *vis-a-vis* most European powers, especially Russia and Britain. When foreign intervention did become an inseparable part of Qajar politics, it resulted in the economic plundering of the country and the retardation of its political evolution. A few Qajar courtiers and highly placed officials amassed great wealth through promulgating the interests of one or the other of the foreign powers. But most merchants and the ordinary masses increasingly suffered because of these very interests. Meanwhile, the economic and industrial advantages that could have been gained through increased contacts with the outside world were minimal. Since each of the two superpowers undermined the other's efforts in Iran, and since commercial treaties were mostly enacted by unscrupulous Qajar officials who gave higher priority to their own personal gains than to the country's economic well-being, whatever benefits Iran could have gained through its foreign ties were lost amid international intrigue and personal greed.

Iran as a Superpower Battleground

While there had been contacts between Iran and the outside world long before the Qajars came to power, often in the form of military ventures and commercial trade, the Qajar era marked the beginning of a colonial relationship between the nominally independent Iran and both Great Britain and Russia. Iran became one of the main battlefields on which superpower rivalry between the two countries was conducted, a rivalry in which some of the most effective weapons were the granting of lucrative loans, acquiring concessions, and exercising influence over the country's economy and over influential personalities within the royal court. In the process, Iran was to be torn between the conflicting interests of Russia and Great Britain and plundered by both domestic and foreign adventurers.

Britain had looked toward Iran with growing interest as early as the Napoleonic era. The possibility that Napoleon might attack either the Ottoman empire or India had led to an increased focus of European diplomatic attention on the Middle East and on Iran in particular.[59] Napoleon would have had to cross Iran in order to attack Afghanistan and possibly even India. Wary of such a prospect, Britain hurriedly signed an Anglo-Persian agreement with Iran in January 1801, in which Fath Ali Shah agreed to attack Afghanistan if the Afghan king decided to attack India.[60]

Iran's relation's with Russia, meanwhile, were marred by military conflicts and border skirmishes from the beginning. Agha Mohammad Khan had repeatedly tried to regain the Georgian territories that Iran had lost to Russia after the death of Nadir Shah.[61] Fath Ali Shah, decided to attack the territory in 1804. The ensuing protracted war with Russia dragged on for some eight years and ended only when Russian forces inflicted heavy blows on Iran's undisciplined and ill-trained soldiers. The Gulistan treaty was signed by the belligerents the following year, as a result of which Iran surrendered much of its northern territory to the Russian empire.[62] Humiliated by his defeat, Fath Ali Shah tried to recapture the territory once again in 1826. But the second campaign proved even more disastrous than the first one, and by 1828 Russian forces had advanced as far south as Tabriz and captured that important city. Thus followed the Turkomonchai treaty of 1828, whereby Iran again lost more of its northern territory to Russia, gave capitulary rights to Russian citizens residing in Iran, and agreed to pay a heavy indemnity to the Russian government.[63]

During the reign of Mohammad Shah, Iran's relations with Russia drastically improved and instead disagreements developed between Iran and Britain. The improvement in relations with Russia was in large part due to the personal dispositions of the new shah and, more significantly, due to the growing commercial trade between the two countries.[64] Instead of attacking Russia, by whom his predecessor had twice been humiliated, Mohammad Shah tried to regain the Afghan city of Herat, which Iran had lost after Nadir Shah's death. Yet

Mohammad Shah was no more successful in regaining Herat than Fath Ali had been in capturing Georgia. From 1836 to 1838 he tried to over run Herat, but was unsuccessful and was repeatedly driven back by Afghan swordsmen.[65] In his campaigns against Herat, the shah met with the determined opposition of Britain, which viewed the fall of Herat as a serious threat to India's security. In 1856 Naser al-Din Shah avenged this loss and successfully captured Herat. But Britain quickly retaliated by attacking Iran's southern shores along the Persian Gulf and occupying Kharq island in 1857.[66] The following year Iran signed a treaty with Britain in which it recognized the independence of Afghanistan and promised not to interfere in its internal affairs.[67]

Naser al-Din Shah's invasion of Herat proved to be diplomatically more significant than may at first appear. The signing of the 1858 treaty with Britain became the prelude to the heavy-handed exercise of British diplomacy and influence in Iran. Initially, this influence was exercised almost exclusively through lucrative concessions granted by the Iranian government to British entrepreneurs and through the loans that Iran itself acquired from Britain.

The sudden and intense hunt for concessions which foreign governments and subjects undertook in Iran was fueled by two concurrent developments. To begin with, Iran had a particular strategic significance for both Russia and Britain. It bordered Britain's prized possession, India, to the west, and Russia to the south. Mirza Hussein Khan's efforts to win foreign, mainly British, concessions in order to finance his modernization efforts significantly polarized an already volatile situation. Secondly, the industrial expansion that took place in the West in the middle and late nineteenth century led to a rapid and consistent hunt for concessions in Iran and in other lesser developed areas as new markets were sought for raw material and imports.

The first such concession had been granted to Great Britain in 1863 for the establishment of an overland telegraph line from the Ottoman border to various Iranian cities.[68] Soon afterward, in 1872, an unimaginably lucrative concession was granted to Baron Julius de Reuter, a naturalized British citizen. Valid for a period of seven years, the concession gave Reuter a seventy-five percent share of all of the country's mines except those with precious stones. In return, he was given the exclusive right to build railways in Iran and to establish a national bank and a customs department. He was also granted the right to bring to the country any number of workers and experts that were needed for his projects.[69]

Not unexpectedly, the Reuter Concession met with considerable opposition both inside and outside of Iran. The internal opposition was spearheaded by the *ulama*, who were outraged at the proposed construction of a railway. They believed that a railway would hasten the intrusion of Western goods and values into Iranian society and would therefore lead to a deterioration of their own social position and authority.[70] Russian opposition to the concession, meanwhile, was based on the premise that it compromised Iran's adherence to equilibrium between Russia and Britain.[71] Faced with these two powerful centers of opposition, the Iranian government was forced to cancel the concession in 1873.

Yet other concessions were granted with uninterrupted frequency. In 1888, Great Britain obtained a concession for the right to navigate in the Karun river. Fearful of the growing commercial and economic penetration of Iran by Britain, in 1889 Russia obtained a promise by the shah not to give the right for the construction of a railway in Iran to any power other than Russia.[72] A further concession was given to Reuter in 1889, this time giving him the right to establish a national bank called the Imperial Bank of Persia, to issue bank notes, and to exploit the country's mineral resources for sixty years.[73] Russia demanded similar privileges and in 1891 acquired the right to establish a new bank in Iran called Banque d'Escompte de Perse.[74]

By far the most significant concession granted by the Iranian government to a foreign interest was that granted to the British-owned Imperial Tobacco Corporation in March 1890. The company was given the sole monopoly to buy, sell, and manufacture all Iranian tobacco inside and outside of the country for a period of fifty years. The Shah was to receive £15,000 annually, in addition to one fourth of the company's annual profits.[75] The detrimental effects of the Tobacco Concession on Iranian merchants, shopkeepers, and tobacco growers were of far more significance than its broader economic and diplomatic ramifications. While the concession itself was significant in accentuating foreign economic dominance over Iran, it was even more important in resulting in the formation of public opinion and nationalist sentiments for the first time.[76]

Because of the pervasive nature of foreign control over Iran's commerce and its natural resources, the first nationwide protests occurred, paving the way for the revolutionary movement of 1905-11. The concession itself was signed in 1889, but its terms were kept secret and the unrests did not begin until the company's agents in Iran began working in 1891.[77] The resulting protests in Tehran and in other major cities so threatened the government that Naser al-Din Shah decided to repeal the concession in January 1892. As a result of the cancellation, the Shah was forced to borrow money in order to pay a sum of £500,000 as indemnity to the Imperial Tobacco Corporation.[78]

The last concession of this kind was signed early in Muzzafar al-Din Shah's reign between the Iranian government and another British millionaire named William Knox D'Arcy. The concession itself was obtained after the British representative in Iran, Sir Arthur Hardinge, bribed influential Iranian politicians, including the prime minister.[79] According to the agreement, D'Arcy's company obtained the exclusive right to exploit natural gas, petroleum, asphalt, and ozocerite throughout Iran except in the five southern provinces for a period of sixty years. In return, apart from the bribes, the Iranian government was to receive £20,000 in cash, the equivalent of this sum in paid-up shares, and sixteen per cent of the company's annual profits.[80]

"Partition of Preponderance" and Loans

Beginning in the 1890s, the intense hunt for concessions in Iran by foreign entrepreneurs was largely abandoned, mainly as a result of the massive, nationwide protests which their lopsided and lucrative nature had ignited. Furthermore, the Boer War had directed much of Britain's military and diplomatic attention toward southern Africa and away from the Middle East. This in turn strengthened Russia's hand in Iranian affairs, albeit temporarily, and allowed it to exercise greater influence over the Qajar court. In order to offset some of this influence, the British Prime Minister, Lord Salisbury, had in 1888 urged Russia to cooperate rather than to compete with Britain in influencing Iranian affairs. Calling his plan the "partition of preponderance," Salisbury hoped to internationalize Iran's position by creating spheres of economic influence within the country for the different foreign powers.[81] A similar move was undertaken by the Iranian government itself in October 1888, when it approached a third power, the United States, and urged it to expand its commercial and diplomatic ties with Iran. This move was undertaken with the hope that Iran's relations with the U.S. would counterbalance the Anglo-Russian predominance in the country. However, President Cleveland refused to break his country's isolationist mold and to become party to the Anglo-Russian rivalry.[82] In the meanwhile, with Britain preoccupied with the Boer War, the Russian position in Iran grew and stayed virtually unchallenged until the turn of the century.

While Britain had sought to secure its economic domination of Iran through concessions, Russia had resorted to the granting of lucrative loans to the country's weak and greedy rulers. In 1900, Russia granted Iran a loan of £2,000,000 so that Mozzafar al-Din Shah could finance his first journey to Europe. The next year Russia augmented its loan by a further £1,000,000. Depleted of any financial resources of its own, the Iranian government secured the loan with receipts generated from all Iranian ports except those along the Persian Gulf.[83] A Russo-Persian commercial convention was held in 1901 and resulted in a trade agreement beneficial to Russia, only to be countered with an Anglo-Persian treaty in 1903 designed to secure Iranian trade with Britain and India.[84] In April of the same year Britain granted Iran a £200,000 loan through the Imperial Bank of Persia, to which a further £100,000 was added in 1904.

Despite such frantic efforts to secure Iran's subjugation through loans and concessions, the era of superpower economic warfare soon came to an end in the early twentieth century and gave way to the overt occupation of the country by foreign forces. This new era of outright foreign intervention was inaugurated soon after the onset of the Constitutional Revolution. With the advent of the Constitutional Revolution, Britain and Russia divided Iran into two spheres of influence. Even when the revolution eventually succeeded in deposing the despotic Mohammad Ali Shah, both Britain and Russia acquiesced in the dethroned shah's efforts at overthrowing the constitutional order, and, when he failed, they occupied the country themselves. The partition of the country occurred in 1907, when in order to counter the growing influence of Germany in the region Britain and Russia decided to cooperate together and formalized their cooperation through an official agreement. According to the agreement, Iran was divided into two spheres of influence and a neutral zone, in which neither party would seek any political or commercial concessions.[85] Russia's sphere was substantially larger and since it included Tehran it was politically more significant. However, the discovery of oil reserves in the regions under British influence soon increased the importance of the British sphere as well.

The Anglo-Russian treaty of 1907 coincided with the occurrence of the Constitutional Revolution and the growing political instability that ensued. It was, in fact, this political instability that gave added significance to the country's partitioning by the two powers. Beginning soon after the Constitutional Revolution and lasting up until World War I, Iran's political troubles became synonymous with its foreign relations. This period marked the beginning of direct foreign interference into Iranian affairs and proved to be only a prelude to even more overt foreign intervention during the Great War.

The Anglo-Russian convention took place a year after the Constitutional Revolution had started. Before the convention, Russian and British goals in Iran had been diametrically opposite to one another. Britain had generally favored the institution of reforms and industrial development in Iran, a process, it hoped, achieved through the commercial concessions that its enterprising citizens acquired from the Iranian government. Consistent with this policy, Britain in the early phases of the Constitutional Revolution supported the efforts of the revolutionaries in trying to impose limitations on the arbitrary powers of the shah and allowed its embassy to be used as sanctuary for the protesters.[86]

Russia, on the other hand, wished to see a continuation of Iran's social and political status quo and to that end it sought to secure the longevity of the Qajars through the granting of loans and the exercise of direct influence over the royal court. The Russians were not as enthusiastic to see the emergence of a reforming government in Iran, especially one that was brought about through a popular revolution. Two main reasons underlied their opposition to the success of the Iranian revolutionaries and their establishment of a parliamentary regime. First, the Russian government was fearful that supporting a revolutionary movement in Iran would have negative domestic consequences, especially in the light of the Romanovs's own domestic difficulties in the early 1900s. Secondly, the establishment of a parliament in Iran would have resulted in a substantial reduction in Russia's influence over Iranian affairs. Since a parliamentary government would have ended the arbitrary nature of Qajar rule, the Russian government would not have been able to continue exercising its paramount influence over Qajar officials.

Thus, Britain's decision to cooperate rather than compete with Russia in Iranian affairs resulted in the loss of the only ally that the Iranian revolutionaries had had. In fact, the revolutionaries were forced to fight the Shah's despotism at a time when he enjoyed the full backing of both superpowers. This Anglo-Russian cooperation proved to be one of the primary causes of the eventual demise of the Constitutional Revolution.

During the intervening period between Mohammad Ali Shah's deposition and the outbreak of World War I, Russia took active measures to overthrow the newly-established Majles. Britain, on the other hand, did so only passively and instead merely supported Russia's initiatives. Russia either assisted the shah or itself directly tried to overthrow Iran's parliamentary government in a number separate instances. On two occasions, the shah ordered Colonel Liakhoff to attack the parliament building. The Russian government also assisted the deposed shah in his attempt to invade Iran and to recapture the throne in 1911, when the ex-monarch set sail from the Russian city of Odessa in July and entered Iran by way of the southern shores of the Caspian.

Russian support for the former Shah continued even after the failed invasion, when it pressured the Iranian government to pay a heavy indemnity to the deposed king. With the military invasion having failed, Russia directed its effort toward creating financial and diplomatic obstacles for the Majles. This strategy crystalized in the form of severe pressure on the Iranian government to fire a recently-hired American national, Morgan Shuster, who had been entrusted with devising a modern budget for the country.[87]

World War I: Outright Occupation

There were no significant changes in Iran's relations with the outside world up until the dawn of World War I in 1914. After the beginning of the war and lasting up until the 1921 coup, which effectively ended Qajar rule, the interventionist policies of Russia and Britain toward Iran were replaced by the country's outright military occupation not only by the two superpowers but also by the Ottoman empire and by Germany. Despite Iran's declaration as a nonbelligerent in the conflict, World War I engulfed Iran in itself as much as it had done Europe. Besides Russia and Great Britain, Germany had also come to realize the importance of the Middle East and tried to increase its influence in Iran under the auspices of its *Dang Nach Osten* (Toward the Orient) policy.[88] This policy was largely unsuccessful and Germany's position in Iran did not gain in strength despite the numerous physicians, technical and military advisors, and commercial representatives that it had sent to the country during the war years. A similarly unsuccessful campaign was undertaken by the United States but was soon abandoned when it met with the opposition of both Russia and Great Britain.

Despite its initial setbacks, Germany was determined to attack Russian and British interests in Iran in order to deflect their attention away from the European theater. To this end, Germany followed a two-pronged objective in Iran: capturing or destroying the British-owned oil installations in Khuzestan, and using Iran as a transit to open a second front in Afghanistan.[89] Britain was as equally determined to protect India from the Axis powers and to keep them away from Iran's oil-rich southern shores. All of this was taking place at a time when the Iranian government was a mere extension of the wishes of London and St. Petersburg, when the Majles was torn by the factionalism of its members, and when the country itself was still a largely tribal domain where the allegiance of the different tribes lay not with the central government but with the foreign powers.

When the war broke out in Europe, Iran hurriedly declared its neutrality in November 1914. Neutrality was seen by many Iranian politicians to be the most effective way to protect Iran's territorial independence, albeit nominally, and to keep foreign troops out of Iran. More importantly, the Third Majles, which had been inaugurated in late 1914, was packed with the pro-British Moderates (*I'tedaliyoun*), and their decision to declare Iran a neutral party was greatly influenced by Britain's desire to keep Iran out of the Turko-German alliance.

From the very beginning, however, Iran's neutrality was completely ignored by all foreign parties involved. Ottoman troops crossed into Iranian territory and Britain deployed some two thousand troops to "guard" the southern oil fields.[90] Nevertheless, the Iranian government was still unwilling to reverse its neutrality and warned its citizens "not to resist the invaders and to uphold (the country's) neutrality. The government," it warned, "will prosecute those violating the neutrality, confiscate their property, and will punish them by hanging."[91] Turkish forces captured Tabriz in January 1915, only to lose it to Russian forces within two days. The Russians advanced all the way into Ottoman territory, but their advance was halted when Turkey captured the Iranian city of Khorramshahr in autumn 1916.

Turkey's initial successes in northern and western Iran were matched by similar advances made by Germany against British forces in the southern and central parts of the country. German influence grew to unprecedented proportions in several Iranian cities such as Isfahan, Shiraz, Kerman, and Yazd, where British diplomats were either attacked or were driven out.[92] Moreover, Germany enlisted the support of four of Iran's increasingly powerful groups. They included the *ulama*, the Democrat (*Dimukrat-ha*) members of the Majles, leaders of the Ashayeri tribe, and the Swedish-officered Gendarmes.[93] The *ulama* and the Democrats supported Germany as an alternative to Britain, while the Ashayeris hoped to use Germany as a counterbalance to the close links between Britain and the Bakhtiari tribe. For their part, the Democrats supported Germany because they believed that Germany would win the war and would emerge as a major global power afterward.[94]

Germany's influence in southern Iran was not lasting and Britain soon regained its pre-war dominance. In January 1916, Britain organized the South Persia Rifles and used them along with its own troops based in Basra to capture one German military stronghold after another. By early 1917, Britain controlled most of southern and central Iran except the mountainous regions near Shiraz and Bushehr, controlled by the Ashayeri tribe. This domination was completed by 1918. With Turkey's defeat in 1917 and Russia's withdrawal from the war after the October Revolution, both armies pulled out of Iran.[95]

The war in Iran ended, but occupation did not. Still fearful of an invasion of India by the Axis powers, Britain extended its occupation into northern Iran in 1918, capturing Mashhad in the northeast in March and Tabriz in the northwest in May. Britain's military presence in Iran was formalized the following year with the signing of the Anglo-Persian agreement. This agreement gave Britain the right to reform the Iranian army and to supply it with modern ammunition, construct a railway in Iran, and reform the customs system. The agreement also guaranteed the provision of a British loan to the Iranian government for financing the terms of the agreement. Immediately after the agreement was signed, Iran's prime minister and the minister of finance each received 250,000 tumon in bribes.[96] World War I ended in 1919, but British forces remained in Iran until 1921 and Britain's influence over the country's politics and economy continued to be paramount for decades to come.

REVOLUTION

The muted evolution of a national political structure under the Qajars was matched by a growth in the level of national consciousness and a growing sense of national identity by large segments of the Iranian population. The overall transformation of the country from a largely tribal territory into a unified and centrally controlled kingdom was accompanied by a growing sense of national consciousness among the kingdom's subjects and by the gradual formation of political sentiments such as nationalism and democracy. Nationalism, admittedly, was a late development in the Qajar era. Demands for democratic rule appeared even later.[97] Both did appear, however, directly as a result of the experiences that the country had undergone during the Qajar era. Along with political autocracy and foreign intervention, revolutions and political crises became the cornerstone of Qajar rule. The Constitutional Revolution was the first revolution of its kind to occur in modern Iranian history. It was directed at curbing the autocratic and arbitrary powers of the Qajar court and sought to bring the affairs of the government under the supervision of an elected parliament, the Majles.

The Timing of the Constitutional Revolution

The question of why the Constitutional Revolution appeared when it did is a perplexin one. There were two fundamental reasons for the appearance of the constitutional movement and eventually the Constitutional Revolution. One was the slow yet steady decline in the powers of Qajar shahs and the progressive decay of political institutions by the late nineteenth century, especially after the death of Naser al-Din Shah. This reduction in the ability of the political elite to adequately govern the country and to maintain a solid hold over the reins of government unleashed forces which were capable of initiating a revolutionary movement.

Secondly, because of the inability of the government to fully enforce its control over society, various opposition groups appeared and began to initiate measures against the regime. These groups included the *ulama*, merchants and traders, and the newly emerging class of intellectuals, the educated elite. The activities of these three groups, their ideologies, their popular appeal, and their political maneuvers were, in the meanwhile, greatly strengthened by the prevailing social and cultural environment that had emerged during the preceding decades. The *ulama* and the merchants had emerged as defenders of Iran's national interests because of their opposition to the Reuter and Tobacco Concessions. Although both groups had opposed the concessions in order to protect their own social and economic interests, their actions made them appear as the defenders of the country's sovereignty, an impression popularized by their vociferous propaganda. The economic nationalism that was generated by the uproar over these concessions added much to the influence and the prestige of the *ulama* and the merchants among the population. At the same time, the modernizing efforts of Amir Kabir and Mirza Hussein Khan had resulted in the appearance of a small number of intellectuals who also wished to put an end to Qajar autocracy and wanted to establish a democracy similar to the one in England.

The increasing contacts between Iran and the West after the 1870s, along with the growth in the number of secular schools and intellectuals, also resulted in a proliferation of intellectual activity before the Constitutional Revolution that eventually contributed to its occurrence. Significantly, all of these developments took place in a political setting that was still predominantly tribal, and tribalism subsequently assumed great importance in the Constitutional Revolution.

It is important to keep in mind that the movement to limit the shah's powers through revolutionary means developed only after the reforms attempted by members of the political establishment failed. Political change under the Qajars took place in two distinguishable phases. Initially, attempts were made to change the political system from within the bureaucracy, as the tenures in office of Amir Kabir, Mirza Hussein Khan, and Amin al-Dowleh represented. These figures tried to make the government machinery more efficient by centralizing the shah's powers and limiting the excesses of the court. Even the emerging cadre of intellectuals, few as they were, sought merely to centralize the shah's powers and to make the government more responsive to the wishes of the people.

The most notable intellectual of this time was a career diplomat named Mirza Malkom Khan. In two important political treatises, Malkom expounded on the structure of an ideal political system for Iran. In both of these writings, entitled *Sheykh va Vazir* (The Shah and the

Minister) and *Ketabche-ye Gheybi* (Invisible Notebook), he advocated
the necessity of implementing reforms, which in the context of the time
meant first and foremost political centralisation and efficiency.[98] "The
organization of the government of the Persia," he is quoted as having
written, "shall be based on absolute monarchy."[99] It was only after it
became evident that these high-ranking officials were trying to reform
the system in vain that a revolutionary movement emerged. In fact, the
frustration of efforts by individuals like Malkom and by other
enlightened bureaucrats might well have been the catalyst for the
Constitutional Revolution.

In 1860, Malkom established a secret society named the
Faramushkhaneh (House of Forgetfulness). The secretive nature of the
society and the elitism of its members prompted many to view it as a
masonic lodge. Many of the members of the secret society were in fact
members in European masonic lodges.[100] However, the
Faramushkhaneh had no formal links with the Freemasonry and was
only intended to be a nucleus around which influential and like-minded
reformists gathered. Political discussions and the exchange of new
ideas were the main activities of the society's members.[101] Naser
al-Din Shah is said to have known about the *Faramushkhaneh* and to
have acquiesced in its existence at first. But, like most other activities
not under his direct control, he soon became suspicious, banning the
society in 1861 and sending Malkom to exile.[102] Two similar "gathering
places" are also said to have been active around this time, one called
the *Majma'e Adamiyat* (Gathering of Humanity) and the other *Jame'h
Adamiyat* (Society of Humanity). Neither had any ties with Malkom
and there is no reason to believe that either of them outlasted the
Faramushkhaneh.[103]

Despite the lack of lasting success by the "secret societies," a
general "awakening," a flurry of intellectual discussion and activity,
began to develop around this time. Members of the *Faramushkhaneh*
and other similar organizations did not adhere to a single and coherent
political ideology. In the late 1890s and the early 1900s, concepts such
as "society," "governance," "sovereignty," and "universal suffrage"
began to be discussed and debated for the first time among a small but
enthusiastic army of intellectuals. Most intellectuals were,
nevertheless, influenced by ideas concerning parliamentarianism and by
the writings of French philosophers.[104] A few notable figures, among
them the historian Ali Akbar Dehkhoda, also became attracted to
socialist ideas and began popularising notions such as "mass strike" and
"scientific socialism".[105]

Yet by far the most dominant doctrine in the Constitutional
Revolution was not a specific ideology but a driving sense of
nationalism fostered after decades of foreign economic and political

domination. The revolution was not viewed as just a movement aimed at curbing the despotism of the monarch; it was seen, rather, as a mechanism through which the overwhelming domination of the country by outside powers could be brought to a lasting end. This sense of nationalism was given much strength and forcefulness when the two groups whose interests were most hurt by foreign intrusion, the *ulama* and the merchants, emerged as the leading cadres of the movement.106

Political associations called *Anjomans* (Societies) had sprung up soon after Naser al-Din Shah's death in 1896. While the *Faramushkhaneh* itself was never revived, it did serve as a model after which the *Anjomans* were based. Spread throughout the country, the *Anjomans* regarded their task as enlightening the people and informing them of the evils of despotism. It was in one of these *Anjomans*, the *Anjoman-e Makhfi* (Secret Society), that a group of intellectuals and clerics decided in February 1905 to launch a nonviolent campaign to end despotism and foreign intervention.107 A month later, Tehran's two leading clerics took refuge (*bast*) in a nearby shrine in protest over the absence of freedom and against royal despotism. While there is no evidence to suggest that the two clerics were members of the *Anjoman-e Makhfi*, it is obvious that they began their protest against the government at the behest of the organization. Considerable excitement was generated throughout the country by this symbolic act of defiance and protest. A number of other events occurred, meanwhile, which heightened popular discontent and precipitated incidents of violence directed against the government. Thus evolved the Constitutional Revolution.

1905: The Involvement of the *Ulama*

Different historians have designated different dates as the starting point of the Constitutional Revolution. Ahmad Kasravi, one of Iran's most notable historians and an authority on the history of the revolution, has declared March 1905 as the revolution's starting point. In that month, the two leading *ulama* of Tehran, Ayatollahs Behbahani and Tabatabai, decided to join forces and to unite their efforts in opposing the policies of the notorious Prime Minister Ayn al-Dowleh.108 A third leading member of the *ulama* in Tehran, Fazlullah Nuri, was left out of the alliance because of his pro-court sympathies and later became one of the main opponents of the constitutional movement. Behbahani and Tabatabai soon began to attract the support of many of Tehran's merchants, who were also dissatisfied with the numerous commercial benefits that Naser al-Din Shah and his premiers had granted to foreign entrepreneurs. With the financial backing of the merchants, the two clerics soon began a movement that changed the very nature of Qajar rule.

The two *ulama* at first expressed their opposition to the court by moving out of the capital as a symbolic gesture and took refuge in a mosque in one of the city's suburbs. Although the move was merely a symbolic act, it was an enormously effective and unprecedented display of discontent against the court by highly influential figures. Tehran's merchants, who had always been responsive to the wishes of the *ulama* in order to maintain their mutually beneficial relationship, closed down their shops and the Bazaar as a show of solidarity, signifying a further act of defiance against the royal court.[109] From the mosque they were in, the *ulama* presented a list of demands to the shah in which they asked for the removal of corrupt and notorious government officials, administrative and bureaucratic reforms, and the establishment of a "House of Justice" (*Edalat Khaneh*). Although the idea of a parliament was at the time not widely held yet, it later grew out of the notion of "House of Justice." Amid much public excitement and anticipation, the Shah accepted the demands of the two *ulama* and promised their swift implementation. A royal carriage was sent to pick up the two clerics, who returned to the capital amid massive popular celebrations.

While the shah at first acceded to the demands of the two *ulama*, it gradually became evident that he was less than enthusiastic in implementing the reforms he had promised and in establishing a House of Justice. Sentiments against the regime and especially against the shah flared once again throughout the country. In Tehran, clandestine leaflets, called Night Letters (*Shab-nameh*), began to be distributed by the *Anjomans* and were posted throughout the city's walls, calling for reforms and an end to absolutism. It was in these Night Letters that the words House of Justice (*Edalat Khaneh*) and parliament (*Majles*) began to be used interchangeably.[110]

In order to appease the public, the Prime Minister continued to issue a string of empty promises. He was to some extent successful in quieting the disturbances, but only temporarily. Ayatollah Tabatabai, for his part, wrote a letter to the Shah complaining about the state of the country and warned that if a Majles were not established "the monarchy will be on the verge of collapse."[111] But the letter was never passed on to the Shah by his ministers and the shah's failure to respond prompted the two *ulama* to leave Tehran again, this time taking sanctuary in the shrine city of Qom. In their support, a number of merchants and Bazaaris in Tehran took sanctuary at the British embassy.

Although taking sanctuary in mosques and in government offices had traditionally been practiced by felons and by those opposing the regime, taking sanctuary in a foreign embassy, particularly that of the

British, was considered to be a serious blow and a source of embarrassment for the government. While the number of protesting merchants who took refuge in the British embassy is not exactly known, one estimate puts the figure at 13,000.[112] The decision of the British Foreign Office to allow the demonstrating merchants into its embassy grounds, meanwhile, demonstrated Britain's approval of the establishment of a less autocratic regime Iran.

Finding himself under increasing pressure from the *ulama* and the *Bazaari* merchants, Muzzafaral-Din Shah agreed to meet all of their demands and initiated a series of conciliatory measures. The principal demand of the revolutionaries had by now become the removal of the reactionary Prime Minister Ayn al-Dowleh and the establishment of a Majles. The Shah twice sent an envoy to Qom to convince the two *ulama* to come back to the capital but in both instances they refused to do so until their demands were fully met. The shah finally relented, and on 15 January 1906 issued a decree calling for the establishment of a Majles. Tehran and other cities erupted in joyful celebrations upon receipt of the news of the granting of the Constitutional Decree (*Farman-e Mashruteh*). The two clerics returned to Tehran and, for some time at least, it seemed as if the revolutionary movement had achieved its main objectives.

The Battle for the Majles

As in previous occasions, however, Muzzafar al-Din Shah's promises were not fulfilled. The Shah himself wanted to see a Majles instituted, but he was gravely ill and his wishes were not carried out by subordinates anxious to preserve their own privileges. The issuing of the Constitutional Decree soon turned out to be only the start of a long battle over obtaining a parliamentary government. With no concrete plans in sight for the inauguration of a Majles and the election of its deputies, political unrest soon erupted again, though this time in the important city of Tabriz.

For some time, conditions in Tabriz had been ripe for political unrest, where a number of sectarian clashes had previously occurred between the Shi'ite Tabrizis, the Sunni Kurds, and the Christian Armenians. Also, the governor of Tabriz, who was also the heir-apparent to the throne, Mohammad Ali Mirza, was highly despotic and had continually aroused the anger of the politically-minded Tabrizis. The extensive commercial links between the city and the Ottoman and the Russian empires had also strengthened Tabriz's merchant classes and had made them particularly resentful of Qajar autocracy.

Early in autumn 1906, Tabrizi merchants closed down their shops as a gesture of protest over the absence of real progress concerning the Majles and many of them took refuge in the British consulate.[113] The shah finally relented and instructions were cabled to all cities regarding the holding of local elections. There were huge celebrations in Tabriz, but once again they proved to be premature. Muzzafar al-Din Shah died on 4 January 1907 and his son, Mohammad Ali, was enthroned a few days later. Although the new shah had reputedly signed the Constitutional Decree along with his father and had taken an oath of loyalty to the new order, he made no secret about his dislike for the Majles as soon as he was crowned.

Majles deputies had in the meanwhile become deeply divided between those who favored secular laws and the drafting of a modern constitution, called the Constitutionalists (*Mashruteh khahan*), and those who wished to see a religiously-based consultative body, called the Religionists (*Mashrueh khahan*). Although both Behbahani and Tabatabai supported the Constitutionalists, Fazlullah Nuri was a staunch supporter of the Religionists and did much to accentuate the cleavage between the two camps. He maintained that constitutional government had no basis in *shari'a* law and defied divine authority.[114] Instead, he argued, Iran needed a political order that was both constitutional and religious, a *mashrute-ye mashrueh*.[115] He particularly objected to two provisions in the constitution, namely compulsory education, which he believed would inculcate children with the corrupt values of the West, and the declaration of equality among all Iranians regardless of their religion.[116]

Nuri's arguments gave direction to a general skepticism that a growing number of clerics were expressing toward the constitutional order. His esteemed position within the clerical establishment prompted many commoners and other clerics to support his claims. The financial reforms that the Majles was trying to implement were also turning many clerics against the new order.[117] These disagreements were in turn reflected in the Majles, which rendered the body highly ineffectual and indecisive and at the same time aroused considerable public doubt over the viability of a parliamentary system. With the Majles unable to govern and the new Shah impervious to the state of affairs, insecurity and fear prevailed over most of the country. It was within this context that the first *coup d'etat* against the Majles took place on 15 December 1907.

In an attempt to overthrow the Majles, the shah summoned the cabinet to his palace and chained and imprisoned the prime minister. He also dispatched troops to surround the parliament building, but gave them orders not to attack the Majles and the deputies. The news of the unfolding coup soon spread to other cities and many people in Tehran gathered in front of the parliament building in order to show their support for the constitution. Sensing danger to his throne and worried by the unexpected reaction of the people, the Shah soon abandoned his efforts, but only temporarily. He tried to overthrow the Majles once again on 23 June 1908, this time successfully.

Although many deputies had tried to improve the relations between the Majles and the court, Mohammad Ali Shah was determined to overthrow the Majles and to crush the fledgling parliamentary system. In early June, he suddenly left Tehran for one of the palaces located in the outskirts of the city. But soldiers soon occupied government buildings and a large number of Cossack troops began to collect under the command of Colonel Liakhoff. The shah declared martial law in Tehran and put Liakhoff in charge of its enforcement. The Colonel and his troops, acting on the orders of the Shah, surrounded the parliament building on 23 June and opened fire on the Majles building and its deputies. Many of the deputies and those who had gathered in their support fled while many others, the two *ulama* among them, were arrested. A number of people were also killed. Liakhoff was installed as the military commander of Tehran and many Constitutionalist leaders were harassed and their houses looted.

Although Mohammad Ali Shah's second coup was successful in suppressing the constitutional order in the capital city, it did not have the same success in most provincial towns, especially in Tabriz and Isfahan. The very day the parliament building was being bombarded in Tehran, irregular militia began taking up arms in Tabriz in an attempt to march to Tehran to force the shah to re-institute the Majles. After some fighting between the militia and loyalist troops, Tabriz fell to the revolutionaries, who were under the command of Sattar Khan. Although the city was taken by the revolutionaries, government troops laid siege to it for a number of months. Starvation and disease spread, resulting in countless deaths. The blockade was finally lifted when Russian troops marched into Tabriz in April, but their rapacious behavior caused as much anguish as the city's siege.

The resistance in Tabriz was only a more dramatic example of similar events taking place in other provincial towns where riots and anti-government revolts had also erupted. Soon the tribal fabric of Qajar rule began to come undue. The Bakhtiari tribe staged a revolt in Isfahan in January 1909. Sporadic and unorganized revolts also occurred in Rasht in February; in Shiraz, Hamedan, Bandar Abbas, and Bushehr in March; and in Mashhad in April. The unrest in Tabriz and Isfahan were, however, by far the most threatening to the government. In Isfahan, leaders of the Bakhtiari tribe assembled some 1,000 tribesmen and after capturing the city began to march north toward Tehran. A similar march was undertaken from the northern city of Rasht, where a group of irregular militia called the *Mujahedeen* had attacked the governor's residence and had captured the city. Joined by the militia who had been holding Tabriz, the *Mujahedeen* also began to march toward the capital. The two rebel armies of southern Bakhtiaris and northern *Mujahedeen* established contacts and decided to combine forces by marching into Tehran simultaneously.

On 23 June the Bakhtiaris marched into Qom and from there on to Karaj, a town only a few miles west of the capital. There they were joined by the *Mujahedeen* and readied themselves for battle against government forces. Through Russian and British diplomats, the leaders of the two armies presented a list of demands to the shah. Their demands included the re-establishment of the Majles, the withdrawal of all foreign troops from Iran, and the disarming of the shah's own irregular army. When the demands of the revolutionaries were not met, the leader of the *Mujahedeen*, Sepahdar A'zam, and some of his soldiers slipped through the Royalist line at night and secretly entered Tehran. Fighting erupted in the city and the next day the leader of the Bakhtiaris, Sardar Asad, also entered the capital. The fighting in Tehran lasted for only a few days, and Mohammad Ali Shah and some 500 of his soldiers took refuge in the Russian Embassy on 16 July 1909.

On the same day, the shah formally abdicated the throne. His twelve-year-old son, Ahmad, was formally crowned two days later and the regency went to a Qajar elder. Liakhoff, who had been fighting for the shah up until then, formally accepted service under the new government that was subsequently set up by the revolutionaries. The leader of the Bakhtiari army, Sardar Asad, became the acting prime minister and Sepahdar A'zam, leader of the *Mujahedeen*, became the minister of war. The constitutional order was once again re-instituted and the Second Majles was inaugurated in November. Some four years after it had started, the Constitutional Revolution had acheived a victorious end.

Notes

1. Ann Lambton, *Qajar Persia* (London: I. B. Tauris, 1987), p. 87.

2. Ibid, pp. 321-322.

3. Ibid, p. 15.

4. Percy Sykes, *A History of Persia*, Vol. II (London: Macmillan & Co., 1930), p. 295.

5. Amineh Pakravan, *Agha Mohammad Ghadjar*, J. Afkaari, trans. (Tehran: de l'Institut France-Iranien, 1953), pp. 214-215.

6. Ibid, p. 220.

7. Robert Grant Watson, *A History of Persia* (London: Smith, Elder, 1866), p. 83.

8. See Ahmad Mirza Azzud al-Dowleh, *Tarikh Azzudi* (Azzudi History) (Tehran: n.p., 1327/1948), pp. 23-25.

9. Lambton, *Qajar Persia*, p. 15.

10. Abdollah Mostoufi, *Tarikh-e Edari va Ejitemai-ye Qajar Ya Sharh-e Zendegani-ye Man*, vol. I (Social and Administrative History of the Qajara or My Autobiography) (Tehran: Zavvar, n.d.), p. 12.

11. Lambton, *Qajar Persia*, p. 14.

12. Watson, *A History of Persia*, pp. 114.

13. Sykes, *A History of Persia, pp. 314, 320*.

14. Ibid, p. 325.

15. Lambton, *Qajar Persia*, p. 96.

16. Ibid, p. 13.

17. Colin Meredith, *The Qajar Response to Russia's Military Challenge, 1804-28*, PhD Dissertation, Princeton University, 1973, p. 47.

18. Ibid, p. 48.

19. Lambton, *Qajar Persia*, p. 24.

20. For Amir Kabir's life and early political career, see Fereidoun Adamiyat, *Amir Kabir va Iran* (Amir Kabir and Iran) (Tehran: Pirouz, 1334/1955), pp. 13-35.

21. Ibid, p. 63.

22. Majid Yektaii, *Tarikh-e Edari Iran* (Administrative History of Iran) (Tehran: Pirouz, 1340/1961), p. 25.

23. Adamiyat, *Amir Kabir*, p. 67.

24. Shaul Bakhash, *Iran: Monarchy, Bureaucracy, and Reform under the Qajars: 1858-1896* (London: Ithaca Press, 1978), p. 78.

25. Ibid, p. 77.

26. Guity Neshat, *The Origins of Modern Reforms in Iran* (New York: Praeger, 1984), p. 43. For a detailed discussion of the *urf* and the *shari'a* laws see Willem Floor, "Change and Development in the Judicial Sytem of Qajar Iran (1800-1925)," Edmund Bosworth and Carol Hillenbrand, eds., *Qajar Iran: Political, Social, and Cultural Change 1800-1925* (Edinburgh: Edinburgh University Press, 1983), pp. 113-147.

27. Neshat, *The Origins of Modern Reform in Iran*, p. 55.

28. Ibid, p. 70.

29. Ibid, p. 79-80.

30. Bakhash, *Iran: Monarchy, Bureaucracy, and Reform under the Qajars*, p. 82.

31. Neshat, *The Origins of Modern Reform in Iran*, pp. 118-120.

32. Bakhash, *Iran: Monarchy, Bureaucracy, and Reform under the Qajars*, p. 113.

33. Ibid, p. 90.

34. Neshat, *The Origins of Modern Reforms in Iran*, p. 137.

35. Bakhash, *Iran: Monarchy, Bureaucracy, and Reform under the Qajars*, p. 113.

36. Ibid, p. 118.

37. Ibid, p. 176.

38. Ehsan Yarshater, "Observations on Nasir al-Din Shah," Bosworth and Hillenbrand, eds., *Qajar Iran*, p. 7.

39. Bakhash, *Iran: Monarchy, Bureaucracy, and Reform under the Qajars*, p. 263.

40. See Hassan Gol Mohammady, *Divan-e Nasir al-Din Shah* (Nasir al-Din Shah's Poems) (Tehran: Pasand, 1363/1984).

41. Bakhash, *Iran: Monarchy, Bureaucracy, and Reforms under the Qajars*, p. 279.

42. Ibid, p. 287.

43. Sykes, *A History of Persia*, p. 374.

44. Ahmad Kasravi, *Tarikh-e Mashruteh-e Iran* (History of Iran's Constitutionalism) (Tehran: n.p., n.d.), p. 23.

45. Bkhash, "The Failure of Reform: The Prime Ministership of Amin al-Dawleh, 1987-8," Bosworth and Hillenbrand, eds., *Qajar Iran*, p. 20.

46. Ibid, p. 25.

47. Ibid, p. 28.

48. Sykes, *A History of Persia*, p. 406.

49. Peter Avery, *Moderrn Iran* (London: Ernest Benn, 1965), p. 128.

50. Edward Browne, *The Persian Revolution of 1905-1909* (Cambridge: Cambridge University Press, 1910), p. 170.

51. Avery, *Modern Iran*, p. 133.

52. Rouhollah Ramazani, *The Foreign Policy of Iran: 1500-1941* (Charlottesville, VA: University Press of Virginia, 1966), p. 95.

53. Sykes, *A History of Persia*, pp. 409-410.

54. Avery, *Modern Iran*, p. 135.

55. Ramazani, *The Foreign Policy of Iran*, p. 39.

56. Lambton, *Qajar Persia*, p. 53.

57. Ibid, p. 100.

58. Ibid, p. 43.

59. Khan Baba Bayani, *Siyasat-e Napoleon dar Iran dar Zaman-e Fath Ali Shah* (Napoleon's Policy in Iran During Fath Ali Shah's Era) (Tehran: Chapp-e Ketab, 1318/1939), p. 4.

60. Ramazani, *The Foreign Policy of Iran*, p. 39.

61. Meredith, *The Qajar Response to Russian Military Challenge*, p. 92.

62. Ramazani, *The Foreign Policy of Iran*, p. 45-46.

63. Ibid, pp. 46-47.

64. Ibid, p. 74.

65. Sykes, *A History of Persia*, p. 332.

66. Ramazani, *The Foreign Policy of Iran*, p. 67.

67. Ibid, p. 49.

68. Ibid, p. 66.

69. Ibid, p. 66-67.

70. Hamid Algar, *Religion and State in Iran, 1785-1906* (Berkeley: University of California Press, 1969), p. 176.

71. Ramazani, *The Foreign Policy of Iran*, p. 67.

72. Ibid, p. 68.

73. Ibid.

74. Ibid, p. 70.

75. Ibid, p. 69.

76. Bakhash, *Iran: Monarchy, Bureaucracy, and Reform under the Qajars*, p. 243.

77. Ramazani, *The Foreign Policy of Iran*, p. 70.

78. Ibid, p. 71.

79. Ibid.

80. Ishtiaq Ahmad, *Anglo-Iranian Relations, 1905-1919* (Bombay: Asia Publishing House, 1975), p. 45.

81. Ibid, p. 39.

82. Ibid, p. 42.

83. Ibid, pp. 48-49.

84. Ibid, p. 49.

85. For terms of the agreement, see Ramazani, *The Foreign Policy of Iran*, pp. 93-94.

86. Ibid, p. 105.

87. Mohammad A. Mahid, *Pazhuheshi dar Tarikh-e Diplomacy Iran*, p. 311.

88. Ibid, p. 307.

89. George Lenczowski, "Forewign Powers' Intervention in Iran During World War I," Bosworth and Hillenbrand, eds., *Qajar Iran*, p. 77.

90. Mahid, *Pazhuheshi dar Tarikh-e Diplomacy Iran*, p. 311.

91. L. Mirashinkoff, *Iran dar Jang Avval Jahani* (Iran in the First World War), A. Dokhaniati, trans. (Tehran: Farzaneh, 1357/1978), p. 43.

92. Avery, *Modern Iran*, p. 101.

93. Lenczowski, "Foreign Powers' Intervention in Iran During World War I," Bosworth and Hillenbrand, eds., *Qajar Iran*, pp. 81-82.

94. Avery, *Modern Iran*, p. 191.

95. Mahid, *Pazhuheshi dar Tarikh-e Diplomacy Iran*, p. 318.

96. Ahmad, *Anglo-Iranian Relations*, p. 318.

97. Richard Cottham, *Nationalism in Iran* (Pittsburgh: University of Pittsburgh Press, 1979), p. 11.

98. Hamid Algar, *Mirza Malkum Khan* (Berkeley, CA: University of California Press, 1973), pp. 93-94.

99. Quoted in Bakhash, *Iran: Monarchy, Bureaucracy, and Reform under the Qajars*, p. 10.

100. Ismail Raeen, *Anjoman-haye Serri dar Enghelab-e Mashruteh Iran* (Secret Societies in Iran's Constitutional Revolution) (Tehran: Javidan, 2535/1978), p. 43.

101. Bakhash, *Iran: Monarchy, Bureaucracy, and Reform under the Qajars*, pp. 17-18.

102. Ibid, p. 20.

103. Ismail Raeen, *Faramushkhaneh va Feramasonry dar Iran* (Faramushkhaneh and Freemasonry in Iran) (Tehran: Amir Kabir, 1357/1978), p. 629.

104. Fereidoun Adamiyat, *Ideolozhi-ye Nehzat-e Mashrute'h Iran* (Ideology of Iran's Constitutional Movement) (Tehran: Payam, 1355/1976), p. 206.

105. Ibid, p. 270.

106. Algar, *Religion and State in Iran, 1785-1906*, p. 242.

107. Lambton, *Qajar Persia*, p. 283.

108. Kasravi, *Tarikh-e Mashruteh Iran*, pp. 85-86.

109. Lambton, *Qajar Persia*, p. 283.

110. Kasravi, *Tarikh-e Mashruteh Iran*, pp. 85-86.

111. Ibid, p. 110.

112. Ibid, p. 158.

113. Browne, *The Persian Revolution of 1905-1909*, pp. 217, 280.

114. V. A. Martin, "The Anit-Constitutional Arguements of Shaikh Fazlallah Nuri," *Middle Eastern Studies* vol. 22, no. 2 (April 1986), p. 183.

115. Ibid, p. 184.

116. Ibid, pp. 186-187.

117. Said Amir Arjoman, "The Ulama's Traditionalist Opposition to Parliamentarianism: 1907-1909," *Middle Eastern Studies* vol. 17, no. 2 (April 1981), p. 180.

3

The Pahlavi Dynasty

The Pahlavi era marked the establishment of a highly differentiated and structurally strong political system in Iran. Under the Pahlavis, Iran became a transitional society, socially and economically as well as politically. Both Pahlavi monarchs engaged in the construction of a solid and comparatively modern state and embarked on a rapid and intense course of modernization. This process was achieved through reinforcing national unification and by establishing modern armed forces. Both shahs succeeded not only in tearing down the old order and establishing a new one, but also in enabling the country to launch primary capitalist production and accumulation, and later in acquiring somewhat of an industrial infrastructure, which had been non-existent.

Nation-building in the Pahlavi era occurred in two historically distinct phases. Initially, during Reza Shah's reign between 1921 and 1941, most of the basic institutions needed for the elementary needs of society were established and put to work. Reza Shah did not so much establish these institutions as he secularized existing ones by transferring their control from the *ulama* to the state, a task in which he often used brutal tactics. During the reign of the second Pahlavi shah, Mohammad Reza, most existing political institutions were made more efficient and modern, and the foundations of the regime were strengthened. However, at the same time as it was reaching the height of power, the state was steadily undergoing atrophy and by the late 1970s died a speedy death.

The political history of Iran continued to embody the three dominant characteristics of autocracy, foreign intervention and dominance, and revolution during the Pahlavi era. In a number of ways, the Pahlavi period was a much more intense and concentrated version of the Qajar era. A number of significant comparisons can be made between the two periods. It has been argued that Reza Shah's twenty-year reign was itself a prolonged revolution, particularly in light of the dramatic changes that he implemented in Iranian politics and society.[1]

However, the basic format of political institutions changed little, although considerable quantitative changes did in fact appear in the bureaucracy and in the economic powers of the state under the Pahlavis. The essentially patrimonial nature of the political system was not altered but rather modernized. Under both the Qajars and the Pahlavis, the political system was composed of an absolutist monarch supported by an array of military and bureaucratic institutions. Under the Qajars, such institutions were primarily made up of the shah's inner circle of ministers and courtiers, an incipient administrative network, and military forces supplied by the different tribes in addition to those under the control of the central government. The institutions on which the Pahlavis based their power were not very different in structure, and only the degree of their efficiency and power varied from those of the Qajars. The bureaucracy, the military, and the royal court continued to function as the primary pillars of the Pahlavi dynasty. Moreover, both the Qajars and the Pahlavis sought to gain popular legitimacy for their narrowly-based monarchies through resorting to tenets embedded in Iran's cultural tradition and heritage: the Qajar shahs continued to portray themselves as the "Shadow of God" on earth, as most Iranian rulers before them had done, while the Pahlavis tried to legitimise their rule by reviving the memory and the splendour of Iran's pre-Islamic past. Despite such efforts, however, neither of the dynasties ever gained widespread legitimacy and continued to survive by relying on patrimonial tribal and kinship loyalties.

Although the Pahlavis succeeded in establishing a state that was politically stronger than that of the Qajars, they were even less successful in obtaining the legitimacy and national acceptance that the Qajars had acquired through their long rule. This failure by the Pahlavis was due largely to the relatively short period in which they tried to nationalize their dynasty, especially in comparison with the Qajars' 140 year reign. Also, neither of the two Pahlavi shahs were ever able to give credence to their claim of divine kingship.[2] While both Reza Shah and his son Mohammed Reza tried ceaselessly to transform their family into a national dynasty, the Pahlavis never became a popular monarchy and their reign rested primarily on the rule of force rather than on popular acceptance and consensus. The Qajars, on the other hand, were never challenged as a dynasty, although each individual Qajar shah at one point or another faced serious rebellions either within his own tribe or by other tribal chieftains.

Another similarity between the Pahlavis and the Qajars was in their efforts to modernize the country socially and economically but not necessarily politically. Admittedly, socio-cultural and industrial modernization was not pursued by the Qajars with any degree of regularity, and occurred only sporadically under Naser al-Din Shah and during the Constitutional Revolution. The Pahlavis, on the other hand, consistently sought to modernize the country's industrial infrastructure and its culture. Yet both dynasties made certain that their reforms and modernizing efforts did not extend into the political realm and that the basic political structure remained unaltered. This lack of political flexibility on the part of both regimes undermined their ability to rectify the numerous systemic shortcomings that were built into the system. Unable to cope with major crises, both systems collapsed when faced with major challenges.

The three recurrent features of Iran's political history--autocracy, foreign intervention, and revolution--marked almost all stages of the Pahlavi era. Under Reza Shah, there was a conspicuous absence of revolutionary upheavals, although there were several regional challenges to the authority of the central government. Revolutionary circumstances did not develop during Reza Shah's reign because the regime initially courted the support of those groups who could form potential blocks of opposition and suppressed them when it no longer needed their support. But even despite the nonexistence of anti-regime uprisings in the first half of the Pahlavi era, foreign intervention and political autocracy were paramount. The largely personal despotism and arbitrary conduct of Qajar officials was replaced by a more systemic institutionalization of political power under the Pahlavis. Instead of emanating from individual political figures, as had been the case with Qajar officials, political power and authority were built into the Pahlavi system and were exercised in a less arbitrary manner than had been the case under the Qajars. Both Pahlavi shahs, nevertheless, continued to be central to the survival of the system that they had established. The longevity of their dynasty thus depended directly upon their continued personal activities and supervision. Foreign interference in the internal affairs of the country also persisted during the Pahlavi era. In certain periods, in fact, outside powers exercised as much dominance over the Pahlavis as they had done over the Qajars.

By the early 1900s, the Qajar dynasty had fallen into ruins and with it the country. Mohammad Ali Shah's repeated efforts to regain the monarchy, supported and encouraged by both Russia and Britain, and the subsequent demands for reparations for his futile venture, had left the country's already depleted treasury in need of even more foreign loans. Political inexperience, and factional and tribal sectarianism, had torn apart the once-united Majles and had rendered it ineffective as a viable political and administrative apparatus.[3] Russian plunders in the north and especially in Tabriz, tribal infighting in the south and south-central areas, and hunger, disease, and strife throughout the country had replaced what only a few years before had been hopes for a better future and a revolution aimed at improving the lives of the citizenry. For his part, the young and timid Ahmad Shah was frightened of the Bolshevik threat that was overpowering the Tzar in the north and feared that the same fate would entangle him.[4] He thus spent much time outside of the country and paid little attention to its affairs.

Within such a context, four potential sources of power existed at the time. First, there was the political establishment itself, composed of an incompetent and factionally torn Majles and an ineffectual Shah. There was also a growing minority of nationalist intellectuals and courtiers, mostly Anglophile in orientation but generally unhurried in pursuing reforms. Third, there were the *ulama*, particularly those who had gained popularity because of their support for the constitutional movement. Since notable clerics like Sheikh Fazlullah Nuri had vehemently opposed the Constitutional Revolution, however, the clerical establishment in general had lost much of it popularity and influence after the capture of Tehran by the revolutionaries and many clerics, including former supporters of the Constitution, had become disillusioned and had withdrawn to the sidelines.[5] Lastly there was the army, more a collection of ineffective armed bands rather than disciplined and well-trained troops. The few flares of military efficiency that did appear did so in troops under foreign command. The British commanded and controlled the South Persia Rifles, set up in the southern regions to combat the area's pro-German tribes; the Gendarmes were under the control of Swedish officers; and the much despised Cossack brigades were mostly Russian-controlled and obeyed Colonel Liakhoff.

AUTOCRACY

In February 1921, the commander of Cossack troops based in Qazvin, Reza Khan, launched a coup by marching his troops toward the capital. On his way to Tehran, he met with a well-known journalist named Seyyed Zia al-Din Tabatabai in Karaj and the two decided to collaborate together in their efforts to improve the country's conditions. Seyyed Zia, who at one point served as Iran's ambassador to the Ottoman Empire, was known for his nationalist and progressive sentiments. Together, Reza Khan and Seyyed Zia pledged to save the country from ruins by serving the people and the shah and by fighting the Bolsheviks. Ahmad Shah, willing to make any concessions necessary to maintain his position, quickly gave in to the coup leaders' demands, appointing Reza Khan as the commander of the army and Seyyed Zia as the prime minister.[6] Fearing further humiliation, the shah left for Europe immediately afterward, content to remain as the country's titular king.

The new cabinet, comprised mostly of nationalist intellectuals of the same persuasion as Seyyed Zia, soon initiated a series of reforms. The prime minister began imposing heavy fines and jail sentences on many Qajar notables known to have accumulated wealth through corruption and other illegal means. Similar to other nationalists before him, he also tried to counter the influence of the two superpowers in Iran by abrogating the Anglo-Persian treaty of 1919 and by trying to augment Iran's ties with the United States. In his efforts to draw Iran closer to the U.S., the prime minister had no more success than the other nationalists before him.[7]

But it soon appeared as if the forging of counter-balancing ties with the United States were not needed. For nearly two decades, it appeared as if the establishment of a new dynasty in Iran had finally put an end to the overt intervention of outside powers in Iranian affairs. It also appeared that the Anglo-Russian domination of Iran was replaced by the establishment of normal and friendly relations between Iran and a number of other Western powers. However, as the Pahlavi dynasty's founder was to painfully discover in 1941, his country was no closer to diplomatic and political independence from the superpowers than it had been under the Qajars.

Reza Khan Takes Power

It did not take long for cracks to appear in the coalition that had brought about the coup and a subtle struggle soon began to develop between Reza Khan and Seyyed Zia. Although at first he did not hold any official cabinet positions, Reza Khan's powers continued to grow because of his efforts to strengthen the army and because of the personal following he was attracting in the process. The army commander's powers grew to such an extent that in April 1921 the prime minister felt compelled to name him as the minster of war.[8] In May, only three months after he had helped launch the coup, Seyyed Zia, seeing his powers increasingly diminished by Reza Khan, left the country for Palestine. Although Reza Khan was left at the helm of power, he did not assume the office of prime minister and instead entrusted it to other politicians whom he practically controlled. The war minister's influence over the cabinet continued to grow, meanwhile, and he subdued his opponents and critics, mostly his former associates, one after another.[9] He further began to cultivate the support of influential figures by setting free most of the wealthy notables whom Seyyed Zia had imprisoned.[10] Having gradually made his existence indispensable to the system, Reza Khan was named prime minister in October 1923 by the shah, who once more left for Europe, allegedly to seek rest and medication for his health.

With his appointment as the prime minister, Reza Khan began exercising a personal autocracy that had not existed since the days of the Constitutional Revolution. He set into motion two processes, one designed to maximize the political, military, and economic powers of the central government, and the other intended to install himself as the ultimate ruler of the country. From the beginning, Reza Khan's powers were virtually unchallenged by Ahmad Shah. In 1923, the prime minister hired an American financial expert, Dr. Arthur Millspaugh, and entrusted him with the task of reforming the country's tax system and giving a measure of order to its finances.[11] The premier himself paid much attention to establishing security and safety in provincial cities and especially in the country's more remote areas. Faced with demands for regional autonomy by the various tribes, he then launched a campaign to re-establish central authority over the tribal areas, personally commanding government troops in battles against the rebellious tribes. In a 1924 campaign against the Lur tribe, he ordered the bombardment of the Luristan region by his newly-established air force. He then won submission first from the Bakhtiaris and later turned southward toward the Mahammareh region, where the local leader, Sheikh Khaz'al, was urging the people to secede from Iran and join the neighboring Arab territories. Having defeated Khaz'al, Reza Khan instituted Farsi as the region's official language, changed its name to Khuzestan, and firmly established central authority over the area and its inhabitants.[12]

Concurrent with these initiatives, the prime minister was engaged in a not-too-subtle effort to undermine Qajar authority and to aggrandize his own powers. Soon after his appointment as the prime minister, Reza Khan began to openly ridicule and discredit members of the Qajar nobility and consistently limited more of their powers and privileges.[13] In 1925, he adopted the last name Pahlavi, the name of Iran's pre-Islamic language, intended to please the nationalist sentiments and to further undermine Qajar popularity. In addition to his support within the army and among reform-minded intellectuals, Reza Khan also began cultivating the backing of the *ulama* and the merchants. His encouragement of the domestic industry and his success in establishing security in most parts of the country won him the support of many merchants. To win over the support of the *ulama*, he also paid homage to religious sites in Iraq after his Khuzestan campaign and frequently invited religious figures to his house in Tehran.[14] Most importantly, Reza Khan refused to declare Iran a republic in the same way as his much-admired counterpart in Turkey had done. The *ulama* feared that a republican government in Iran would be as detrimental to

Islam as it was proving to be in Turkey.[15] Reza Khan was first attracted to the idea of republicanism, but in 1923 declared that after having

> exchanged ideas with the religious authorities, ... we came
> to the conclusion that it would be better for the welfare of
> the country if all effort to promote a republican form of
> government were halted.[16]

These maneuvers resulted in a steady rise in the popularity and powers of Reza Khan while those of other institutions, especially the monarchy, consistently withered. In October 1925 the Majles voted to depose Ahmad Shah, and two months later, on 12 December, by an overwhelming majority, it voted to install Reza Pahlavi as the new Shah. Of the votes cast, 115 were in favor, about thirty delegates abstained, and only four opposed the bill. Thus establishing the Pahlavi dynasty, Reza Shah once again resumed Iran's age-old tradition of monarchical absolutism.

As Reza Khan's subsequent actions were to demonstrate, he was not a religious man by any means and his overtures to the religious establishment early in his reign stemmed from practical political considerations rather than religious convictions. When considered within the broader context of his rise to political power, Reza Khan's initial approach to the *ulama* becomes part of a pattern he utilized in repeated instances on his way toward monarchy. As a Cossack commander, he already had the support and the backing of the country's only viable military unit. He then allied himself with reform-minded intellectuals and veteran politicians of the Constitutional era and gained their support and assistance, only to dispense with them once they were no longer needed. The *ulama* were naturally Reza Khan's next allies. So long as the *ulama* maintained their independence from the state, held onto considerable judicial authority, and enjoyed insurmountable social influence and prestige, their support and acquiescence was essential to the success of any political initiatives. Once Reza Khan had become Reza Shah and no longer needed the *ulama* for granting religious legitimacy to his actions, he began reducing their numerous powers one after another. Whether these shifting and temporary alliances were part of a calculated plan by Reza Khan to reach the throne or were merely prudent measures he took as the opportunity arose is open to debate. What is certain is that he was driven by both personal ambition and by a desire to change his stagnant country.

While autocratic rule was nothing new to Reza Pahlavi, his ascension to kingship gave that practice added weight and new vigor.

Dr. Millspaugh, the American financial advisor hired to inject some order into Iran's financial system, said of the shah:

> He was a creature of primitive instincts, undisciplined by education and experience, surrounded by servile flatterers, advised by the timid and the selfish. He was sincerely and deeply moved by the sorry conditions of his country, conscious of his own strength, and supremely self confidents.[17]

The Shah as Government

The Shah himself soon became the whole system, personally supervising even the most trivial of the government's functions. He concentrated on four areas: building an efficient government machinery and a unified army; obliterating the threat posed to national unity by the different tribes; establishing a new and modern economic infrastructure; and "Persianizing" the Iranian culture along its pre-Islamic lines. In pursuing these goals, he built up a state based on two principal foundations. They included the army, with himself at the helm, and a growing administrative apparatus comprised of numerous bureaus and departments. In order to increase the efficiency of the government and the military, one of the new shah's first acts was to remove the corrupt officials who were left over from the Qajar era.[18] He dealt as ruthlessly with those subordinates found guilty of inadequate performance as he did with those suspected of conspiring against him. Early in his reign, a number of military plots to assassinate him were uncovered and their perpetrators were harshly punished.[19]

The shah, a career military officer all of his adult life, was a reserved man, rather isolated, and unable to confide in others. Like his son years after him, he believed that only through his direct, personal control over the political process would the country be saved from chaos and from lapsing into communism, which was then seen as a momentous force poised to spread well beyond the Soviet Union's borders.[20] Reza Shah viewed this form of authoritarianism as necessary not only in terms of maintaining a strong personal hold over the reins of power, but also in the effective imposition of central government authority over the entire society.

To this end, he strove ceaselessly to make the two potential sources of opposition to the central government, the religious classes and the tribes, completely subservient to the government. The religious establishment was subjected to a two-prong attack. On the one hand, the government's tireless efforts to secularize the country socially and culturally meant the replacement of traditional and religious values with those prevalent in European societies and cultures. More pointedly, the government enacted several laws designed specifically to secularize the judicial functions of the *ulama*. Since a provision in the 1906 Constitution prohibited the passage of laws that were considered to be contrary to the *Shari'a* (Islamic law), the new set of secular laws that were passed were labelled as "provisional." Furthermore, the government took over a number of the judicial functions of the *ulama* and restricted them from acting as judges in the country's courts.21

In governing the country, Reza Shah gave special priority to the tribes. Since the days of the Constitutional Revolution, most tribes had flaunted the central government by refusing to pay taxes, being subject to the military draft, disarming themselves, or adopting the Farsi language and the Persian culture. Of the country's numerous tribes, the Bakhtiaris, Boyr Ahmadis, and the Shahsavans were the most belligerent in their opposition to the imposition of central authority. Reza Shah attacked tribal rebellions head-on, of which there was a sudden flare in the spring of 1929 and again in 1930. He was successful in quieting the tribes, however, only after he imprisoned many of their leaders and forced others to reside in the capital city and away from their tribal followers.22

Reza Shah left no doubt in anyone's mind as to who the sole source of power in Iran was. He embodied the new regime and personified its goals and aspirations. At the same time, he was tactful enough to employ the services of a number of influential and respected figures in carrying out his reforms. In order to give his regime a semblance of democracy, he permitted the appearance of a number of political parties in 1927. Similar to the Majles, which Reza Shah had effectively turned into another department within his government, these parties were mere bureaus where the regime's official doctrines and policies reigned supreme. They included the *Iran-e Nou* (New Iran) party, whose motto was "Loyalty to the Shah, Devotion to progress," the *Tajaddod* (Modernity) party, headed by the minister of education, and the *Taraqqi* (Progress) party. Of the three, only the latter was comprised of men not entirely supportive of the shah's programs, although they never gained enough popular support or political clout to be considered a formidable force.23

The collaboration of reform-minded intellectuals with the regime, a development arising more out of mutual social concerns rather than political interests, was most evident in the literary field. Beginning in the mid-1930s, the Shah began a campaign to eliminate the influence of Arabic from the Farsi language and literature.24 In this pursuit, he was helped greatly by the efforts of some of Iran's most noted literary scholars. Renowned men such as Ali Akbar Dehkhoda, Ahmad Kasravi, and Sadeq Hedayat wanted to "Persianize" Iran's culture as much as possible by "purifying" it from the vestiges of the Arab conquest. As a result, a plethora of literary works appeared praising Iran's pre-Islamic past and glorifying the virtues of its ancient religion of Zoroastrianism.

Economic Modernization to the Forefront

A further area on which Reza Shah focused much of his attention and efforts was the country's economy. Ever since his days as the minister of war and later as the prime minister, he had concentrated on building up Iran's textile, steel, and armament industries, and on expanding and improving the country's roads. While the shah had sought the expertise of a foreign national in sorting out the country's finances (i.e., Dr. Millspaugh), he was unwilling to subject Iran to the same kind of financial enslavement to foreign powers as the shahs before him had so readily done.

The needed revenues for financing the numerous projects were raised through four means. First, largely through the efforts of Dr. Millspaugh, the collection and administration of tax revenues were drastically improved and, as a result increased in volume. Reza Shah did not so much impose new taxes as he made the collection of old ones more efficient.[25] The government also sold much of the land it owned in order to raise capital, and continued to collect sizeable tariff fines and at times even confiscated the property of those he suspected of plotting against him or found guilty of improper conduct. At the same time, economic and industrial cooperation between Iran and Europe's newly-emerging powerhouse, Germany, began to expand at an accelerated pace. This industrial cooperation was crystallized in 1926 by work on the Trans-Iranian Railway project, an ambition frustrated for nearly seventy-five years due to rivalry between Russia and Britain. The project was financed exclusively by internal revenues raised domestically, but its actual construction was carried out by contractors from diverse Western nations such as the United States, Germany, and Scandinavian countries. The project was completed in 1938 amid much national rejoicing.[26] By the time of his departure from the Iranian political scene in 1941, Reza Shah had overseen the establishment of some 150 new factories and the control of government monopoly over most industrial goods and consumer products.[27]

Yet the country's relatively rapid pace of economic growth was not without negative ramifications for the public at large. A new aristocracy came into being as a result of the government's granting of contracts to individuals and entrepreneurs. Many members of the old aristocracy, meanwhile, especially those residing in the provinces, declined in fortune and lost much of their wealth. Some of the younger merchants--no longer trading solely in traditional goods and commodities such as tea and other herbs--amassed fortunes by importing the materials needed for the numerous public projects under way. To these privileged few were added a minority of army officers who had won the shah's favor and had subsequently acquired considerable wealth.[28]

Despite the prosperity of these few, however, the bulk of the population suffered economically. There was heavy taxation on those with average earnings, and there were few opportunities for economic improvement outside of the capital city. As a result, there was a short supply of foreign exchange and a glaring concentration of wealth in Tehran, and in very few hands.[29] The country's almost complete technical and industrial reliance on Germany also proved costly, especially in later years during the World War II, when most German technical experts were needed to run Germany's own war machine.[30]

Secularization in the Service of the State

Perhaps the most acute impact of Reza Shah's reign was felt by Iranian culture and society. Inspired by the secularization of Turkey by Kemal Ataturk, Reza Shah embarked on an intense program to ingrain three principles into Iranian life: a complete dedication to the state and to nationalist values; the adoption of Western technology and industry; and the abandonment, it not the outright ridiculing, of traditional, mostly religious, beliefs and practices.[31] His efforts to break down the overwhelming social and cultural influence of the religious classes started mainly after 1925, when his position was secure enough to afford him the power to take on the religious establishment. He gave special priority to education and introduced a series of far-reaching reforms in the educational system. In 1921, the Ministry of Education drew up the country's first full plan for elementary and secondary education.[32] French educators were brought in to supervise Tehran's Teachers' Training College, and by the end of Reza Shah's rule thirty-five more such training centers had been established throughout the country.[33] Beginning in the 1930s, some 1,500 students were given state scholarships to study in the West, among them Crown Prince Mohammad Reza, with nearly eighty percent of them being sent to France and the rest to England, Belgium, and Switzerland.[34] These efforts toward educational improvement reached a high in 1934, when the University of Tehran was established. Earlier, as a further blow to the *ulama*'s strict adherence to Islamic rites, the government had permitted human dissection at the Tehran Medical College, demonstrating again the new direction in which the energetic ruler wished to take his country.[35] These and other efforts designed to bring about the rapid secularization of the country were given some doctrinal cohesion in 1939, when the shah established the Organization to Guide Thought (*Sazman-e Parvaresh Afkar*), modelled after the Nazi and other fascist propaganda machines of the time in Europe.[36] The social status of women was also targeted for change, further undermining the traditional roles ascribed to them by the religious establishment. In the field of education, the number of girls' schools rose from a mere forty-one in 1910 to 190 in 1929 and 870 by 1933. In the same years, the number of girls enrolled in schools rose from 2,167 to 11,489 and eventually to 50,000 in 1933.[37] Although child marriage were still prevalent, in 1924 eighteen was set as the legal age of majority. Although there was a lull in the years between 1925 and the early 1930s in implementing reforms, they were once again pursued with renewed vigor after 1934. In 1931 women had been given the right to file for divorce suits under special circumstances. In 1935, the government ordered the wearing of European hats, dubbed "Pahlavi caps," and it had earlier forbidden the use (and more often the abuse) of grandiose personal titles.[38] Women entered the University of Tehran along with male students in the first year of its operation, 1936, and in February of the same year they were officially forbidden to wear the traditional black veil, the *chadur*. The forced unveiling of women stirred much uproar and disquiet among the *ulama* and even among most elderly women, although there had always existed a desire among the more educated social classes to ban the *chadur*.[39] While the ban was zealously implemented during the Reza Shah's reign, it waned as soon as the monarch was deposed in 1941. The widespread return of the veil after Reza Shah's departure was not so much the result of a dismantling of his coercive police apparatus as it was due to the persistence of deeply entrenched social values and religious biases.[40]

Reza Shah's Downfall

Reza Shah's pro-German sympathies led the British to remove him from power soon after the outbreak of World War II in 1941. Despite the forceful nature of his rule, most of Reza Shah's policies were suddenly reversed soon after his ouster. His social policies, which had aroused the greatest degree of resentment and discomfort among the traditional classes--particularly among the *Bazaari* merchants and the *ulama*--were especially subject to the strongest criticisms and the sharpest reversals. Women began appearing in the streets in their black *chadurs*, and many of the intellectuals who had praised Reza Shah for his secular and progressive ideas now began attacking his reign and his legacy as having been one of Iran's darkest dictatorships.[41] At the same time, the seemingly unassailable position of monarchy that the shah had created rapidly fell apart under the highly tenuous rule of his twenty two-year old son and lost a considerable degree of its power to the prime minister's office. Criticism of "past mistakes" were heard from all corners of society, and a national euphoria, similar to that of a population having just launched a successful revolution, prevailed over the country.

To understand why Reza Shah's policies were so abruptly and fundamentally reversed soon after his departure from the Iranian political scene, it is important to keep in mind the haphazard nature of his plans to modernize the country and his sole reliance on coercive means to achieve his modernizing ends. Although most intellectuals and men of letters were vociferous in their support of Reza Shah's social policies, they were never able to popularize their ideals and existed, until the end of Reza Shah's reign and even well into the reign of his son, in a social and cultural vacuum. The intellectuals' inability to give credence and popular support to Reza Shah's initiatives was due partly to their own elitist outlook in relation to others in society, on whom they often looked with pity and contempt, and partly from the shah's own refusal to allow the expression of unsolicited and independent views and opinions.

What resulted was a set of alien and largely offensive regulations, held intact not by the virtue of their popularity but because of the coercive powers of the central government. Once the government's principal source of power--the shah--had been removed, there was little reason for the people to continue abiding by the laws that they considered to be contradictory to their religious and cultural values. In the end, once the Second World War broke out, Reza Shah's reforms faded as quickly as did his seemingly invincible authority.

Mohammad Reza Shah's Reign

At the beginning of his reign, the young Mohammad Reza Shah wielded little real authority and the country remained occupied by Allied forces throughout the war. The Majles, which Reza Shah had effectively emasculated if never completely eliminated, and the office of prime minister once again became dominant over the position of the shah. Ever since the Constitutional Revolution, political power had alternated between the royal court and the office of prime minister. With Reza Shah, this dichotomy had ceased under his supremacy. When Mohammad Reza Pahlavi assumed power in 1941, the system of constitutional monarchy was revitalized and continued to function until 1953. Princess Soraya, who was married to the shah from 1950 to 1957, maintains that the monarch deliberately relaxed the political atmosphere that his father had created and purposefully granted extensive liberties to the Majles. Having been impressed by the democracy he had witnessed while in boarding school in Switzerland, she quotes the Shah as having said:

> I saw with my own eyes the advantages of a democratic education. From then on I was inwardly in revolt against my father, and I took an oath to myself that as soon as I came to power I would do everything differently from the way he did.[42]

Given the circumstances of the time, it is doubtful that the young shah could have gathered autocratic powers even if he had wanted to. Moreover, the shah never took any active measures to promote democracy. The apparent political resurrection of the Majles was not part of a deliberate move by the shah but rather a result of his inability to keep the prime minister and the parliament politically subordinate. The powers of the legislature grew to such an extent that in 1951 Prime Minister Mohammad Mussadiq initiated policies that threatened the very foundations of the regime. Even after Mussadiq was overthrown by the American Central Intelligence Agency in 1953, the prime minister's office was still responsible for the political and the administrative running of the country. The shah's personal hold on political power was solidified only in 1965, when he chose Amir Abbas Hoveida as his prime minister. Nevertheless, while the 1953 coup reinstated the power of the monarchy, it did not immediately consolidate the shah's personal rule and in fact it heightened his unpopularity among important social strata. Mussadiq had enjoyed widespread public support and was seen to have been removed by a combination of foreign intervention and forces inimical to the aspirations of the majority of the people. From 1953 to 1965 a succession of prime ministers followed, each enjoying some individual political leverage, although this depended more on the throne than on a timorous and corruptly elected parliament.

After the 1953 coup, the conditions that emerged inside the country and in the international arena afforded the Shah the opportunity to concentrate on building a strong state and on solidifying his personal rule. Internally, the coup seemed to have removed the last vestiges of opposition to political absolutism, namely liberal nationalists loyal to the 1906 Constitution.[43] In fact, a coordinated campaign to oppose the regime and its policies was not to occur until a decade had passed, when in 1962-63 the *ulama* opposed the government's proposal to institute universal suffrage and the "White Revolution."

Internationally, the Shah's efforts to solidify his rule benefitted greatly from the intense superpower rivalry of the Cold War, because of which the United States gave Iran lucrative economic and military assistance in order to strengthen its anti-communist monarch.[44] With the absence of domestic opposition and with foreign support, the shah energetically began to establish new state institutions and modernize existing ones. In the process, the state became more centralized as it acquired more and more political power, grew less tolerant of opposition activities and employed harsher measures to subdue its opponents, and at the same time became diplomatically, militarily, and psychologically dependent on the support it received from the United States.

The shah continued vigorously to pursue the social and economic modernization programs that his father had initiated. The younger Pahlavi was much more successful in implementing his reforms because he had considerably more favorable geopolitical circumstances. Furthermore, Reza Shah had already muted if not actually obliterated a number of the obstacles which his son would have otherwise faced in modernizing the country. Like his father, Mohammad Reza's efforts to modernize Iran socially and culturally met with stiff opposition from the *ulama*. Unlike his father, however, he was not faced with the problem of trying to impose central authority over the various tribes, curtailing the powers of the Qajar aristocracy, and building up an industrial and economic infrastructure from scratch. In trying to unify the country and reassert the powers of the central government, Reza Shah had relied extensively on the military as the primary tool for achieving his goals. While the military continued to play a pivotal role during Mohammad Reza Shah's reign, the task of modernizing the country was largely entrusted to the bureaucracy. The armed forces continued to grow in strength and hardware at a staggering rate under the latter Pahlavi, but so did the bureaucracy become more cumbrous and sluggish and the government's administration more inefficient.

The Shah as Government, Again

The state that developed under the second Pahlavi monarch had three principle foundations.[45] First, there was the person of the shah. By installing himself at its apex and by making all other institutions dependent on his court, the Shah became an integral part of the state. The second source of power for the state was its administrative network: the cabinet, the bureaucracy, the Majles, and the state-sponsored political party called the *Rastakhiz*. Lastly, the state relied on a number of military and para-military institutions, the most notable of which were the armed forces and the secret police, SAVAK.

By far the most significant foundation of Mohammad Reza Pahlavi's reign was the shah himself. During his thirty-five year reign, he underwent a marked transformation from a largely powerless and ineffectual monarch to a central and inseparable part of the state. Early in his reign, the shah lived in relative modesty and made a deliberate effort to keep his court free of unnecessary pomp and luxury.[46] His frugal attitude changed as he grew in power after the 1953 coup, and the royal court became famous, or rather infamous, for its extravagant luxury. The shah, never able completely to overcome his childhood shyness, always appeared as cold and distant to those even closest to him.[47]

The monarch personally assumed onerous duties and consumed himself in the daily running of the country. His primary preoccupation was with issues pertaining to foreign affairs, economy, and the military. He held weekly audiences with most cabinet members, during which he was presented with reports about the ministries' activities in the preceding week. Theoretically, all of the ministers' inquiries were to be channelled through the prime minister's office, and they were to be referred to the Shah only if the prime minister was unable to handle them. However, if the prime minister's decisions were contrary to the wishes of a particular minister, the minister often appealed directly to the shah and after having won the shah's support relayed his orders to the prime minister. The prime minister as well as the ministers of foreign affairs and war were in constant contact with the monarch. Junior ministers were not permitted to have royal audiences, except in the official ceremonies during which they presented their credentials.

All ministerial appointments were made by the Shah, with loyalty to the crown being the most important qualification. Based on the advice and the information he received from his cabinet and his top military commanders, the Shah also personally made all political and military decisions and allowed no room for individual initiatives or coordinated efforts by any of his subordinates.[48] In military affairs, the Shah personally made all strategic and tactical decisions. He could also promote or demote any military officer regardless of rank or seniority, and he required his personal permission for even the landing or take-off of all military planes.[49]

Besides the military, the monarchy relied on a number of institutions which were all part of the state bureaucracy. These included the cabinet, the *Rastakhiz* party, and the Majles--which the shah, like his father, effectively turned into a government bureau. The *Rastakhiz* (Resurgence) party was formed in 1975 and was supposed to have been a "great political and ideological school, able to engender the civic spirit necessary for administrative reform."[50] But the party's rigid and highly centralized organisation, coupled with its politically-motivated activities aimed at maximizing the powers of the state, soon revealed the shah's attempt to further legitimize his regime and to strengthen his traditional political authority in the face of the country's social and economic modernization. Amid failure to attract popular support and much criticism, the Shah dissolved the party in 1978 and later admitted that its creation had been an error.[51]

Unlike his father, who always remained a soldier at heart, the shah tended to rely more heavily on the bureaucracy than on the military, at least up until the revolutionary crises of 1978-79. The bureaucracy served as a mechanism through which the government's policies were carried out and new recruits were brought into the system. Through several agencies and programs, the regime often made extensive efforts to assimilate notable members of the intelligentsia into itself. These efforts often resulted in the appointment of individuals such as university professors and journalists to high-ranking bureaucratic posts and in the formation of semi-official "think tanks" that were in one way or another connected to the royal court. More importantly, an extensive bureaucratic network, which by now reached into even the remotest towns and villages, carried out the government's policies, although it was plagued with inefficiency and corruption in virtually all of its strata.

Supporting the whole system were the various military and security institutions, notably the secret police, called SAVAK, and the armed forces. Infamous for its brutality and condemned worldwide for torturing the regime's opponents, SAVAK was designed to infiltrate the different guerrilla movements and to arrest their key leaders, crack the allegedly extensive Soviet spy network in the country, and to keep an eye on the regime's own employees in order to ensure their loyalty to the state and to the shah. Despite its feared reputation and apparent deadly efficiency, several people with intimate knowledge of the secret organization have argued that SAVAK was in reality inept and inefficient, unable to even fulfill the basic functions that were entrusted to it.[52] While the shah used the bureaucracy rather than the military as the institution through which he ruled the country, he never kept the two very far apart from one another. In two occasions, during the 1953 coup and the 1978-79 revolution, the armed forces were marshalled to keep the regime intact, a task in which they were successful in the first instance but failed in the second.

Yet by the time the reign of Mohammad Reza Shah was drawing to a close, the Pahlavi state had largely lost its military character. This overall change in the role of the military was symptomatic of the evolution of the Pahlavi dynasty. Initially, Reza Shah had used the military to establish his authority both in the capital city and throughout the country. Once this authority was no longer threatened militarily, the armed forces were directed toward defending the country from outside aggression. To this end, the regime launched an ambitious military procurement campaign aimed at turning Iran into a regional superpower. In his quest for military superiority, the shah was helped by the wealth generated through rising oil revenues and by favorable international developments and geo-political circumstances.

Land Reform: A Plan Gone Awry

As the Shah gradually strengthened his hold on power in the 1950s and the 1960s, and largely at the behest of the Kennedy administration in Washington, the government began to implement a series of social and economic reforms. One such reform, the Land Reform plan of the 1960s, is worth mentioning in detail because of its dramatic social consequences and its centralizing effects on the state. In 1961, the government launched a widely publicized Land Reform program as part of a "White Revolution." The "revolution's" main purpose was to minimize the economic powers, and thus the political influence, of rural-based landlords by confiscating their land and distributing it among the peasantry.[53] These reforms were also intended to create a sizeable peasant-dominated base of support for the regime.

Despite some initial progress and benefits for a number of peasants, the plan was broken down into stages and was eventually reversed, leaving most peasants without land or even a place to live. Migration to the cities consequently accelerated as the reforms started to look like a thinly-veiled campaign to nationalize land belonging to peasants and farmers. The bewilderment of the cultivators, meanwhile, after their hopes had been raised to a high pitch in 1961, resulted in a reassertion of influence by the former land owners.

Additionally, numerous traumatic demographic and social ramifications ensued. A new urban-based economic class, composed primarily of propertyless, unskilled, and unemployed rural immigrants, developed. These immigrants flooded the cities in the hope of securing a lasting occupation and being eventually assimilated into the urban mainstream. The growth of this socio-economic class altered existing patterns of relationships among other classes and introduced new values and expectations both to the immigrants as well as to the original urban population. Rapid social change took place, not as a result of the premises of the regime's "revolution," but largely because of the eventual failure of its principal initiative, land reform. These dramatic ramifications were to prove highly detrimental to the Pahlavi regime in the middle to the late 1970s.

FOREIGN INTERVENTION

With the end of the Qajar era, Iran's foreign relations underwent significant transformations. Consistent with his unceasing efforts to transform Iran's traditional mold and to turn it into a modern nation-state, Reza Shah abandoned the Qajar' long-standing policy of subservience to the superpowers and re-oriented the country's foreign policy in a manner intended to maximize Iran's national interests. An increasing level of compatibility also grew between the country's foreign policy goals and commitments on the one hand and its means and capabilities on the other.[54] The most clear example of Iran's departure from its traditional foreign policy was its cancellation of the Anglo-Persian agreement of 1919, its successful maneuvers to get Soviet troops out of the northern provinces, and its annulment of capitulary rights previously granted to the citizens of Britain, France, Belgium, the Netherlands, Austria, Czechoslovakia, Sweden, and Italy.

Foreign Policy Shift

Several domestic as well as external factors contributed to this dramatic shift in Iranian foreign policy. The most obvious factor was Reza Shah himself, for he was determined to put an end to the unending and flagrant violations of Iran's sovereignty by its northern neighbor and by Great Britain. Equally important was a general tendency among both the British and the Soviet governments to allow the development of a strong central government in Iran, thus giving unprecedented freedom to Iranian leaders and policy-makers to shape and determine their country's foreign policy.[55] The Iranian government also initiated a *rapprochement* with a third, "distant and disinterested" power, Germany, and to a lesser extent the United States, in an effort to counter the pervasive influences of Britain and the Soviet Union. It is significant to note that in the first years of his ascent to power, when Reza Khan did not yet have much control over the country's foreign policy, most decisions regarding diplomacy were made by nationalist and reform-minded politicians of the Constitutional era.[56] It would be erroneous to suggest, however, that such diplomats functioned autonomously and without the prime minister's explicit consent.

While the change in dynasties brought an end to the overt control of Iran's political destiny by Russia and Britain, it did not by any means result in its complete economic and diplomatic emancipation from the superpowers. Upon assuming power, Reza Khan was faced with two pressing foreign policy dilemmas: the Soviet occupation of the north and their support for the *Jangali* movement, and the British-supported secessionist movement of Sheikh Khaz'al in Khuzestan. The actual presence of Soviet troops on Iranian soil was the more pressing of the two problems, but through skillful diplomacy the Iranian government was able to persuade the Soviets to withdraw their forces.[57] Reza Khan then attacked the *Jangalis*, whose leader, Kuchik Khan, had set up the autonomous Republic of Gilan in the north. In the absence of Soviet troops, the *Jangali* resistance collapsed and Kuchik Khan froze to death while trying to escape from government forces. The Khuzestan secessionists were similarly defeated and their leader was forced to reside under Reza Khan's watchful eyes in Tehran.

Despite the apparent improvement in diplomatic relations with the Soviet Union, Soviet-Iranian relations were still far from being mutually beneficial. Trade between the two countries grew at an astronomical rate, with Iran's exports to the USSR rising from 2,600,000 tumon in 1921 to 24,400,000 tumon in 1925.[58] However, because of the controlled nature of the Soviet economy, Iranian merchants found themselves at a far less advantageous position in comparison to their northern counterparts who exported goods to Iran.[59] Furthermore, a series of issues pertaining to Iran's relations with Britain and with other nations continued to darken prospects for a genuine Soviet-Iranian *rapprochement*. They included the unprecedented growth in Iran's relations with Germany, its hiring of American financial advisers, who were given considerable authority in reorganizing the country's finances, and the Soviet Union's own desire to augment its influence in northern Iran. Additionally, while Reza Shah succeeded in settling Iran's border disputes with all of its other neighbours (Afghanistan, Turkey, and Iraq), he was unable to achieve a similar agreement with the Soviet Union.[60]

As part of an overall strategy to interest third party governments in Iran as a counterweight against Anglo-Soviet dominance, Reza Shah consistently sought to increase Iran's contacts with other Western powers. The ideal choices for ties with "distant and disinterested" powers in Iranian affairs were the United States and Germany. While the U.S. was reluctant to break its isolationist mold and to expand its diplomatic relations in the Middle East, Germany was extremely eager to do so, if only to challenge the two superpowers' influence in the region. Germany's relations with Iran thus grew markedly under Reza Shah. Also, while the Shah never abandoned his aversion toward foreigners, his extreme nationalism drew him closer to the Germany of the 1930s and further away from Britain. Massive numbers of German advisors and technical experts were brought in to help and to supervise the country's modernization. By 1939, Germany had become Iran's number one trading partner.[61]

Despite the apparent emergence of Iran as an equal among European powers, the outbreak of the war in Europe brought about the collapse of Iran's diplomatic achievements over the past two decades, its sovereignty, and even its monarchy. When hostilities broke out in Europe, Iran declared itself neutral in the conflict, as it had done during World War I. The neutrality declaration was made with the hope to keep Iran out of the conflict. For Iranian policy-makers, alliance with either side was not a desired alternative: they neither sympathized with the British or the Soviets, nor did they trust Germany's intentions and future policies toward Iran.[62] Yet this neutrality declaration was as nominally respected as was the one issued in 1914. As in before, Iran's vital strategic position, serving as a supply-bridge for the Soviet forces that had been attacked by Germany, rendered its neutrality in the conflict unacceptable to the Allies. On 25 August 1941, Soviet and British forces simultaneously invaded Iran from the north and the south respectively, with the Soviets bombarding the cities of Anzali, Ghazian, and Qazvin. After a hopeless effort by the army to repel the invaders, the Iranian government declared "cease-fire" with the Allies two days after their invasion. Three weeks later, amid much propaganda attacks against his "brutal and avaricious rule" by the British,[63] the shah abdicated in favor of his son. Thus came to an end an era in Iran's foreign policy, and more importantly, in its political history.

For some time after Reza Shah's abdication, Iran's foreign policy remained in shambles, a mere reflection of its desperate domestic situation. The country remained occupied throughout the war, and even after the war ended the Soviet Union refused to withdraw its troops from Azarbayjan. The shah later complained that in the 1940s the Soviet and British ambassadors to Tehran presented him with lists of candidates whom both superpowers wanted to see elected to the Majles.[64] To this were added Soviet-backed secessionist movements in Azarbayjan and Kurdistan provinces and Soviet demands in late 1942 for oil concessions in the northern provinces.[65] These Soviet demands set into motion U.S.-Soviet competition for Iranian oil and ultimately resulted in the Cold War.[66] As it had done after World War I, the Majles was able to utilize skillful diplomacy to rebuff the Soviet Union on the oil concession issue and to convince the northern giant to withdraw its troops from Iranian soil.[67] Once Soviet troops withdrew from Iran in 1946, the central government easily crushed the Azarbayjan and Kurdistan Republics and re-imposed its authority in those regions.

The events that occurred immediately following the war served as catalysts that drew Iran increasingly closer to the Western camp. The Soviet Union had done much to discredit itself among Iranian leaders by its demands for oil concessions and by its support for secessionist movements. Meanwhile, the British became more sensitive to Iran because of the brewing unrest in India, while the United States became more aware of the economic and strategic importance of the oil-rich Middle East. Strengthening American ties with Iran during this period of Soviet occupation was the development in the late 1940s of close personal relations between the shah and American leaders, a development which lasted up until the end of the Pahlavi dynasty in the late 1970s.[68]

Although preoccupied with the Indian independence movement, Britain was soon to face another crisis in Iran. On 15 March 1951, the Majles passed a bill nationalizing the British-owned and controlled Anglo-Iranian Oil Company (AIOC), which had for years been controlling Iranian oil. Earlier that year, a newly-formed coalition of small parties called the National Front (*Jebhe Melli*) had gained a majority in parliamentary elections and their leader, Dr. Mohammad Mussadiq, an ardent nationalist, had become prime minister.[69] Mussadiq espoused on a policy he called "negative equilibrium", according to which no outside power was to be allowed to have even the slightest influence on Iran's social, economic, and political affairs.[70] He steadfastly refused to compromise with the British over the AIOC's nationalization and was at first successful in gaining the sympathy of the American government. This support was terminated, however, with the inauguration of General Dwight Eisenhower as president in 1952. The new American administration was highly suspicious of communist intrigues in Iran and was much more susceptible to arguments made by American oil companies eager to share in the spoils of Iranian oil.[71] But the Soviets looked to Mussadiq with no more fondness, preferring to see a weak post-war Britain in Iran rather than the possibility of American influence there.[72] Furthermore, Stalin's death in 1953 and the resulting confusion and lack of direction in USSR's foreign policy and in the international communist movement prevented the Soviet Union from coming to Mussadiq's help when he needed it the most.

In March 1953, the CIA coordinated a coup that overthrew Mussadiq and firmly reestablished the shah's autocratic powers. The idea of launching a coup in Iran aimed at overthrowing Mussadiq and reversing his policies had originated with the British government, which had then persuaded the United States to carry it out. The coup resulted in the establishment of an oil consortium comprised of the newly-formed National Iranian Oil Company and several other Western companies, an arrangement only marginally more beneficial to Iran than had been the case under the AIOC.[73] Diplomatically, the coup was followed by massive American military and economic aid to the Iranian regime as part of the Eisenhower Doctrine's policy of building up strong and stable anti-communist regimes around the world. During the Eisenhower administration, Iran received more than $1 billion in U.S. aid (Table 1). In a further effort to reinforce its pro-Western orientation, Iran joined the Baghdad Pact in 1955 and signed a bilateral agreement with the U.S. in 1959. Devising a policy of "positive nationalism" as a replacement for Mussadiq's "negative equilibrium", the Shah proceeded to conduct as many trade and diplomatic agreements with other, mainly Western and pro-Western, countries as possible. "Positive nationalism," in the shah's words, "meant that we make any agreements which are in our own interests, regardless of the wishes or policies of others."[74]

Table 1. U.S. Technical Aid to Iran, 1951-56 (millions of dollars)

Fiscal Year	Aid
1951	1.3
1952	23.6
1953	23.2
1954	84.8
1955	75.5
1956	73.3

Source: James Bill, *The Eagle and the Lion*, p. 124.

Iran's relations with the United States grew steadily amid precarious and often hostile relations with the Soviet Union. After the coup, the Soviet government viewed Iran's heavy reliance on the West for its security and military build-up with particular disquiet. There was a continuous stream of protest notes from Moscow to Tehran and Washington regarding Iran's growing pro-Western bent. The USSR's primary aim in the 1950s and the 1960s was to pressure Iran to stay out of bilateral pacts and alliances such as the Baghdad Pact and the 1959 bilateral agreement with the U.S. In pursuit of this goal, the Soviet Union often used a combination of economic enticements on the one hand and threats and hostility on the other.[75]

The shah, meanwhile, used Iran's relations with the Soviet Union as a leverage with which he hoped to gain unconditional American military and technical support.[76] He used this tactic with particular success during the Johnson administration, when he convinced the American president to reverse Kennedy's push for social and economic reforms in Iran. President John Kennedy had emphasised the need for reforms in Iran and in other Third World countries as an antidote to revolutions of the kind that had taken place in Cuba.[77] He particularly advocated the necessity of such reforms in Iran, especially in light of a stern warning by Khrushchev regarding the inevitability of the shah's downfall.[78] Thus followed the Shah's 1961 Land Reform plan and the "White Revolution." But the advocacy of reforms was largely abandoned by Lyndon Johnson, who was highly impressed by the shah's pomposity and with whom he had a close personal as well as professional relationship. Entangled in an ugly war in Vietnam, Johnson showed his appreciation for the shah's regional and international support of U.S. positions by providing Iran with numerous types of American military hardware and assistance.[79]

America's *carte blanche* to the Shah was considerably augmented (and given doctrinal cohesion and consistency) under the Nixon-Kissinger

Doctrine. Based on the principle of "multi-polarity," this doctrine aimed to develop regional middle powers under American auspices. Brazil, Indonesia, Zaire, and Iran were chosen for this purpose.[80] These countries were to provide stable regional conditions which would facilitate an orderly devolution of American power, thereby creating a "linkage policy" in which superpower detente would take place.[81] In the case of Iran, the large extent to which the aims of the Nixon-Kissinger Doctrine and the interests of the Shah concurred singled out U.S.-Iranian relations as the paradigmatic application of Washington's foreign policy approach. Obsessed with the Soviet threat and with the omnipresence of communist-inspired intrigues and conspiracy against his reign,[82] the shah was more than eager to serve as the United States' "middle power" in the region.

Iran thus became the largest single recipient of American military hardware, loans, and other forms of assistance. Up until 1978, U.S. trade with the whole of Latin America and Africa together totalled $3.2 billion and $8.8 billion with South Korea. U.S. trade with Iran, however, was more than $10 billion, most of which took place after 1972.[83] In 1973 the shah proudly boasted that "we can get anything non-atomic that the U.S. has."[84]

With Jimmy Carter's election in 1976, the Nixon-Kissinger Doctrine was ostensibly abandoned and replaced by a new and supposedly more farsighted approach to foreign policy. Hoping to "remove reasons for revolutions that often erupt among people who suffer from persecution," the newly-elected president declared that he was "determined to combine support for our more authoritarian allies and friends with the effective promotion of human rights within their countries."[85]

In specific relation to Iran, the Carter administration's objective was to compel the Shah to become more observant of human rights without destabilizing Iran or jeopardising the close relations between the two countries.[86] There was, consequently, great pressure on the Iranian government to "reform" itself if it wished to maintain its privileged relations with Washington. In early 1977, a high-ranking official of the Carter administration reportedly remarked that "this is a new administration. If the shah thinks he will get anything he wants in the arms field, he is in for a big surprise."[87] In 1978, for the first time in many years, the United States refused to sell Iran electronically enhanced F-4 aircraft.[88] Similarly, there was a considerable row in the U.S. Congress over the ill-fated proposal to sell AWACS planes to Iran. The shah, who was always searching for signs in the American diplomatic language for his security or demise and who was paranoid about U.S.-Soviet masterplans to partition Iran, was greatly disillusioned by his diplomatic setbacks in Washington and reluctantly started to initiate some domestic reforms beginning in 1977.

Iran's Role in the Cold War

In retrospect, American policy-makers became increasingly aware of Iran's vital importance within the emerging international equation soon after the 1953 coup. This realisation was brought on partly by Britain's gradual decline in power and international stature after World War II, particularly in regions east of the Suez. More importantly, the "northern tier" countries--Afghanistan, Iran, Iraq, and Turkey--had begun to assume paramount importance because of the Cold War. Consequently, regardless of the changes in the direction of American foreign policy from one administration to another, Iran's special geo-political and strategic position *vis-a-vis* the Soviet Union always accorded it a pivotal role in Washington's various diplomatic formulas. Iran became one of the primary recipients of American military aid under Eisenhower's Point Four plan; it was central to Kennedy's efforts to promote reforms in the Third World and to create an "Alliance for Progress;"[89] the shah became the main beneficiary of the Nixon-Kissinger Doctrine of multi-polarity and served as the United States' principal proxy in the Middle East; and the Iranian regime became one of the primary targets of the Carter administration's efforts to promote human rights among America's "authoritarian allies."

While Iran's relations with the Soviet Union grew in the 1960s and the 1970s as well, they did so with far less intensity and regularity. Whenever there were signs that the U.S. may hesitate in its military sales to Iran, the Shah would initiate a *rapprochement* with the Soviet Union, only to cool his enthusiasm as soon as he had reached his American objective. Underlying this reluctance to improve relations with the Soviet Union, as far as the shah was concerned, were the USSR's support for Egypt's Nasser (a potentially serious threat to the Shah and to other pro-Western leaders of the region), the continuous activism of members of the communist *Tudeh* party based in the Soviet Union and in other Eastern Block countries, and the ever-present suspicion of Soviet territorial ambitions in northern Iran.

The Pahlavi era marked the beginning of the end of Iran's overt domination by foreign powers. It was a period in which the country's foreign relations grew substantially more sophisticated and subtle, itself symptomatic of the general increase in the complexity of the political system as a whole. No longer were the court and the entire government at the mercy of one or both of the superpowers, and even the once omnipresent British imperial might was giving way to less blatant economic domination by the United States. The Iranian regime, meanwhile, grew and thrived, as it found mutually shared ideological and strategic medians with successive administrations in Washington. It was poised, as the shah liked to boast, to become "The Japan of the

Middle East." But the shah's Japan turned out to be only an apparition, a false dream based on fallacious economic policies and inherently brittle political institutions. When crisis came, it came with force and swept away the regime with unimagined might.

REVOLUTION

The Constitutional Revolution of 1905-11 had resulted in a significant but temporary curtailment of Qajar autocracy. It had, however, ultimately borne little fruit as it fell prey to the avarice of Mohammad Ali Shah and later the complete disregard of Reza Khan. Yet for almost all Iranians, regardless of their ideological persuasions, the Constitutional Revolution is still seen as a proud historical example of how a seemingly invincible dynasty and a despotic monarch were brought to their knees, however temporarily, and made obedient to the will of the people. Few Iranian historians have since been able to write about the Constitutional Revolution without glorifying it or making mythical figures out of its principal actors.[90] However, whatever glory there was soon faded away at the hands of autocracy, leaving its imprint on Iranian history not as an actual era but as a mere historical footnote. And such an experiment in the exercise of popular will was not to occur for another seven decades, and even then it was to be as impermanent.

Under the Pahlavis, developments in two historical periods served to mute the expression of political sentiments other than the regime's. The first was the authoritarian reign of Reza Shah. From 1925 to 1941, the government permitted only the propagation of beliefs that were in concert with the official state ideology. All ideologies and beliefs that did not embody elements of militarism and chauvinistic nationalism were considered to be subversive and their propagators were prosecuted. As a result, there was a flurry of anti-government sentiments directed against the deposed monarch and his collaborators soon after Reza Shah's abdication in 1941. While the government that came to power immediately after his departure was ineffective and even less popular, it did not face a revolutionary situation because of an absence of groups actively seeking to bring about its collapse.

The second phase of Pahlavi dictatorship occurred after the fall of Mussadiq in 1953 and lasted until the outbreak of the 1978-79 revolution. In the early 1960s, a serious and potentially crippling crisis enveloped the regime and nearly resulted in its downfall. But it was effectively remedied by a combination of sheer force and concessionary reforms. A revolution did not occur at the time because those opposing the regime did not want to overthrow it or to curb its powers but merely sought to repeal certain laws. Furthermore, the state was not weak or in any way vulnerable and enjoyed complete diplomatic and strategic support from abroad. But all conditions necessary for the development of a revolution were present in the late 1970s, and a combination of internal political collapse and widespread and unyielding opposition proved fatal to the Pahlavi state.

Reza Shah Silences His Opponents

Reza Shah's authoritarian reign had brought on a period of complete silence on the part of political activists and opponents of the regime. The shah's main opponents were not political activists as such but rather tribal *khans* and regional leaders, such as Sheikh Khaz'al and Kuchik Khan, who refused to submit to the powers of the central government. The shah effectively suppressed the many tribes that sought autonomy and ensured their submission through military means.

But he also ensured that there were no organized or even unorganized activities that might somehow pose a threat to his rule. The women's rights movement was a clear example. Although the shah wished to see improvements in the social status of Iranian women, he was not willing to allow a women's rights movement to develop independent of government control. In the early 1930s, he dismantled all independent women's organizations and banned the publication of their magazines.[91] Even more drastic limitations were placed on the *ulama*, whose powers were dramatically and consistently reduced and taken over by the central government. The shah's most far-reaching nonpolitical reforms were in the areas of education and law. Consistent with the overall secularization of the country, Reza Shah nullified most of the educational and judicial responsibilities that had traditionally been entrusted to the *ulama* and introduced increasing government control in other areas where the clergy continued to exert some influence.[92] In the process, the powers and the influence of the central government grew at the expense of the only significant institution that was still outside of complete government control. *Bazaari* merchants had also maintained their independent status *vis-a-vis* the central government, although they had not been able to acquire sufficient political or financial powers to pose any serious threat to the regime.

Challenge to Mohammad Reza

While Mohammad Reza Pahlavi was as ruthless as his father in suppressing his opponents, he was less successful in maintaining an unchallengeable hold on power. Three times in his reign--during Mussadiq's prime ministership, in the early 1960s, and beginning in 1977--the shah saw the very foundations of his rule threatened by events which ultimately culminated in a successful revolution in 1979. The Mussadiq era had been one of political turmoil and unrest, but it was neither a revolutionary episode, nor did the premier intend to make anything of the kind out of his tenure in office even if he had not been deposed by the CIA. Much disquiet also developed in 1962, when the *ulama* residing in Qom got news of the passage of a bill in the Majles that extended the right to vote to women and to religious minorities.[93] The religious authorities reacted quickly by sending telegrams and open letters to the shah and the prime minister and by preaching in mosques, arguing that the law undermined the integrity of Islam and the independence of the country. Among such telegrams, those sent by a little-known ayatollah named Rouhollah Khomeini were most poignant and sarcastic. He suggested that the prime minister travel to Qom, "so that if there are any misunderstandings that cannot be put into writing they be discussed verbally." The government finally repealed the law, after which Khomeini thanked the shah in a telegram but reminded him that "of course, the protection of Islam is what the Moslem people of Iran expect from Your Excellency."[94]

Khomeini did not stop his attacks against the regime and continued to preach against the shah from a seminary school. In March 1963, the government retaliated by occupying the seminary and arresting Khomeini. During the occupation, some theology students died, thus inciting the *ulama* to launch a vociferous campaign against the regime. Khomeini was soon released, but was detained again after he renewed his sharp attacks against the regime. News of his arrest a second time triggered riots and demonstrations in Qom, Tehran, Shiraz, Mashhad, and Kashan, during which several people died and many were wounded. After a few days the unrest finally subsided as the presence of government troops in the streets deterred further demonstrations. Khomeini spent another six months in detention in 1963, this time for calling for a boycott of Majles elections. In October 1964 he was finally exiled, residing first in Turkey but moving to the Shi'ite holy city of Najaf in Iraq the following year. With much encouragement from the Kennedy administration, the Shah had in the meanwhile gone ahead with a series of social and economic reforms and had initiated his "White Revolution."

Conditions conducive to the development of revolutionary circumstances appeared again in the late 1970s.[95] The Carter administration's emphasis on human rights, the shah's growing preoccupation with his image in the international media, and his apparent intentions to pass along the reins of power over to his son in the near future prompted him to introduce a series of reforms. Instead of reforming the dictatorial nature of his reign, however, the shah merely dismissed his prime minister of thirteen years, Amir Abbas Hoveida, and gave some marginal freedom to moderate opposition groups, permitting, for the first time since the early 1950s, writers and essayists to promote the virtues of freedom. But such reforms only served to further the regime's demise.

Reforms and the Revolution

There were two fundamental reasons why the regime's reforms expedited the brewing revolution. First, the reforms initiated by Hoveida's successor, Jamshid Amuzegar, were primarily cosmetic and were mostly administrative rather than political. The primary aim of these superficial reforms was to appease the U.S. Congress and the Carter administration. Equating "reforms" with an easing of restrictions on political activities, Amuzegar merely facilitated the polarization of anti-regime sentiments throughout the country. Furthermore, the prime minister's efforts to curb inflation resulted in a sudden rise in the level of unemployment, especially among rural immigrants and other members of the lumpen proletariat. His bureaucratic "housecleaning," meanwhile, meant that many high-ranking bureaucrats were made redundant or were demoted, thus depriving the regime of a potentially significant base of support.

Secondly, neither the shah nor the liberal administration in Washington were willing to implement the extensive and fundamental reforms that the emerging groups of revolutionaries were beginning to demand. Instead of reforming the structure of his regime and the nature of his rule, the shah decided to modify his response to opposition activities. When the shah was finally willing to yield to some of the demands for reforms (e.g., limitations on his powers, abolition of SAVAK, and the release of political prisoners), the revolutionaries settled for nothing less than the total overthrow of the Pahlavi regime.

Concurrent with the regime's own internal dismemberment, the 1978-79 revolution was caused by the efforts of groups opposing the regime. Such groups included the political parties and the guerrilla organizations, secular intellectuals, and the *ulama*. Following the 1953 coup, the two political parties, the *Tudeh* and the National Front, were harshly suppressed and most of their members were either imprisoned or exiled. Neither was able to play a significant role in the revolutionary movement. The two guerrilla organizations--the *Mujahedeen*, inspired by a radical interpretation of Islam, and the communist *Fadaiyan*--were also largely inactive in the 1970s as most of their leaders had been identified and subsequently arrested by SAVAK. Of intellectuals, only a handful dared to speak against the government and to criticize its policies, but most of what they had to say could not be read or even be understood by their overwhelmingly illiterate audience.

The *ulama*, on the other hand, had the most accessible facilities through which they could reach the masses: the mosques. Furthermore, the regime's ceaseless attacks against the *ulama* because of their social conservatism had resulted in their popular identification as defenders of democracy and as victims of despotism. The *ulama* could also mobilize by far the largest numbers of people to demonstrate against the regime. This was due to the culturally rich nature of their revolutionary message and its appeal to the general masses and especially to rural immigrants. Also important was the inevitable transformation of funeral processions and other religious ceremonies into anti-government demonstrations, and the government's own reluctance to further popularize the religious establishment by directly attacking it.

When the government finally tried to discredit the main religious figure thought to have been behind the unrest, Khomeini, its efforts only backfired and turned the obscure ayatollah into a national hero. In a newspaper article alleged to have been written by someone in the Ministry of Court, Khomeini was branded as a foreign agent and was accused of being an insane reactionary.[96] By mentioning Khomeini's name and by slandering him, the government had provided the restive masses with a symbolic figure around whom they could rally and base their movement. Khomeini was also compelled to leave his Iraqi exile, in the belief that the further he was from Iran the less troublesome to the regime he would be. The ayatollah travelled to France and, despite what the Iranian government had expected, continued his vociferous denunciation of the shah and attracted even more attention.

At the same time, a growing number of Iranian intellectuals living abroad began to collaborate with the ayatollah in an orchestrated effort to overthrow the shah. The alliance of these intellectuals with Khomeini arouse partly because of their ideological affinity with him and partly because they saw in the Ayatollah a real opportunity to finally topple the regime. Combined with the government's own ineptitude and clumsy handling of the deepening crisis, the cluster of revolutionary leaders centered around Khomeini's new exile in Paris began directing the revolutionary movement in Iran.

The psychologically distraught shah, dependent more than ever on American advice and support, was not to receive any decisive aid from his American patrons. The Carter administration was bitterly divided over the Iranian crisis and was unable to decide whether to encourage the shah to stage a military coup or to press forward with reforms.[97] Many high-ranking U.S. officials visited Iran to assess the situation first-hand and to assure the shah of their government's full support. But such assurances were hardly gratifying to the shah, who wanted the United States to make the necessary decisions for him.

Collapse of the Dynasty

While the shah and his American friends were trying to figure out how best to contain the brewing crisis, the revolution was gaining irreversible momentum. As a last desperate move to save his collapsing dynasty, in January 1979 the shah appointed a member of the National Front party, Dr. Shapour Bakhtiar, as prime minister and relegated most of his personal powers to him. The shah left Iran on 16 January 1979. Bakhtiar, calling himself a "social democrat of the European tradition," was soon expelled by a reactivated National Front and his cabinet was denounced as being "illegal" by Khomeini.[98] Khomeini asked another notable National Front member, Mehdi Bazargan, to form a provisional cabinet and to assume the prime minister's post. Bakhtiar repeatedly tried to meet with Khomeini personally, hoping apparently to work out a compromise, but his efforts all failed. He was also having difficulty enforcing his authority over the military, especially since most commanding generals were reluctant to obey anyone but the shah himself. Desertions and signs of disquiet had also reached unprecedented levels among conscript soldiers, who for months now had been enforcing martial law regulations and had often been forced to open fire on street demonstrators. The crisis came to a head on 10 February, when mutinous Air Force technicians took control of an air base in Tehran. When Bakhtiar ordered the military's high command to bombard the base the following day, the commanders refused his orders, citing the military's "neutrality in the political conflict."[99] The military commanders' decision was soon read over the radio, immediately after which the prime minister and most military commanders themselves went into hiding. Some of the military leaders were later found and arrested by mobs and by the rejuvenated guerrillas, many of them brought before summary trials and executed. Bazargan, the provisional prime minister, appointed a new chief of staff for the army and ordered the dismissal of most military commanders loyal to the shah. Elections were held in March in order to elect new deputies to a parliament, soon to be followed by a national referendum on whether to establish an "Islamic Republic." The new system of government was approved by 98.2 percent of the votes cast. The collapse of the Pahlavi regime was thus completed, and its successor was popularly legitimized. The Islamic Republic of Iran was officially established on 11 April 1979.

Notes

1. Roger Savory, "Social Development in Iran during the Pahlavi Era," George Lenczowski, ed, *Iran Under the Pahlavis* (Stanford, CA: Hoover Institution Press, 1978), p. 88.

2. See, for example, the shah's attempt to claim divinity in a revealing interview in Oriana Fallaci, *Interview With History* (New York: Liveright, 1976).

3. Anthony Parsons, *The Pride and the Fall, Iran 1974-1979* (London: Jonathan Cape, 1984), p. 151.

4. Donald Wilbur, *Riza Shah Pahlavi: The Resurrection and Reconstruction of Iran 1978-1944* (Hicksville, NY: Exposition Press, 1975), p. 39.

5. Said Amir Arjomand, "The *Ulama's* Traditionalist Opposition to Parliamentarianism: 1907-1909," *Middle Eastern Studies* vol. 17, no. 2 (April 1981), p. 186.

6. Donald Wilbur, *Riza Shah Pahlavi*, p. 47.

7. Ibid, p. 51.

8. Peter Avery, *Modern Iran* (London: Ernest Benn, 1965), p. 253.

9. Ibid, p. 255.

10. Wilbur, *Riza Shah Pahlavi*, p. 69.

11. Avery, *Modern Iran*, p. 263.

12. Wilbur, *Riza Shah Pahlavi*, p. 100.

13. Ibid, p. 75.

14. Avery, *Modern Iran*, p. 264.

15. Shahrough Akhavi,*Religion and Politics in Contemporary Iran* (Albany, NY: SUNY Press, 1980), p. 29.

16. Quoted in Wilbur, *Riza Shah Pahlavi*, p. 79.

17. Arthur C. Millspaugh, *Americans in Persia* (New York: Da Capo Press, 1976), p. 26.

18. Wilbur, *Riza Shah Pahlavi*, p. 118.

19. Ibid, p. 120.

20. L.P. Elwell-Sutton, "Reza Shah the Great: Founder of the Pahlavi Dynasty", Lenczowski, ed, *Iran Under the Pahlavis*, p. 45.

21. Avery, *Modern Iran*, p. 284.

22. Wilbur, *Riza Shah Pahlavi*, p. 146.

23. Ibid, p. 122.

24. Avery, *Modern Iran*, p. 285.

25. Amin Banani, *The Modernization of Iran 1921-1941* (Stanford, CA: Stanford University Press, 1961), p. 114.

26. Ibid, p. 134.

27. Elwell-Sutton, "Reza Shah the Great: Founder of the Pahlavi Dynasty," Lenczowski, ed, *Iran Under the Pahlavis*, p. 32.

28. Avery, *Modern Iran*, p. 273.

29. Wilbur, *Riza Shah Pahlavi*, p. 177.

30. Banani, *The Modernization of Iran*, p. 132.

31. Ibid, p. 45.

32. Ibid, p. 92.

33. Ibid, p. 94.

34. Wilbur, *Riza Shah Pahlavi*, p. 146.

35. Avery, *Modern Iran*, p. 290.

36. Wilbur, *Riza Shah Pahlavi*, p. 189.

37. Eliz Sanasarian, *The Women's Rights Movement in Iran* (New York: Praeger, 1982), p. 62.

38. Avery, *Modern Iran*, p. 273.

39. Sanasarian, *The Women's Rights Movement in Iran*, p. 64.

40. Ibid.

41. L. P. Elwell-Sutton, "The Iranian Press, 1941-1947." *Journal of Persian Studies*, pp. 65-66.

42. Soraya Esfandiary, *The Autobiography of H.I.H. Princess Soraya*, C. Fitzgibbon, trans. (London: Arthur Barker, 1963), p. 68.

43. Richard Cottam, *Nationalism in Iran*, (Pittsburgh: University of Pittsburgh Press, 1979), p. 288.

44. Hossein Bashiriyeh, *State and Revolution in Iran*, (London: Croom Helm, 1984), p. 19.

45. Focusing on "class analysis," Bashiriyeh identifies five (economic) foundations for the regime: (1) state control of financial resources; (2) success of economic growth program; (3) creation of "an equilibrium of classes through their economic control"; (4) patron-client relations with the upper-bourgeoisie, and; (5) expansion of the coercive forces of the state (*State and Revolution in Iran*, pp. 29-30). While such methods were in fact used by the state to expand its control over society, they did not form the "foundations" of the regime as such.

46. See, for example, Esfandiary, *The Autobiography of H.I.M. Princess Soraya*, pp. 62, 70.

47. Ibid, p. 49.

48. Khosrow Fatemi, "Leadership by distrust: The ShahModus Operandi," *The Middle East Journal*, vol. 36, no. 1, (Winter 1982), p. 49.

49. Ibid, p. 51.

50. Mohammad Reza Pahlavi, *Answer to History* (New York: Stein & Day, 1980), p. 124.

51. Ibid.

52. Anthony Parsons, Britain's last ambassador to Iran before the revolution, is one such observer. He maintains that SAVAK paid too much attention to students while ignoring the clergy (*The Pride and the Fall*, pp. 33-34).

53. Ann Lambton, *The Persian Land Reform 1962-1966* (Oxford: Clarendon Press, 1969), pp. 60-61.

54. Rouhollah Ramazani. *The Foreign Policy of Iran: 1500-1941* (Charlottesville, VA: University Press of Virginia, 1966), p. 171.

55. Ibid, p. 198.

56. Ibid, p. 173.

57. Ibid, p. 190.

58. Ibid, p. 196.

59. Ibid, p. 222

60. Ibid, p. 223.

61. Ibid.

62. Ibid, p. 228.

63. Quoted in Ervand Abrahamian *Iran Between Two Revolutions* (Princeton, NJ: Princeton University Press, 1982), p. 165.

64. Pahlavi, *Answer to History*, p. 70.

65. For a detailed discussion of Soviet-Iranian relations in this period, see Faramarz Fatemi *The U.S.S.R. in Iran* (London: Thomas Yoseloff, 1980), Chapters 2 and 3.

66. James Bill, *The Eagle and the Lion: The Tragedy of American-Iranian*

Relations (New Haven, CT: Yale University Press, 1988), p. 30.

67. Shahram Chubin and Sepehr Zabih, *The Foreign Relations of Iran: A Developing State in a Zone of Great-Power Conflict* (Berkeley, CA: University of California Press, 1974), pp. 38-39.

68. Bill, *The Eagle and the Lion*, p. 39.

69. For a full treatment of Mussadiq's tenure in offices, see Sepehr Zabih, *The Mussadegh Era* (Chicago: Lake View Press, 1982).

70. Abrahamian, *Iran Between Two Revolutions*, p. 189.

71. Bill, *The Eagle and the Lion*, p. 85.

72. Chubin and Zabih, *The Foreign Relations of Iran*, p. 48.

73. Homa Katouzian, *The Political Economy of Modern Iran 1926-1979* (New York: New York University Press, 1981), p. 202.

74. Pahlavi, *Mission For My Country*, p. 125.

75. Chubin and Zabih, *The Foreign Relations of Iran*, p. 48.

76. Ibid, p. 63.

77. Bill, *The Eagle and the Lion*, p. 132.

78. Ibid.

79. Ibid, pp. 176-177.

80. Robert Litwak, *Detente and the Nixon Doctrine: American Foreign Policy and the Pursuit of Stability* (Cambridge: Cambridge University Press, 1984), p. 135.

81. Ibid, p. 78.

82. Pahlavi, *Mission For My Country*, pp. 294-6.

83. Gary Sick, *All Fall Down: America's Tragic Encounter with Iran* (New York: Random House, 1985), p. 18.

84. Quoted in Litwak, *Detente and the Nixon Doctrine*, p. 141.

85. Jimmy Carter, *Keeping Faith* (London: Collins, 1982), p. 143.

86. Michael Ledeen and William Lewis, *Debacle: The American Failure in Iran* (New York: Alfred Knopf, 1981), p. 77.

87. Quoted in ibid.

88. Ibid, p. 85.

89. Bill, *The Eagle and the Lion*, p. 131.

90. Ahmad Kasravi is the most vivid example of this category of notable Iranian historians who glorify the Constitutional Revolution and discuss its actors in a selective manner. See his *Tarikh-e Mashruteh-e Iran* (History of Iran's Constitutionalism) (Tehran: n.p., n.d.)

91. Sanasarian, *The Women's Rights Movement in Iran*, p. 67.

92. Akhavi, *Religion and Politics in Contemporary Iran*, p. 38.

93. Ali Davani, *Nehzat-e Rouhaniyun-e Iran* (The Struggle of the Iranian Clergy) Vol. 3 (Tehran: n.p., n.d.), offers a fully documented account of the 1963 disturbances.

94. Quoted in ibid, p. 91.

95. For a detailed treatment of the background and the causes of the 1978-79 revolution, see Mehran Kamrava, *Revolution in Iran: Roots of Turmoil* (London: Routledge, 1990).

96. *Ittela'at* (17 Day 2536/7 January 1978), p. 7.

97. Mehran Kamrava, *Revolution in Iran*, p. 41.

98. Ibid, pp. 45-6.

99. Ibid, p. 50.

4

The Islamic Republic

The success of the revolutionary movement ushered in a new era in Iran's political history. The 1978-79 revolution represented by far one of the most dramatic departures from the traditional mold of Iranian politics, at least in appearance if not in substance. For the first time ever in Iranian history, a revolution had been launched and had resulted in the permanent termination of dynastic rule in the country. Even the Constitutional Revolution, that lasting and almost mythical milestone in Iranian history, had not achieved so much by not only curbing the autocracy of the crown but by overthrowing it all together. The dreams and ideals of the many thousands who had risked their lives by chanting revolutionary slogans in the daily street demonstrations had finally come true. Revolution filled the air in Tehran and other Iranian cities. The house of the Middle East's most powerful ruler, supported by a superpower and a sophisticated military of its own, had crumbled at the hands of the revolution. Twenty-five hundred years of monarchical despotism had finally come to an end, and, supposedly, a new era of personal and political liberties had begun.

While the dramatic events of January and February 1979 marked the end of the Pahlavi dynasty, for the new powerholders the real revolution had just begun. The movement against the Shah had been launched by a mostly unorganized and *de facto* coalition of groups with highly divergent ideological persuasions. The personification of Ayatollah Khomeini as the embodiment of the movement against the shah did not necessarily endear the clergy to most other, nonreligious revolutionary groups, notably the *Fadaiyan* and the *Mujahedeen* guerrillas. These guerrillas had played a pivotal role in the final days of the shah's reign by attacking several military installations in Tehran and in other cities. They now wanted a share of power in the post-revolutionary era. Similarly, most of the secular intellectuals who had rallied to Khomeini's support and who had emerged as prominent figures within the revolutionary movement did not share Khomeini's narrow interpretation of Shi'ite principles and developed increasingly sharp differences with the Ayatollah and his emerging block of new allies. What resulted was an ugly but inevitable breakup of the anti-shah coalition, a bloody and violent jockeying for positions, and eventually the emergence of one of the camps, that of Khomeini and his ardent followers, as the revolution's prime beneficiaries.

The 1978-79 revolution removed once and for all the system of monarchy from Iranian history and politics. But this permanent change in the system of government did not fundamentally alter the form of *governance* practiced in Iran. The Shah was removed, all of his loyal supporters were purged and many were executed, a new government machinery replaced the old, and nearly every single policy of the old regime was reversed. But the former regime's most ample characteristic, autocracy, continued to be equally prominent in the new order. The revolution, in essence, succeeded in achieving all of its peripheral goals. It changed names, titles, and personalities. It banished many individuals and glorified others. But it failed in its most fundamental goal and challenging task of establishing democracy in Iran. When the dust raised by the revolution was finally settled, there were little substantive differences between the political systems of the pre- and the post-revolutionary eras. That one political feature which many of the revolutionaries wanted to be rid of, autocracy, continued to remain intact. Autocracy was, in fact, exercised in post-revolutionary Iran with a zeal rarely evident during the reign of the Pahlavis.

While autocracy continued to persist through the 1978-79 revolution, so far there have not been marked signs of a revolution against the relatively young Islamic Republic. Several developments since the revolution appear to invalidate such an assertion. The Kurdish rebellion in quest of self-autonomy and the relentless and bloody campaigns of groups like the *Mujahedeen* to eliminate the regime's key leaders represent two examples of an apparent embryonic revolutionary movement against the regime. Yet in one way or another, such developments are all outgrowths of the 1978-79 revolution itself. Although the *Mujahedeen* claim to be spearheading a "second revolution," for them the "first" revolution never really ended: they never attained the freedom of expression and the political power they had sought under the shah. As for the *Tudeh* party and the *Fadaiyan* guerrillas, for the *Mujahedeen* the revolution had been "pirated" by groups even more brutal than the shah.[1]

If the *Mujahedeen* or other groups have not made substantial progress toward initiating a "second revolution" in Iran, it is certainly not due to a lack of efforts. Besides the *Mujahedeen*, groups opposing the new order include remnants still loyal to the previous regime, the communist *Tudeh* party, and the Maoist *Fadaiyan* guerrillas. Outside of Iran, supporters of the dethroned Pahlavi dynasty have been the most vocal opponents of the regime. Due to their close relationship *vis-a-vis* the former regime, most "monarchists" have considerable financial resources at their disposal. But because of their concentration outside of the country, their activities against the regime have occurred solely among Iranian expatriates living abroad. Furthermore, despite their common adherence to a monarchical system, the pro-monarchy groups are divided among themselves and form a number of contending factions with serious cleavages. Two of the ex-shah's prime ministers lead their own resistance fronts, while a third is led by the shah's son, former Crown Prince Reza Pahlavi, who later proclaimed himself as Iran's legitimate king.

The activities of the two former premiers, Ali Amini and Shapour Bakhtiar,[2] have been limited to issuing grandiose but hollow warnings and threats to Tehran's new leaders. The ex-shah's son has been unable to achieve a whole lot more. Although his supporters are relatively more enthusiastic than those of either Amini or Bakhtiar, he has been unable effectively to distance himself from the corrupt legacy of his father's rule. His own initiatives and pronouncements also lack conviction and tenacity. Furthermore, his semi-organized political apparatus, put in charge of spearheading a new revolution in Iran, has been plagued by internal dissension and disagreements among its principal policy-makers.[3]

After more than a decade of theocratic rule, the monarchists have grudgingly accepted the fact that the reestablishment of monarchy in Iran is all but an impossibility. After years of promising an impending takeover by a supposedly royalist military, pro-monarchy leaders have in recent years become more hesitant to make such definite promises. Like most others seeking to overthrow the Islamic Republic, those hoping to reinstate monarchy in Iran have reluctantly accepted the fact that the ayatollahs running the country today are much stronger and more shrewed than most observers had originally thought. Pro-monarchy politicians have also realized that despite some measure of support among expatriates who left Iran after the revolution, hardly anyone inside the country wishes to see a return to the old, exclusionary system of monarchy. Contrary to what many monarchists had hoped, there have been no signs of a popular uprising in Iran against the ayatollahs in the same way as there were against the Shah.

Apart from the monarchists, and considerably more serious than them, are groups which took active part in the revolutionary movement but were soon disenchanted with the emerging clerical power-block. They include the communist *Tudeh* party, the *Fadaiyan*, and the

Mujahedeen guerrillas. Although all three groups have been more active in the Iranian political scene than the monarchists, they have also been unable to make any significant headway in overthrowing the Islamic regime. Soon after the revolution, the *Tudeh* and a faction of the *Fadaiyan* aligned themselves with the new regime and subsequently lost a great deal of prestige and popularity among their communist followers. While the parties justified their alliance with the clergy on grounds of the new regime's "anti-imperialist" character, many saw it as an opportunist maneuver and a sign of weakness.4 For its part, when the regime no longer needed their alliance, it executed and imprisoned many noted communist figures. One of the *Tudeh*'s original theorists, Ehsan Tabari, was forced to write apologetic columns in Tehran's pro-regime daily newspapers ridiculing communism and praising the virtues of Islam, adding much to the dismay and the disillusionment of Iran's communist intelligentsia.5 For the time being at least, communism has been effectively eliminated as a viable political force in Iran.

The *Mujahedeen* have had a somewhat different history since the revolution. Soon after the new regime began its ruthless campaign to quiet those objecting to its conformist policies, the *Mujahedeen* emerged as the main group vowing to overthrow it through a second revolution. The group's leaders escaped to France and its members inside Iran launched a highly successful terror campaign against the regime's key leaders. But the regime proved to be resilient to armed insurrection and it quickly found capable replacements for the influential figures who the *Mujahedeen* were assassinating. Realizing the ineffectiveness of their efforts, the *Mujahedeen* shifted tactics. Their leader, Masoud Rajavi, signed a peace treaty with Iraq and eventually moved there when he was expelled by the French government. The *Mujahedeen* justified their move by arguing that the Iranian regime's overthrow could be achieved through its military defeat in its war with Iraq. The organization's guerrillas thus began fighting Iranian forces alongside Iraqi soldiers in the hope of expediting Iran's defeat and the subsequent collapse of the regime.

Regardless of its tactical or strategic merits, the *Mujahedeen's* move to Iraq and their military cooperation with the Iraqi army cost them much of the popularity and support they had gained soon after the revolution. Although the Iranian regime may not necessarily be popular among most Iranians, strong nationalist sentiments continue to prevail in Iran and cooperation with Iraq during the war was popularly perceived as outright treason. Furthermore, as part of an "ideological revolution" within the organization, Rajavi married the divorced wife of one of his lieutenants and elevated her to the position of "co-leader" within the organization.6 Whatever the ideological motives behind this move, it also adversely affected the popularity of the *Mujahedeen* and made the organisation appear to the public as a family dynasty run by leaders more hungry for power than either Khomeini or the Shah.

To this day, all three of the potential opposition groups active against the Islamic Republic continue to operate in a political and social vacuum, void of any meaningful popular support. The monarchists hope for a U.S.-sponsored coup to put them back in power (in the same way as they were in 1953), while the pro-Soviet *Tudeh* party hoped that Iran's improved relations with the former Soviet Union will result in an easing of restrictions on its activities. With the collapse of the Soviet Union in 1990-91, the *Tudeh* lost its major international patron and, consequently, its hope for becoming a major player in Iranian politics in the near future. The *Mujahedeen*, on the other hand, kept on engaging in military operations against the regime in the contested areas along the Iraqi border, hoping to achieve what Iraq's formidable forces were unable to do in a bloody eight-year war. In July 1988, the *Mujahedeen* (in collusion with the Iraqi army) scored seemingly impressive but temporary military gains against Iranian forces. But it quickly became evident that Iran's military setbacks were part of a planned tactical retreat which trapped the *Mujahedeen* behind Iranian defense lines and resulted in a significant military defeat for the guerrillas.

So long as the current political constellation of the Islamic Republic remains intact, a "Second Revolution" remains an elusive dream at best. For such an event to occur, not only do the positions of the different groups opposing the regime need to change radically but also the very populist and inclusionary underpinning of Tehran's theocracy need to be dramatically altered. In order for a revolution to succeed, in Iran or elsewhere, an opposition group needs to have more power than the ruling elite. Ever since the Islamic Republic was established in 1979, its opponents have been steadily losing their power and popularity while the regime has grown both in its coercive capacities as well as its populist base of support. As long as the regime itself continues to be the most powerful political force in the country, any changes that may appear in Iran will only be initiated from within the existing political system.

Iran's post-revolutionary regime is an essentially populist one, relying on the popular appeal of Islam for its legitimacy and allowing certain approved forms of political participation such as parliamentary debates and elections. One observer has branded the Islamic Republic's political system as a "theocratic populist" one,[7] while another maintains that it is based on "neo-Shi'ism."[8] Whatever the actual terminology used in describing it, there is overall agreement that the Islamic Republic is an authoritarian and populist regime.[9] A combination of these two characteristics--inclusionary forms of political participation and weak opposition forces--have so far prevented the appearance of serious and mass-based uprisings against the new order. Those seeking to overthrow the Islamic Republic have so far been either remnants of the former regime or those groups who participated in the revolution but are now excluded from power. There is yet to appear an opposition movement whose roots lie in the politics of the post-revolutionary era. It is, perhaps, only a matter of time before such a movement appears, considering the authoritarian nature of the regime and its inability to indefinitely hold on to Islam as a legitimizing ideology. For the present, the Islamic Republic can be best understood through examining its autocratic nature and the internal factionalism that threatens its cohesion.

AUTOCRACY

There were three separate mechanisms through which Ayatollah Khomeini and his increasingly narrow group of followers established their hegemony over the post-revolutionary regime. These three mechanisms were the Friday Prayer ceremonies, the Islamic Republic Party (IRP) (*Hezb-e Jomhuri-ye Islami*), and the Majles. All three mechanisms served as tools through which the popular appeal that the *ulama* had acquired during the revolution was steadily transformed into institutionalized political power. They also facilitated the political ascension of individuals who were staunchly loyal to Khomeini and who vehemently opposed other, mostly secular, figures and groups who had also taken part in the revolution. Consequently, in the early years of its existence all three institutions became the principal foundations upon which the Islamic Republic was based.

Friday Prayers and the *Ulama*

The Friday Prayer ceremonies were a unique blessing naturally bestowed on the clerical establishment. Immediately after the start of the revolutionary movement, all provincial Friday Prayer Imams declared their complete allegiance to the revolution and to Ayatollah Khomeini. During the publicly held Friday Prayer meetings, they exalted the ayatollah and his clergy-dominated support base by discrediting the communists, the "liberals," and whoever who was not completely supportive of Khomeini. Soon Khomeini personally began appointing the Friday Prayer Imams, and they became known throughout the country as "the representatives of Imam Khomeini." Once Khomeini's powers were fully entrenched and his authority unchallenged, the functions of the Friday Prayers changed. In place of routinizing the *ulama*'s powers, they became one of the means through which the ruling clergy propagated their views in support of the government and announced important policy decisions to the public. Such important announcements are usually made in Tehran, where the position of Friday Prayer Imam has often been filled by the government's highest political officers, such as Presidents Khamenei and Rafsenjani. Nevertheless, important announcements were also made by provincial Friday Prayer Imams, the most significant being the announcement of Ayatollah Montazeri's appointment as Khomeini's designated successor by the Qazvin Friday Prayer Imam in 1985.[10]

The Rise and Fall of the Islamic Republican Party

A second mechanism through which the Iranian regime maintained its popularity and support among the public (up until June 1987) was the Islamic Republic Party. The IRP was established for the specific purpose of attaining political power for the *ulama* and then giving legitimacy to clerical rule. Soon after the collapse of the Pahlavi regime, a group of clerics came to the realization that a political party was needed to redirect the popular enthusiasm generated during the revolution into an organized, institutional support base. Prior to the Shah's departure from Iran, a Council of Revolution (*Shoura-ye Enghelab*) had been created by prominent revolutionary activists who had gathered around Ayatollah Khomeini in order to coordinate anti-regime activities both inside Iran and abroad. While the Council functioned as a policy-making body for the revolutionaries, a number of factors prevented it from becoming a means for the clergy to acquire hegemony over the post-revolutionary government. Besides its being intended only as a coordinating body for the formulation of a revolutionary strategy, the Council of Revolution included individuals who held views and persuasions which greatly varied from those of Ayatollah Khomeini and other clerics who had rallied behind him. Of the Council's thirteen members, only six were clerics while the remainder included individuals such as Mehdi Bazargan and AbolhassanBanisadr, both of whom had shown an aversion to direct clerical rule in the post-Pahlavi era. Consequently, the clerics needed another mean by which they could attain power in the new government. While still in exile in France, Ayatollah Khomeini had argued that the *ulama* will not be allowed to participate in "running the country" after the revolution[11] and had nominated a secular figure within the National Front, Mehdi Bazargan, to head a provisional government. Fearing total seclusion from the country's political life, six clerics (all of whom were members of the Council of Revolution) quickly formed a political party with the specific aim of consolidating control over the various branches of the government and its ministries. The new party, called the Islamic Republic Party, was established in February 1979 by Ayatollahs Rabbani-Amlashi, Beheshti, and Musavi-Ardebili, and Hujjatoleslams Bahonar, Khamenei, and Hashemi-Rafsenjani.[12] The founding members soon formed a Managing Committee and wrote letters to thirty prominent secular and religious figures inviting them to join the IRP. Almost all high-ranking ayatollahs rejected the new party's invitation while some twenty individuals joined it. The party soon began publishing a daily newspaper, called *Islamic Republic* (*Jomhuri-ye Islami*), and launched its climactic quest to power.

The political evolution of the new party can be divided into three approximate phases. The first phase lasted from the IRP's initial formation in 1979 up until the setback it suffered during the first presidential elections in 1980. In this period, the party faced considerable difficulties in achieving a measure of political credibility and in gaining the trust of Ayatollah Khomeini. As a result, it was not successful in establishing control over the political machinery as quickly as its founders had hoped.[13] A number of reasons underlined the IRP's initial setbacks and its inability to achieve a speedy hegemony over the post-revolutionary government. To begin with, the IRP was forced to fight political and ideological battles on four fronts: against Bazargan and his provisional government; against Banisadr, another secular figure whose lack of party organization was somewhat compensated for by his considerable personal popularity throughout the country; against secular nationalists and other supporters of the once-powerful National Front; and against the guerrilla organisations, especially the *Fadaiyan* and the *Mujhedeen*.

The IRP's difficulties were further compounded by Khomeini's lack of enthusiasm regarding the formation and the functions of the new party and his mistrust of the political skills and the know-how of the IRP's founders. While still in Paris, Khomeini had in fact objected to the formation of a party by the clergy and had deliberately refrained from appointing clerics to the provisional government.[14] This same lack of trust led Khomeini to abstain from endorsing the IRP's candidate during the first presidential elections and to support Banisadr's candidacy instead.[15]

The slow progress of the IRP and its clerical leaders in gaining political power did not last long and was soon replaced by an aggressive and energetic revival, one that took place at the expense of the party's opponents. Thus began the second phase of IRP's development, during which Ayatollah Beheshti's shrewed and capable leadership of the party enabled IRP-affiliated clerics to obtain not only important positions within the government but, more significantly, to gain the trust of Ayatollah Khomeini. Having lost the executive branch to the increasingly intransigent Banisadr, the IRP then concentrated its efforts on getting its members elected to the Majles. Earlier, the IRP had been able to occupy more than half of the seventy-two seats in the Assembly of Experts (*Shoura-ye Khebregan*), elected in August 1979 in order to draw up the country's new constitution. The Assembly had twenty-seven secular members and forty-five clerics, about thirty-six of whom were either members of the IRP or were closely affiliated with it.[16] The party was even more successful in the Majles elections of March 1980, managing to get eighty percent of its candidates elected to the body.[17] Of a total of 270 seats, more than 130 of the elected deputies were from the IRP, forty were supporters of Banisadr, and some seventy were either independent or were affiliated with the National Front.[18] The IRP's dominance over the legislature was completed when Hashemi-Rafsenjani, one of the party's founders and its Deputy Secretary General, was elected as the Speaker of the Majles.

The gradual advancement of IRP-affiliated clerics came at the expense of secular nationalists such as Bazargan and Banisadr. Bazargan and his cabinet had earlier resigned in frustration on 5 November 1979, a day after the American embassy in Tehran was occupied and its personnel were taken hostage by students vowing to obey no one but Ayatollah Khomeini. With the Majles under its control, the IRP set out to add the executive branch to its sphere of influence through the office of the prime minister. According to constitutional procedures, the president appointed a prime minister, but his appointment was subject to the approval of the Majles.[19] Exercising effective control over the Majles, the IRP's leaders became determined to ensure that the prime minister was either a member of their party or was sympathetic to its goals and policies. IRP members in the Majles thus refused to accept the credentials of Banisadr's nominees for the office. The President tried to outmaneuver the IRP by nominating Ayatollah Khomeini's son, Ahmad, but the elder Khomeini disapproved and maintained that "the nation can be better served if those related to me stay out of the government."[20]

In August 1980, Banisadr was finally forced to nominate Mohammad Ali Raja'i. Although Raja'i was not an IRP member himself, he was closely affiliated with it and enjoyed the full support of its powerful and influential leaders such as Beheshti and Rafsenjani.[21] Raja'i appointed a fourteen-man cabinet, seven of whom were from the IRP.[22] This heightened the growing friction between President Banisadr and his small clique of moderates and the clerical leadership of the IRP and ultimately Ayatollah Khomeini. Banisadr's fall from power in June 1981 signaled the effective domination of the IRP over the executive.

Parallel to the growth of IRP's political power was a dramatic rise in the level of its popularity throughout the country. This popularity was the result of the growing religious fervor which had taken root across Iran after the fall of the monarchy. Moderate figures from the National Front had proven to be incapable of coping with the tumult of post-revolutionary politics. The *Mujahedeen* and the *Fadaiyan* guerrillas had openly endorsed demands made by the Kurdish and the Turkmen ethnic minorities for self-autonomy and had thus given the IRP grounds for a vehement propaganda campaign against themselves. Banisadr was also at a disadvantageous position *vis-a-vis* the IRP since he lacked the support of a political party or a similar organization which could mobilize popular support in his favor. The IRP, meanwhile, had as many as 60,000 to 70,000 people affiliated with it in different ways throughout Iran, with the notable exceptions of the city of Tabriz and the Kurdistan region.[23] In Tabriz, the more moderate Ayatollah Shariatmadari, who was accused of plotting to overthrow Khomeini in 1983 and put under house arrest, had always enjoyed considerable influence and the IRP was incapable of attracting supporters from among his followers. The Kurdistan region had also been a traditional base of support for the communist-oriented Kurdistan Democratic Party (KDP) (*Hezb-e Demokrat-e Kurdestan*). Soon after the revolution, the KDP had begun demanding autonomy for Kurdistan and had embarked on a bitter campaign of armed struggle against the regime. The IRP, meanwhile, had ready access to the extensive communication network of mosques needed to solicit the support of the people since most clerics either belonged to the party or supported its objectives. Additionally, most of the more prominent clerics who were affiliated with the party were often leaders of the Friday Prayer sermons, thus being afforded with yet another forum through which they could propagate their cause and attract supporters. The transformation of the pulpit into a powerful political unit, a process put into motion during the revolutionary movement, was finalised after the revolution, and, in fact, greatly facilitated the IRP's political dominance in 1980 and 1981.

The second phase of IRP's life was not as extensive as some of its leaders might have liked. By the mid-1980s, the very viability of the party was beginning to be questioned. While the ouster of Banisadr had paved the way for the IRP's domination of the executive branch, it had also resulted in an open guerrilla warfare between the *Mujahedeen* and the regime. In their bloody campaign against the regime and its most vociferous proponent, the IRP, the *Mujahedeen* assassinated one party official after another. Before long they had killed Dr. Hassan Ayat, the party's main ideologue, and the influential Ayatollah Beheshti, one of the IRP's founders and its energetic Secretary General.

With Beheshti's removal, IRP's life entered into a third phase, lasting from July 1981 to June 1987. This third stage was marked by the party's continuous decline, brought about by two factors. First, with the growing entrenchment of the post-revolutionary government, individual personalities gained dominance within the regime, and consequently abandoned the party organization because they did not need it to help them attain and hold power. Having served its purpose as an instrument for attaining state power, the IRP had outlived its utility and become increasingly obsolete. Related to this development was growing factionalism within the IRP's highest ranks, epitomized by the bitter rivalry between its second Secretary General, President Ali Khamenei, and its Deputy Secretary General, Majles Speaker Rafsenjani. The party's demise came to a head by its disbanding by Khomeini, which came in the form of a positive reply to a joint request made by Rafsenjani and Khamenei regarding dissolving the party. The Majles Speaker and the President wrote to Khomeini that:

> ... it is felt that the existence of the party no longer has the benefits of its early days and, on the contrary, party polarisation under present conditions may provide an excuse for discord and factionalism, damaging the unity of the nation. It may even waste energies for encountering one another.[24]

Once its goals of acquiring power were achieved, the IRP's functions had changed from one of attaining power for the clerical establishment into becoming a sphere of influence for individual personalities and officeholders. While the IRP was initially a relatively powerful instrument for the exertion of power, it later became a source of contention and disagreement within the regime, so much so that former Prime Minister Musavi, one of the party's Central Committee member, was rumored to have resigned from his position in the party.[25]

Another means through which autocracy was reestablished in post-revolutionary Iran was through the new regime's constitution. Provisions were built into the constitution that ensured the personal dominance of Ayatollah Khomeini, and subsequently his emerging block of clerical followers, over the new system. This was done through two specific constitutional mechanisms: the Majles, which was ironically viewed as the strongest institution capable of preventing the reappearance of dictatorship, and the theological concept of *faqih*, one elaborated by Khomeini himself and adopted by the new constitution almost verbatim.

The Majlis Revived

Following the victory over the Pahlavi regime, a general feeling prevailed among the revolutionaries that a strong parliament would provide an effective safeguard against the reappearance of a dictatorial political system. Extensive constitutional powers were given to the Majles, therefore, and numerous provisions were created to ensure its leverage over other government branches. Three factors lay behind the desire to ensur the constitutional superiority of the Majles over the offices of the prime minister and the president. First, in the intellectual tradition of modern Iran, democracy had always been equated with greater powers for the parliament. Thus, during the Constitutional Revolution, intellectuals seeking to put an end to monarchical absolutism devised a constitution in which the Majles had considerably more powers than the crown. This was repeated during Dr. Mussadiq's tenure in office from 1951 to 1953, when he curbed the powers and the privileges of the Shah. Following the 1978-79 revolution, i t was similarly believed that a strong Majles would guarantee the evolution of a democratic political system.

Secondly, while the executive branch was suspected of having the potential to become an absolute center of power, a collective parliamentary body was perceived to be less susceptible to such a tendency. It was felt, in fact, that a powerful parliament would offset any authoritarian tendencies that may be inherent to the executive branch. Finally, by the time the constitution was being drafted, Banisadr already occupied the presidency following a major electoral setback for the IRP. With seventy-six percent of the votes cast in Banisadr's favor, the IRP and its allied clerics wanted to secure an even stronger foothold through which they could exert control over the government. When an Assembly of Experts was elected to draw up a constitution, it was replete with IRP candidates. The Assembly thus gave greater constitutional powers to the Majles not only on ideological grounds but also because of immediate, practical considerations. By having its candidates gain a majority in the upcoming Majles elections, the IRP could then mount an effective campaign to undermine Banisadr's presidency and augment its own influence within the government.

The *Faqih:* Theocracy Personified

The precursor to the Majles, the Assembly of Experts, also provided the official mean through which all institutions and offices of the new regime were made subservient to the person of Ayatollah Khomeini. In drawing up the new constitution, the Assembly of Experts declared Khomeini to be the sole *faqih*, the country's supreme jurist-consult. Khomeini had elaborated on the concept of *Velayat Faqih* (literally translated as "Governance of the Religiously Learned") in a book he had written in 1971 under the same title. In his book Khomeini outlined in detail the executive, judicial, and the legislative functions of government in an ideal Islamic community. Such a community, he argued, will be governed by a *kalif* or a *faqih*, someone learned in the religious sciences, until the return of the hidden Imam Mehdi. The *faqih* is responsible to see that the Moslem community's laws and mode of life correspond to Islamic principles. Such a person needs to be pious, possess a deep understanding of justice, and be knowledgeable about laws and other legal matters. The *faqih* needs to be not only an administrator, he must also be a legislator, a judge, and an army commander at the same time. He must be both a ruler and an onlooker over the whole system.[26]

Being replete with clerical supporters of Khomeini, the Assembly of Experts incorporated the concept of *faqih* into the republic's constitution and designated Khomeini as the first holder of the position. In his own writings, Khomeini had not specified the details of how someone could become a *faqih*, merely stating that whoever possessed a *faqih*'s qualities could claim to be one.[27] This ambiguity was at least theoretically clarified by the Assembly of Experts. Popular consensus was declared to be the sole means for any qualified theologian to become a *faqih*. Having attained that status through his mass-based popularity, Khomeini was designated by the Assembly to be the Islamic Republic's first *faqih*. If no person is believed qualified enough by a majority of people to become the *faqih* after Khomeini's death, then a popularly-elected council of three to five theologians will either take over the *faqih*'s functions or will appoint someone to that position.[28] Yet the actual decision as to who would succeed Khomeini as the *faqih* was not made by an elected council. After considerable speculation about whether to appoint an individual to the post or to hold elections for a replacement council, Ayatollah Hussein Ali Montazeri, a former student of Khomeini and his protege, was announced to have become the *faqih*'s designated successor in November 1985. Khomeini was officially referred to as the "Leader" (*Rahbar*) and his heir apparent labelled as the "Deputy Leader" (*Nayeb-e Rahbar*).

Just as Khomeini had theorized in his book, the Assembly of Experts granted sweeping constitutional powers to the *faqih*. He was empowered to be the supreme commander of the armed forces, declare wars or accept peace with other countries, and appoint the country's highest ranking judicial authorities. He was also required to appoint the clerical members of the Council of Guardians (*Shoura-ye*

Negahban), a body with complete authority over the Majles. The Council of Guardians is made up of a collection of legal and theological experts responsible for reviewing and approving the credentials of the elected deputies. The Council is also empowered to either approve the bills passed by the Majles or to send them back for modifications. More significantly, the constitution gives the *faqih* the power to reject the inauguration of a popularly-elected president if the *faqih* determines that the president-elect is not fit for office. Similarly, the *faqih* can dismiss a president from office with the approval of the Majles and the Supreme Court.

Such constitutional provisions dramatically facilitated the reappearance of political autocracy in post-revolutionary Iran. Officially, Khomeini, as the *faqih*, was granted powers more extensive than even the shah's.[29] The ayatollah and his emerging block of followers in the Majles and in the IRP were able to utilize the position of *faqih* to exclude some of their former revolutionary allies from power. Initially, the Council of Guardians refused to approve the credentials of a number of deputies elected to the Majles who were known supporters of either Banisadr or the National Front. Thus the influence of those not enthusiastic about Khomeini's absolute rule was kept in check in the Majles. During the first presidential elections of 1980, the IRP also successfully maneuvered to have the *Mujahedeen*'s presidential candidate, Masoud Rajavi, disqualified on grounds that his organization had objected to constitutional provisions regarding the *faqih*. Eventually, Khomeini and the IRP stripped the popularly-elected president of his authority through relying extensively on the constitution. When the war with Iraq broke out, Khomeini had relegated his constitutional powers as the commander in chief of the armed forces to President Banisadr. In an effort to oust Banisadr, in June 1981 Khomeini first relieved him from command of the armed forces and, with the full approval of the IRP-dominated Majles and the Supreme Court, dismissed him from the presidency. Banisadr's ouster from office was, in essence, a most official *coup d'etat*.

With Banisadr removed from the presidency, Khomeini's ascension to autocracy was completed. Up until then, the President had consistently criticized and opposed the policies being pursued by the cabinet and the Majles. In his efforts to gain some leverage against the IRP's extensive organizational network throughout the country, Banisadr had consistently tried to capitalize on his personal popularity among students and professionals through his newspaper and by giving frequent speeches. Yet his popularity proved to be only a minor obstacle for his opponents, who through the IRP and the Majles undermined the president whenever possible.

The manner in which Banisadr was removed proved even more

important than the reasons for his removal. Contentions and serious disagreements had developed between Banisadr and principal figures within the IRP ever since the party was first established. But Khomeini, while favoring the clerical block of the IRP over the secular president, did not involve himself in the conflict and refused to take sides until the last minute. Khomeini came out in opposition to Banisadr only after the IRP's efforts to oust the president had gained considerable momentum. This pattern of last-minute intervention was to become Khomeini's standard *modus operandi* later on. In the subtle but persistent factional conflicts that later developed within the regime, the *faqih* always abstained from intervening in support of one faction over another until he either sensed who the clear winner of the conflict would be or determined that his intervention was necessary in order to avoid a deadlock.

FACTIONALISM

The mammoth unity of February 1979, that unprecedented demonstration of solidarity between men and women, politicians and commoners, proved as impermanent as it was intense. The priorities of the revolutionary project had suddenly shifted, almost overnight. The principal goal was no longer to topple the Pahlavis but to construct a new polity, and not just any polity. The growing direction of the post-revolutionary regime toward Islam was assuming a finer point every week, month, and year that the new regime added to its life. The question of political correctness was no longer one of Islam or the ways of the others, that of the collective "infidels"--the communists, the "liberals," and the *Mujahedeen*. That was settled long ago, soon after the Ayatollahs began their crusade to purge, imprison, and kill those who were misguided and unwilling to repent. With age came the growing sophistication of the regime and hence the growing subtlety of the political question itself: which brand of Islam, or, more accurately, whose Islam, was to guide the new theocracy toward national salvation? This was the question that the ayatollahs began asking themselves in silence but with increasing frequency, one whose relevance assumed greater poignancy as the patriarch Imam's age drew him closer to his ultimate fate.

While factions did and in fact still continue to exist within the Islamic Republic, pinpointing them is made difficult by the fluidity of the system and by the elusive nature of the factions themselves and their respective proponents. This difficulty is further compounded by the dispersion of factions throughout the different organs of the government and the subtlety of the factional conflict between the various groups. Nevertheless, factions do exist within the regime and some of the government's most visible members have repeatedly called for "unity of word as well as deed" in order to lessen the frictions caused by factional infighting.[30]

Due to the political and the organizational configuration of the regime, the boundaries of each faction are often not clearly identifiable and at times the positions that the factions take overlap depending on the nature of the issues at hand. This elusiveness of factional delineations is further exacerbated by the very patrimonial bases on which the regime rests. Less powerful figures who have neither a secure base of support nor the patronage of influential allies are often forced to change allegiances and switch alliances in order to maximize their political longevity. This built-in necessity to alternate between allies and rivals and to adopt different positions on different issues itself serves to further deepen existing factional and ideological rivalries.

But to mistake the increasingly hostile cleavages which began separating once-unanimous clerics on purely ideological grounds is to fall into a trap nourished by none other than stewards of the Islamic Republic itself. It is true that alternative interpretations of specific Islamic concepts provided locus for the activities of fringe groups such as the *Hujjatiyeh* and the *Fadaiyan-e Islam*. But often the sources of intra-elite conflict among the new rulers were neither religious nor in any sense necessarily doctrinal. What separated groups of ayatollahs and their respective followers from one another were such issues as the role of the government *vis-a-vis* the economy, the question of political succession, and the extent to which exporting the revolution abroad was considered feasible and prudent. Equally important were a number of non-ideological factors: the clash of personalities among the clerics themselves; variations in ethnic background, class, and place of birth; and the degree of privileged access to the person of Khomeini.[31] Added to all of this were the shrewd hands of the Great Leader himself, the masterful political engineering of the Imam designed to keep his "children" not only in line but at one another's throats as well. Whatever his moral or ethical shortcomings, Khomeini was surely a politician of the first order.

Khomeini and His Divided Followers

Khomeini constructed an elaborate internal system of checks and balances within each ministry, bureau, and department. He knowingly placed personal rivals in competing positions in virtually every level of the government and maintained equally cordial relations with both. Through such a manipulative duality, he hoped to achieve two primary goals. His main concern was to ensure that political actors in potentially influential positions did not succeed in acquiring too much power and that anyone emerging as a power broker within the regime did so only with his explicit consent. Secondly, by placing rivals within the higher echelons of the administrative apparatus and by cultivating ties with all sides, Khomeini hoped to gain as much information as possible regarding even insignificant developments in the government.

To the very end, the Imam was bent on knowing exactly what his lieutenants were up to. This tactic had once been employed by the shah, although the monarch had applied this divisive scheme mostly to the military, where he had hoped to reduce the possibility of a coordinated coup by his generals. But in Khomeini's theocracy, practically every official with an influential position had an opponent placed in an equally powerful office. In some cases, Khomeini *created* positions and offices in order to counterweight the influence of another figure. Most often, such appointees were given the title "Representatives of the Imam" if there were no other existing positions through which they could counterbalance the influence of another figure: President Khamenei was designated as the head of the Supreme Defense Council, while his rival at the time, Majles Speaker Rafsenjani, became the "Imam's Representative" to the same body and was later elevated to the position of Commander in Chief. The Minister of Revolutionary Guards, Mohsen Rafiqdoost, was countered by a personal rival, Mohsen Rezai, appointed as the Commander of Revolutionary Guards. Each provincial Friday Prayer Imam had to contend with an IRP provincial head. And almost all deputy ministers in the various ministries got along neither with one another nor with their respective bosses.

Added to the divisiveness perpetuated by Khomeini in order to keep an eye on his subordinates were inherent factional rivalries due to ideology and interests among the various political actors themselves. This factionalism was practiced mainly through the very medians which had helped the *ulama* hegemonize post-revolutionary politics, namely the Majles, the IRP, and the Friday Prayer ceremonies. It was through these organs that competing orientations toward matters of economic policy, diplomatic course, and political succession found their expression.

Broadly, three distinctive camps developed. On one side were revolutionary diehards, toughened by the violence of the post-revolutionary years and bent on pursuing their dogma not just at home but also abroad. These were foot soldiers of the ultra-conservative expressions of the new order, a cadre of turbaned revolutionaries having finally come of political age and unwilling to let go. They included such abashedly reactionary groups as the Qum-based Theological Teachers'

Association (*Moddaresin-e Qom*), the *Hujjatiyeh*, and the *Fadaiyan-e Islam*. These were, for all intents and purposes, those elements within the Iranian government which the Western media had simplistically come to label as the "radicals" or "extremists."

On the other side were those who did not see the revolutionary merits of continued anti-American rhetoric, those who believed that some sort of accommodation with the Great Satan was a necessary part of the post-revolutionary and post-war construction. For them, revolutionary dogma was useful not as a viable tool for furthering the revolutionary project but as a weapon for opposing real or perceived enemies of the self. These were pragmatists, ruthless realists wisened by a cunning ability to ride the shifting sands of revolutionary politics. To the Western eye their conciliatory gestures made them appear as "moderates." But in reality the only moderation of men like Hashemi-Rafsenjani, first the Speaker of the Majles and later president, and Khamenei, president and later Khomeini's successor, was not in their revolutionary temperament but in their realization that to survive in the international system hostage-takings and loud noises do not offer lasting remedies.

And somewhere in between these two groups were a bunch of fiscal liberals, high-placed administrators, and bureaucrats who found the new underpinnings of the state in tune with their doctrinal agendas. In the beginning at least, the government had begun nationalizing a host of industries and enterprises, from banks and insurance companies to large factories and other private operations. Up until the war's end in 1988, during which the government's share of industry had steadily grown, the political arena belonged to these men, individuals like the former Prime Minister Musavi, who found themselves in chronic conflict with *Bazaari* merchants and other fiscal conservatives. Lacking political ambition and tenacity, however, these doctrinaire bureaucrats have in recent years all but withered from political life.

Motazeri's Political Ascent

One of the principal figures within the regime's factional drama was Ayatollah Hussein Ali Montazeri, a man who Khomeini installed as his designated successor in 1985 but later removed in 1989. Montazeri had emerged as the principal clerical spokesperson for the interests of fiscal conservatives soon after 1982, by which time the *ulama* had come to dominate the post-revolutionary regime. As one of Khomeini's old theology students and his faithful lieutenant ever since, Montazeri burst onto the national political scene soon after the revolution. He was appointed by Khomeini as the Friday Prayer Imam of Qom and in 1980 also became the supreme guide of the country's theological colleges, thus being able to appoint representatives to councils that ran these colleges.[32]

Later in the same year, Khomeini addressed Montazeri by the title of Grand Ayatollah (*Ayatollah uzma*), thus elevating the latter's status to only one rank below that of himself and making him eligible to become his successor. Ayatollah Khomeini also delegated greater religious and political authority to his former pupil, authorizing him to appoint members to the Supreme Judicial Council and putting him in charge of the secretariat of the Friday Prayer Imams.[33] Bolstered by the official media and by his own active interest in the daily affairs of the government, Ayatollah Montazeri soon emerged as one of the most powerful clerics, if not indeed as the second most powerful, after Khomeini. While there were at times challenges to his authority, Montazeri gradually overcame them and his official position as Iran's "Deputy Leader" for some time appeared secure and above reproach.

Like most others within the regime, Ayatollah Montazeri did not fit into a specific political and ideological category and it is difficult to definitively place him in the Islamic Republic's spectrum. This lack of clarity arouse from the fact that Montazeri expressed radical diplomatic views on the one hand and economically conservative views on the other. At the same time, he continuously called for a normalization of bureaucratic and administrative procedures and for a softening of revolutionary zeal by responsible officials. Economically, he consistently advocated lifting restrictions on the private sector, a view often voiced as subtle opposition to Prime Minister Musavi's efforts to curb inflation and to aid the "disinherited" (*mostazafan*) at the expense of *Bazaari* merchants. "If the government," Montazeri theorized

> becomes more active in giving more room to the private sector for goods distribution and confers the distribution of non-essential goods to the private sector, . . . certainly many of the problems concerning the new personnel, excessive hiring by the government and related procedures will no longer be a responsibility of the government and the government will be able to carry out its essential duties.[34]

He also maintained that

> . . . as much as possible, the government must not intervene directly in work that is outside of its jurisdiction, such as the distribution of minor and non-essential merchandise. . . It is the businessman or merchant himself who has both greater incentive to trade in and deliver merchandise to the one who

> really needs it. . . . In my view, if the government turned most
> domestic and foreign trade over to the . . . commercial and
> business classes . . . the people would be happier.[35]

Such statements indicated not only Montazeri's desire to see a less
restricted market economy, but also his disapproval of policies pursued
by Prime Minister Musavi. Musavi had repeatedly called for a
campaign to alleviate the economic deprivation of the masses and to
eliminate the profiteering of essential goods by merchants.[36] Former
President Khamenei, who at the time was in the same factional camp
as his prime minister, reinforced this policy by declaring that "fighting
poverty and supporting the oppressed are among important goals of the
Islamic revolution of Iran."[37] Such attacks on the entrepreneurial
classes drew equally sharp criticism by Montazeri, who gradually
emerged as the main spokesperson for the interests of the *Bazaaris*. In
one of his sharpest remarks ever, he urged the people that

> . . . if someone wishes to introduce Marxist economics in the
> guise of Islam to society, it is necessary for others to explain
> this deviation and distortion and not allow others to be
> misguided.[38]

Despite Ayatollah Montazeri's advocacy of a more open market and
less interventionist economic policies by the government, he repeatedly
called for the export of the Islamic revolution abroad. This radical
approach to foreign policy resulted in Montazeri giving frequent
audiences to a stream of foreign students, diplomatic dignitaries, and
Iranian diplomats stationed abroad. In one such meeting with Foreign
Minister Ali Akbar Velayati, Montazeri argued that "we must utilise
every opportunity to contact the people of the world in order to promote
the true face of the revolution and its divine and populist goals."[39] He
also announced the opening of a special bank account set up for aiding
and strengthening various Islamic movements,[40] claiming that other
Moslems' "problems are our own."[41]

A prominent feature of Montazeri's radical approach to foreign
policy was his conspicuously soft and at times non-existent criticism of
the United States, especially in light of revelations in the summer of
1987 about secret U.S.-Iranian contacts. This abstinence from lashing out
at the "Great Satan" assumes considerable significance when considered
in the context of the broader factional groupings within the regime.
More doctrinaire elements such as Prime Minister Musavi and President
Khamenei did not welcome U.S.-Iranian contacts and argued that the
possibility of further liaisons in the future was only minimal.[42] On
numerous occasions, however, Former Majles speaker and later president

Rafsenjani declared that as soon as the United States abandons its "mischiefs" it could establish normal relations with Iran.[43] Montazeri's silence *vis-a-vis* Tehran's unending anti-American rhetoric indicated his closer affinity with Rafsenjani. Furthermore, it highlighted Montazeri's pragmatic realism and his belief in the uselessness and possibly adverse consequences of spreading propaganda against the United States. This was consistent with Montazeri's calls for a greater role by merchants in foreign trade. Aware of the heavy dependence of Iran's industrial infrastructure on the West and on the U.S. in particular, Montazeri was possibly leaving the doors open for the resumption of commercial relations between Iran and the United States in the future, especially when he was to become the *faqih* himself after Khomeini's death. On other similar matters, Montazeri's statements classified him in the same league as other pan-Islamic groups. He often called for Moslem unity and action, claiming that the "indifference of the Moslems is under no circumstances justifiable."[44] Christian missionaries, he once argued, have dominated Africa and must be counterbalanced by a campaign to familiarize more Africans with Islam.[45]

Ayatollah Montazeri's fervently radical foreign policy found its expression along with a surprising advocacy of the normalization of governmental procedures and processes. In this respect, Montazeri basically argued that the Islamic Republic was well established and the regime was firmly rooted within society. Consequently, the government needed to routinize the political process and to abandon revolutionary zeal and excesses, welcome constructive criticism instead of dismissing it as mere counter-revolutionary sentiment,[46] and pay more attention to the country's shortcomings.[47] He also called on the government to offer incentives in order to attract Iranians living abroad, replace slogans with constructive efforts,[48] hire more qualified officials,[49] pay greater attention to the emotional and psychological needs of the people, and work harder to win the population's satisfaction.[50]

In pursuit of such goals, Montazeri tried to become involved in the process of government as much as possible without appearing to be intervening directly in the affairs of the executive branch and thus further upsetting the prime minister and the president. In his numerous meetings with various government officials, he frequently gave "recommendations" and advice.[51] Clearly, Montazeri's directives regarding the government's appropriate policies were not particularly flattering to the prime minister or the president. Montazeri's recommendations about more cautious and conservative behavior by government officials were in fact criticisms of the zealous pursuit of avowedly revolutionary goals on behalf of the "oppressed and the deprived" by cabinet ministers and other highly-placed officials.

Conservative Clergy and the Government

In the same faction as Montazeri belonged another group of clerics with strong ties to most of Qom's theological schools. Called the Theological Teachers' Association (TTA) (*Moddaresin-e Qom*), this group of conservative clergy were highly critical of the government in general and of former Prime Minister Musavi in particular. This criticism was often voiced in the form of sharp verbal attacks by the group's nominal head, a Majles deputy from Qom named Ayatollah Azari-Qomi, or in the form of sharply worded commentaries in the group's newspaper, *Resalat*.[52]

However, despite their highly vocal profile against the government and their vociferous denunciations of Musavi's cabinet, the Qom TTA did not by itself constitute a significant block of opposition to the government. This lack of real significance and political viability was epitomized by the very vociferous nature of the group: if the TTA had sufficient means and resources at its disposal to achieve its goals, such as the patronage of influential political figures or control over important state institutions, it would have quietly used them to undermine Musavi's premiership or to block his policies instead of criticising him openly. The TTA could have achieved its objectives more effectively through the use of important institutions or the active support of influential personalities instead of risking Khomeini's wrath by openly attacking the government.

Several reasons underlie the TTA's relative insignificance within the broader context of Iranian politics. First, as already mentioned, none of the regime's notable figures with a personal following were members of the group or supported it unreservedly. Similarly, those tied to the TTA were not necessarily well-known personalities and did not have extensive revolutionary credentials. Secondly, the TTA's propagation of strict application of *shari'a* law never found much appeal among broad segments of society and resulted in its ideological isolation. Consequently, the only base of support the TTA could lay claim to were theology students (*tullab*) in Qom and perhaps some in Mashhad. Additionally, while the TTA supported the private sector and favored a reduction of the government's role in the economy,[53] it was unable to forge a strong alliance with *Bazaari* merchants or with other economically powerful segments. This absence of a *Bazaar*-TTA alliance arose largely from the *Bazaari's* estimation that the TTA was politically insignificant and that an alliance with it could be unnecessarily troublesome. The *Bazaaris* were at times subject to extensive pressure by the Musavi government and feared that any overt overtures with the largely ineffectual TTA could only further antagonize the prime minister.

Apart from the Theological Teachers, the more dogmatic elements within the regime included three additional groups: the *Fadaiyan-e Islam*, the *Hujjatiyeh* Society, and the *Bazaaris*. While the views and positions of those affiliated with the *Fadaiyan*-e Islam and the *Hujjatiyeh* were based almost entirely on doctrinal grounds, that of the Bazaaris was based almost exclusively on their economic interests. Furthermore, the Bazaaris represented a more fluid and amorphous block of political interest because of their highly informal structure and also because of their position within the society at large. Both the *Fadaiyan-e Islam* and the *Hujjatiyeh* Society, on the other hand, were political organizations which participated in the political process, or at least tried to do so. It is significant to point out the nominally organised nature of these "political organizations" and the extensive degree of the informality which permeated their structures and their functions. They were, nevertheless, distinguishable from the *Bazaaris* in that while both the *Fadaiyan-e Islam* and the *Hujjatiyeh* were motivated by doctrinal considerations, the Bazaaris tried to influence the political process because of and through their economic powers.

The *Hujjatiyeh* Society was established in the mid-1950s as an anti-Bahai society in Mashhad by a young theology student. While it attracted a number of followers in the early stages of its life, especially among the theology students of Mashhad and Qom, the society was unable to expand its support base among wider segments of society. Although despised by most religious fundamentalists, Bahaism gradually lost its appearance as a major threat to Islam in the late 1960s and the early 1970s. The Society merely lingered through the two decades preceding the revolution, even suffering a splinter in 1974. Those who remained in the Society adopted the name *Hujjatiyeh* and reactivated it in the late 1970s. Following the revolution, the general anti-Bahai environment that had been created as a result of the ensuing religious fervor left the *Hujjatiyeh* with little purchase in claiming to be a uniquely anti-Bahai movement. The Society therefore intensified its propaganda activities against the country's Bahai minority but for the most part eschewed direct political activities. Its constitution was devised accordingly, proclaiming the society to be a nonpolitical, cultural charity organization.

Within only a few years, the influence and the power of the *Hujjatiyeh* Society drastically declined and by 1985 it had practically ceased to exist. Given the organizational nature of the *Hujjatiyeh* and the doctrinal views of its members, it is surprising that the Society was able to maintain a semi-active profile for as long as it did. To being with, the *Hujjatiyeh*'s doctrine was fundamentally opposed to the concept of *velayat-e faqih* and, by implication, to Khomeini. The Society had based its ideology on the classic premises of Shi'ite quietism, believing that all political activity until the return of the Hidden Imam Mehdi is futile. It thus refuted Khomeini's justification of acting on behalf of the "disinherited." This doctrinal disagreement at times turned into open clashes between *Hujjatiyeh* members and Khomeini's supporters.[54] One such incident took place in 1983, when a group of Khomeini supporters disrupted and eventually shut down an exposition that the *Hujjatiyeh* Society had sponsored in commemoration of Imam Mehdi's birth.[55]

While organizationally the *Hujjatiyeh* no longer existed after 1985, the fluid nature of Iranian politics did not prevent its supporters and sympathizers from continuing to influence the system in different ways. However, this influence was by no means extensive. Ali Akbar Parvaresh, allegedly a member of the *Hujjatiyeh*, was the minister of education from 1981 to 1985. He could have used his influence to ensure that certain aspects of the *Hujjatiyeh*'s ideology were reflected in school textbooks. Also, those civil servants who supported the *Hujjatiyeh*'s ideology could, and at times did, cause bureaucratic obstacles for policies devised by the president or by the prime minister. Such measures, however, were mostly inconsequential politically and did not reverse the Society's declining importance. The pressures brought on the president and the prime minister were mostly not from the *Hujjatiyeh* but were from other, significantly more powerful sources. Theological beliefs about Mehdi's imminent return, meanwhile, took a back seat during Khomeini's highly active and supreme reign.

The elusive *Hujjatiyeh* Society found an ally in another equally secretive group, the *Fadaiyan-e Islam*. Like the *Hujjatiyeh* Society, little is known about the nature and the political power of the *Fadaiyan-e Islam* group. Similarly, the fluid nature of the organization made it difficult to identify its affiliated government officials or those sympathetic to its goals and objectives. Nevertheless, there were *Fadaiyan-e Islam* supporters and even members in the cabinet, in the Majles, in the IRP, and in most other state institutions. Furthermore, while those affiliated with the *Fadaiyan-e Islam* might not have actually held government positions, the informal nature of the political system enabled them to exert influence over the political process in one way or another. Similar to the *Hujjatiyeh* Society, however, the *Fadaiyan-e Islam*'s significance in the regime's broader factional drama was only marginal.

The *Fadaiyan-e Islam* reached the height of their activism and popularity in the 1940s, the 1950s, and briefly after the success of the revolution, in the early 1980s.[56] The group was reactivated soon after the revolution by Hujjatoleslam Sadeq Khalkhali. Khalkhali was appointed as a revolutionary judge by Khomeini and soon became famous for his summary execution of countless drug traffickers, criminals, and members of the former regime. He revived the *Fadaiyan-e Islam* and was alleged to have organised an international hit-squad comprised of the group's activists in order to assassinate the remaining members of the Pahlavi family. Khalkhali's excesses in trying to eliminate "corruption on earth" led to his eventual dismissal as a revolutionary judge. He then became a Majles deputy from Qom. Ever since, the *Fadaiyan-e Islam* have ceased their activities, at least formally.[57] Although the group maintained offices in Tehran and in Qom, its supporters and sympathizers were dispersed throughout different institutions. More specifically, former members of the *Fadaiyan-e Islam* could be found in the Majles and the cabinet, in the theological schools of Qom and Mashhad, in the revolutionary courts, in the press, and even among Iranian students abroad.

In addition to their own offices, members of the *Fadaiyan-e Islam* entered the IRP in order to be elected to the Majles under the regime's auspices.[58] This method proved relatively effective and resulted in the election of a number of Majles deputies loyal to the *Fadaiyan-e Islam*. Furthermore, at one point at least two former cabinet ministers, Habibollah Asghar-Owladi, former minister of commerce, and Ahmad Tavakoli, former labor minister, were said to have been members of the *Fadaiyan-e Islam*. Former education minister Ali Akbar Paravaresh, reportedly a *Hujjatiyeh* member, was also said to have been supportive of the *Fadaiyan*.[59] Asghar-Owladi and Tavakoli abruptly resigned from their posts in 1983, and Paravaresh was not included in future cabinets.[60] All three were accused of having favoured the Bazaaris and free enterprise over the nationalisation of trade and business. These dismissals were a prelude to a significant reduction in the powers of the *Fadaiyan-e Islam* not very different from the decline in the power of the *Hujjatiyeh*.

The printed press offered yet another mean through which members of the *Fadaiyan-e Islam* propagated their views and positions. In more recent years, at least until the transfer of the control of the *Keyhan* and *Ittela'at* dailies over to the Imam's (Khomeini's) Office (*Daftar-e Imam*), *Fadaiyan-e Islam* members had much influence over both newspapers. Prior to his assassination in 1980, in fact, a notable figure within the *Fadaiyan-e Islam* headed the powerful Keyhan Organization.[61] In addition to its own publication, called *Manshour-e Baradari* (The Brotherhood Charter), which had very limited circulation and readership, the group also had some influence within the editorial board of *Jamhouriy-e Islami*, the organ of the IRP. Although the IRP was banned in June 1987, the publication of its organ has not been interrupted. None the less, the direct control of *Keyhan* and

Ittela'at   by the Imam's Office led to a further decline in the political fortunes of the *Fadaiyan*.

A similar reduction in the powers of the group took place in the revolutionary courts as a result of the dismissal of Sadeq Khalkhali as a special revolutionary judge. Prior to Khalkhali's removal, he had granted influential posts to members and supporters of the *Fadaiyan* in revolutionary courts and committees. This trend was largely reversed after Khalkhali's dismissal, soon after which most of his appointees were also purged.[62] What remained of the *Fadaiyan-e Islam* after these purges were only a few ideological sympathizers who, not having any overly powerful positions within the regime, tried to inject their views from the sidelines. A final component of the more conservative elements within the regime were the *Bazaaris*. While the *Bazaaris* themselves did not represent an independent faction pressing a particular political position, they were the cause of much of the factional conflict within the regime. Since the economy was one of the main dividing issues among the various factions, the *Bazaaris* were placed at the center of the regime's factional cleavages. Although they were unable to marshall the support of a decidedly political force, they did succeed in forming a powerful economic interest group. Because of their highly controversial nature within the regime, the *Bazaaris* were as much subject to praise and support from within the regime as they faced criticism and condemnation. Ayatollah Montazeri, the *Hujjatiyeh* Society, and the *Fadaiyan-e Islam* all favored and actively advocated a reduction of the government's control over the economy and hence a freer hand for the *Bazaaris*. Furthermore, while none of the deputies of the Council of Guardians ever voiced unreserved support for the *Bazaaris* or the upper classes in general, they repeatedly rejected bills passed by the Majles which called for the confiscation of lands owned by large proprietors and their redistribution to the needy. Along with others, the influential and usually quiescent Ayatollah Golpaygani also lent his support to those opposing such measures.[63] Nevertheless, the Bazaaris' opponents within the government were found in equally influential positions. Their most prominent opponents included the Speaker of Parliament and later the President, Rafsenjani, and former Prime Minister Musavi. Rafsenjani tended to criticize the *Bazaaris* less on doctrinal grounds than on their economic practices which contributed to higher inflation rates, especially the hoarding of foodstuffs and other essential goods. Musavi, on the other hand, criticized the *Bazaaris* with an ideological zeal that was uncommon within the regime.

The economic divide which led to disagreements within evolving factions ran both ways. Alongside fiscal conservatives were a group of officials who advocated seemingly more egalitarian economic policies and a more anti-Western foreign policy. The main proponents of this faction were former President Khamenei, who later succeeded Khomeini as the *faqih*, former Prime Minister Musavi, and the informal *Hezbollah* group and its supporters in various state institutions such as the Majles, the IRP, and among the Friday Prayer Imams. These more doctrinaire individuals tried to forge ties with other groups and institutions in order to strengthen their own position.

Khamenei, for instance, who was among the most influential of the group, tried to turn the IRP and the army into personal power-bases for himself. He had been elected President in October 1981, subsequently emerging as one of the most prominent figures of the radical faction within the Islamic Republic. Throughout his two-term presidency, he continually advocated radical land reform and vigorously implemented the government's nationalization of foreign trade, with clear disregard for Montazeri's "suggestions" and the *Bazaaris'* interests. His anti-American rhetoric and opposition to efforts to end the war with Iraq were also in sharp contrast to Rafsenjani's efforts in the opposite direction. Besides the IRP, Khamenei successfully cultivated strong ties with the regular military during the long war with Iraq. As a result, the dissolution of the IRP proved not to be as significant a blow to Khamenei's political fortune as it could have been.

Throughout his presidency, one of Khamenei's most important characteristics was his fierce advocacy of greater government control over the economy. As late as March 1987 he declared that "fighting poverty and supporting the oppressed are among the most important goals of the Islamic Republic."[64] In numerous policy proposals, support for the "oppressed" was always high on the President's agenda. He often maintained that

> if the government does not establish policy, then there are chances of abuse, corruption, and the enrichment of a small group of wealthy individuals in the private sector. The government is accountable in this respect, therefore, and cannot endure such activities. It has to establish policies regarding these issues.[65]

Khamenei himself strongly denied that his position on the economy led to discord between himself, Rafsenjani, and Montazeri. The very need to deny the existence of frictions itself indicated that differences (if not necessarily sharp disagreements) did in fact exist among the three factional leaders. Nevertheless, while standing in sharp contrast to Montazeri's "suggestions," Khamenei's advocacy of interventionist economic policies significantly coalesced with the views of Rafsenjani. For reasons enumerated below, however, Rafsenjani and Khamenei did not join forces to solidify their mutual interests until much later, when Khomeini was out of the picture.

Khamenei had constantly tried to reactivate the IRP and to raise its stature and prestige among both the public and government officials. Prior to the dissolution of the IRP by Khomeini, Khamenei's speeches were permeated with grand descriptions of the party's services and sacrifices.[66] His goal was to turn the party into a personal base of support, thus giving himself a solid political backing after the expiration of his second term of office in 1989. He similarly took an active interest in the ceremonial aspects of the regular military, not only praising the army's role in the war at every opportunity but also taking part in military ceremonies and marches and frequently visiting troops in the front. Being the head of the Supreme Defense Council, Khamenei used even insignificant occasions to heighten his visibility within the armed forces in an apparent attempt to gain their support. In a speech in 1983, he proclaimed:

> (One) cannot find many instances in our history when being part of the armed forces is so honorable, because our armed forces are now defending our country's honor, independence, and territorial integrity. . .[67]

Clearly, Khamenei could not rely solely on the armed forces as a source of political support, especially following the effective depoliticization of the military after the revolution. His cultivation of strong ties with the military was designed specifically to counter a similar bond between Rafsenjani and the Revolutionary Guards. In the end, despite his efforts to cultivate close ties with the military, and in fact largely because of it, Khamenei was passed over by Khomeini for the post of commander in chief, which went to Rafsenjani.

Rafsenjani: A Political Pragmatist

Whereas Khamenei and Montazeri personified factional groupings whose positions were derived from doctrinal orientations, whether mostly economics-based or out of different expectations for the growth of the revolution abroad, Rafsenjani personified the pragmatists. He was among a group of revolutionaries whose agendas often took a back seat to the changing dictums of political correctness. Within the Islamic Republic, Rafsenjani's political wiliness and brute realism was second to only that of Khomeini himself. As such, he emerged as one of the major players in the regime's factional conflicts. At the outset, he consistently tried to place himself above the factional disputes and to appear as if he were uninterested in the divisive configurations within the regime.

Being the first and most powerful speaker of the Majles, he gradually became highly supportive of Montazeri, praising his acumen, perceptiveness, and dedication. He also developed a substantial support base among the Revolutionary Guards, counterbalancing Khamenei's popularity within the regular military. His brother also for a time headed the Radio and Television Organization, a potentially powerful medium at Rafsenjani's disposal. Although Rafsenjani vehemently attacked the *Bazaaris*, he was hesitant to fully endorse the initiatives of either Prime Minister Musavi or President Khamenei. At the same time, he was one of the only figures within the regime to openly advocate the normalization of ties with the United States, thus placing himself at odds the prime minister and his cabinet.

Because of an absence of pronounced ideological orientations--apart, of course, from adherence to the Islamic order and the concept of the *faqih*--Rafsenjani is considerably less easy to place within the regime's political spectrum, and embodied characteristics found in both of the opposing factions. He often masterfully utilized pragmatism, refusing to circumscribe the scope of his actions by rigid doctrines and beliefs. His positions were taken with an eye toward maximizing his own interests and political longevity. Once Montazeri's position as the successor to Khomeini was secured, Rafsenjani began praising him, calling him "the strongest arm of the revolution after the Imam and . . . the hope of our nation."[68] Nevertheless, while Montazeri supported the Bazaaris, Rafsenjani did not. "Our enemies," Rafsenjani once declared in reference to the entrepreneurial classes, "through . . . hoarding (goods) and creating long lines have created tensions and hardship."[69] He also called for a strengthening of the Foundation for the Oppressed (*Mostazafan*) and its need to confiscate industrial complexes belonging to wealthy industrialists.[70] His conciliatory position towards the U.S. has already been alluded to. This further signified Rafsenjani's pragmatism as he realized that Iran could significantly enhance its war efforts and the subsequent reconstruction if it adopted a less hostile attitude toward the administration in Washington.

All three factions were kept under considerable pressure by Khomeini for some time. This pressure was especially intensified in 1987 after the disclosure of secret Iranian contacts with the United States. The entire story about the secret meetings was disclosed with the arrest of an alleged relative of Ayatollah Montazeri, Mehdi Hashemi, who was opposed to normalizing diplomatic ties with the "Great Satan." For sometime thereafter it appeared that Montazeri was in serious trouble, especially as his calls for a radical approach to foreign policy made him a ready suspect for supporting Hashemi. Montazeri soon disassociated himself from Hashemi and called for his full punishment. The "Deputy Leader" again resumed giving advice on different matters after a brief lull and appeared to have weathered the incident. Rafsenjani, the real force behind the American initiative, seemed to have also emerged as a winner and proceeded to pursue his intents publicly. In a rare display of friendliness towards the United States, Rafsenjani confidently stated:

> We are not happy to have caused trouble for Reagan and the White House. We did not initially intend to (harm the US). The U. S. can prove its goodwill by releasing our assets . . . We will then mediate with the Lebanese people for the release of (American) hostages.[71]

Rafsenjani continued making such conciliatory statements throughout 1987 and 1988. Yet when the regime's relations with the U.S. again deteriorated through the course of the war with Iraq, Rafsenjani became increasingly critical of the United States, though again temporarily. He was reported to have called the American president "a bull that has horns but has no brains."[72] He also claimed that "we would point part of our artillery at the Yankees and take Americans captive with their hands on their heads to camp with humiliation."[73] Although such statements were in part reactions to the overt presence of American warships in the Persian Gulf (and a reply to similar statements from Washington), they also reflected erratic changes in Rafsenjani's conduct according to changing situations. Rafsenjani's views about the United States were not likely to change within a month, but the stability of his domestic positions and political strengths were. After encountering obstacles and resentment to his comparatively unorthodox foreign policy, Rafsenjani reversed his position and began advocating a "revolutionary" position once again.

The Factions Under Pressure

There were two sources of pressure on the various factions. Firstly, weary of public discontent and in mutual competition to win favors with the Imam, each faction tried to maneuver itself so that it could augment its popular supportbase. Locked in such a war of positions, the factions often merely modified their orientations in order to heighten their public support. A second source of pressure on the different factions was Ayatollah Khomeini himself. Khomeini made a practice of placing contending individuals and factions in close proximity and in a working relationship with one other. It was, in fact, difficult to see personalities within the regime who had interrelated positions or similar powers but who were not ideologically or personally at odds with one another. Through extensive use of this practice, Khomeini kept in check the powers of the different factions, exerting selective pressure whenever necessary and forcing others to become more in tune with his own wishes and directives. This, in essence, led to a further centralization of political power in the person of the *velayat-e faqih* at the expense of everyone else. The factions could fight all they wanted, but ultimate power rested with noone but the Imam himself. He was both the perpetuator and the supreme arbitrator of the regime's factional drama, a master at the game of divide and conquer. To the very end, he remained central to the political process, not long before his death removing his old pupil from the position of Deputy Leader and future *faqih*.

But Khomeini's death in June 1989 brought little of the much-anticipated political chaos and confusion. An unexpectedly smooth transfer of power to a new Imam soon took place, almost as if by prior arrangement. President Khamenei, having served his second and final term in office, became the *faqih* while Majles Speaker Rafsenjani was elected as the new president. Montazeri went into political oblivion, even his massive portraits on city walls disappearing almost overnight. Khomeini's legacy was perpetuated both in form and in style. The position of the *faqih*, one which Khomeini had theorized about and later occupied, remained as the basic premise of the political order. Perhaps more importantly, the regime continued to rely on a religious brand of patrimonial populism, a brilliant arrangement through which the political agendas of the revolutionary project were carried forward and the entire system was maintained.

POLITICS OF PATRIMONIAL POPULISM

In essence, the political system that evolved under Ayatollah Khomeini's stewardship was strikingly similar to that of the shah's. Up until his death, Khomeini kept his theocratic system intact through first the force of his personality and charisma and then through a series of patrimonial networks made up of Friday Prayer Imams, the "Imam's Representatives," local clergymen, and so on. Similar to the Shah, Khomeini kept his lieutenants at a distance, perpetuating cleavages and rivalries among them, and opting for the support of one group over another only after the drawn-out struggle dragged on or seemed to produce results contrary to his wishes. Both the shah and Khomeini embodied the political systems over which they presided, and privileged access to them by subordinates was a rare and significant advantage. However, whereas the Shah sought to legitimise his rule through coercion and the extension of patrimonial networks throughout society, Khomeini did so by relying on the popular appeal of Islam and by instituting populist policies. Under the Islamic Republic, participation in the political process was no longer the perfunctory obligation that it had been during the monarchy. Owing its very genesis to acts of collective behavior, the new regime did not curtail the brewing demands for political participation and instead channelled them toward augmenting its own legitimacy. The incorporation of the masses into the political process began with the popular referendum of March 1979, whereby the new system was approved by some ninety-eight percent of the voters, and grew increasingly more intense with the meteoric rise of the IRP, the mobilizing sermons of the Friday Prayer Imams, open debates in the Majles, and with each successive parliamentary and presidential election.

Gradually, the fusion of the masses into politics resulted in the growth of an incredibly strong post-revolutionary state, capable of outlasting the crippling effects of violent internal purges, terrorist assassinations, a costly war, and, eventually, Khomeini's death. Whereas the monarchy withered away with the shah's departure from the scene, the Islamic Republic survived Khomeini's death with little difficulties. It is the establishment of inclusionary, populist politics that has so far been the most lasting contribution of the 1978-79 revolution. In the process, what has emerged is a state with a degree of strength and power unsurpassed in Iranian history.

Ayatollah Khomeini's emergence as the sole source of power in the Islamic Republic warrants further investigation, for, after all, the revolution directed much of its energies toward the obliteration of personal autocracy from Iranian politics. More specifically, it is important to see what factors underlie the unimpeded rebirth of personal patrimonialism after being so violently overthrown by the revolution. Clearly, a large part of the equation was the ayatollah himself, who slowly gained power through subtle and careful maneuvering. Why did Khomeini try so ceaselessly (and effectively) to become the ultimate source of authority in the Islamic Republic? His intents cannot simply be discounted as political avarice and lust for personal aggrandisement. Khomeini was too shrewd a politician simply to want to augment his already extensive powers. He had already successfully achieved this goal as early as 1982, when all "nonbelievers" and even those "believers" with potential for undermining the *faqih's* authority were eliminated through internal purges or assassinations. Khomeini's practice of keeping the factions in check was derived from a more fundamental realization: that ongoing factional infighting could potentially erupt into open warfare once he departed from the scene. Thus, by reducing the powers of all factions, he tried to make it difficult for the various camps to effectively overpower each other and that no faction did so without his personal blessing.

Clearly, factional rivalries and purposely manipulated divisiveness continually hampered the evolution of clear policies by the government and frustrated whatever progress had been achieved in a particular direction. This disarray was most poignant and its consequences most disruptive in regards to areas where vital policy decisions needed to be made. There were considerable disagreements and ultimately indecisiveness over the government's foreign policy, the basic economic model to be adopted for the country, and other vital issues such as when and how to end the war with Iraq. Largely because of its internal debates and indecisiveness over the adoption of a government-controlled or a free market economy, a decade after the revolution the government had yet to devise medium and long-term development plans.[74] From 1985 onward, Khomeini called every year the year that the war with Iraq would end. Yet the war continued until late August 1988. Pragmatists such as Rafsenjani continually sought to improve Iran's relations with the U.S. and with other Western powers, only to meet obstacles and at times even embarrassment at the hands of those opposing the "Great Satan."

As long as he was alive, Khomeini was the ultimate authority in the Islamic Republic, the supreme arbiter of all conflicts, and the master without whose knowledge and consent no decisions were made. With the system so extensively dependent on his personality and his presence, whether anyone will be able to fill the void after his death remains to be seen. Yet shrewd as he was, Khomeini himself determined who his successor would be (i.e., Khamenei) long before he left the political scene. He also made certain that Rafsenjani and other pragmatists have the upper hand over the more doctrinaire and radical elements. Khamenei's effectiveness as a *faqih* and Rafsenjani's political longevity as his lieutenant are two crucial tests the Islamic Republic will undergo in the post-Khomeini era.

Notes

1. See, for example, the*Mujahedeen* organization's *Majmueh E'lamiye-ha va Mouze-giriha-ye Siyasi-ye Mujahedeen-e Khalq-e Iran*, Vols. I and II (Collected Communiques and Political Positions of the People's *Mujahedeen* Organisation of Iran) (Tehran: *Mujahedeen*, 1358/1980); *Fadaiyan* guerrillas's *Kar no. 30* (12 Sharivar 1358/ 3 September 1979), p. 1.

2. Bakhtiar was found murdered in his home in Paris in August 1991. For his political platform, see Shapour Bakhtiar, *Mabani-ye Andishe-haye Siyasi va Barname-haye Ejraii* (Principles of Political Thoughts and Executive Programs) (Paris: n.p., 1983).

3. The director of Reza Pahlavi's "Political Office," Holaku Rambod, resigned in July 1988. Coinciding with the Iran-Iraq cease-fire agreement, Rambod's resignation was said to be based on his belief in the futility of

opposing the Islamic Republic. See *Sangar* no. 332 (Paris). p. 1. *Sangar* is published by Reza Pahlavi.

4. Noureddin Kianouri (head of *Tudeh*'s Central Committee), "For Unity Among Patriotic Forces," *World Marxist Review* (July 1981), pp. 15-19.

5. *Ittela'at* (14 Esfand 1366/5 March 1987), p. 1.

6. *Ittelaiyeh Daftar Siyasi va Komiteh-ye Markazi Sazman-e Mujahedeen-e Khalq-e Iran* (Communique of the Political Directorate and the Central Committee of the People's *Mujahedeen* Organisation of Iran) (Auver-sur-Oise, France: 10 March 1984).

7. Kambiz Afrachteh, "The Predominance and Dilemmas of Theocratic Populism in Iran," *Iranian Studies* vol. XIV, nos. 3-4 (Summer-Autumn 1981), p. 193.

8. James Bill "Power and Politics in Revolutionary Iran," *Middle East Journal* vol. 36, no. 1 (Winter 1982), p. 31.

9. Richard Cottam, "The Iranian Revolution," Juan Cole and Nikki Keddie, eds., *Shi'ism and Social Protest* (New Haven, CT: Yale University Press, 1986), p. 57.

10. *The Middle East* (February 1986), p. 11.

11. Ayatollah Khomeini's press conference, Paris, 9 November 1978.

12. *Iran Press Digest*, 28 February 1983.

13. Ibid.

14. *Iran Press Digest*, 13 March 1984.

15. *Iran Press Digest*, 3 April 1984.

16. Dilip Hiro, *Iran Under the Ayatollahs* (London: Routledge & Kegan Paul, 1985), pp. 119-120.

17. *Iran Press Digest*, 8 March 1983.

18. *Iran Press Digest*, 1 June 1980.

19. *Constitution of the Islamic Republic of Iran*, Article 124.

20. *Enghelab-e Islami*,   no. 311 (1 Mordad 1359/23 July 1980), p. 1. *Enghelab-e Islami* (Islamic Revolution) was published by Banisadr.

21. *Jomhuri-ye Islami*, no. 338 (9 Mordad 1359/31 July 1980), p. 16. *Jomhuri-ye Islami* (Islamic Republic) was the organ of the Islamic Republic Party.

22. *Iran Press Digest*, 10 April 1984.

23. *Iran Press Digest*, 15 March 1983.

24. Islamic Republic News Agency (IRNA), 2 June 1987, as quoted by *Foreign Broadcast Information Service Near East & South Asia* (*FBIS-NESA*), 2 June 1987.

25. *Iran Press Digest*, 8 January 1985.

26. Rouhollah Khomeini, *Velayat Faqih* (Governance of the Religiously Learned) (Qom: n.p., 1350/1971), p. 80.

27. Ibid, p. 109.

28. *Constitution of the Islamic Republic of Iran*, Principle 5.

29. Sepehr Zabih, *Iran Since the Revolution* (London: Croom Helm, 1982), p. 38.

30. *Keyhan*, (1 Mehr 1363/23 September 1984), p. 2

31. Nikola Schahgaldian, *The Clerical Establishment in Iran* (Santa Monica, CA: Rand Corp., 1989), p. 35.

32. Hiro, *Iran Under the Ayatollahs*, p. 265.

33. Ibid.

34. *Bours* (Tehran: 24 Day 1364/14 January 1985), pp. 1, 4.

35. *Sobh-e Azadegan* (6 Sharivar 1363/28 August 1984), p. 12.

36. Speech on Iranian radio on 15 April 1987 as quoted by *FBIS South Asia* (SA), 16 April 1987.

37. IRNA, 7 March 1987, as quoted by *FBIS-SA*. 9 March 1987. After assuming the position of the *faqih*, Khamenei toned down his advocacy of greater government control over the economy.

38. Speech on Iranian radio on 13 April 1987 as quoted by *FBIS-SA*. 14 April 1987.

39. *Sobh-e Azadegan* (18 Day 1364/8 January 1985), p. 16.

40. Ibid.

41. Speech on Iranian radio on 22 April 1987 as quoted by *FBIS-SA*, 23 April 1987.

42. Speech on Iranian radio on 1 March 1987 as quoted by *FBIS-SA*, 2 March 1987.

43. Speech on Iranian radio on 20 April 1987 as quoted by *FBIS-SA*, 21 April 1987.

44. IRNA, 9 February 1987, as quoted by *FBIS-SA*, 11 February 1987.

45. Speech on Iranian radio on 10 April 1987 as quoted by *FBIS-SA*, 13 April 1987.

46. *Keyhan* (27 Shahrivar 1363/18 September 1984), p. 22.

47. *Sobh-e Azadegan* (24 Azar 1363/15 December 1984), p. 2.

48. Speech on Iranian radio on 20 April 1987 as quoted by *FBIS-SA*, 22 April 1987.

49. *Sobh-e Azadegan* (2 Aban 1362/26 October 1983), p. 46.

50. *Keyhan* (4 Shahrivar 1365/26 August 1986), p. 17.

51. See, for example, Montazeri's recommendations to the Commander and the Minister of Revolutionary Guards in *Sobh-e Azadegan* (24 Azar 1363/15 December 1984), p. 2.

52. *Iran Press Digest*, 1 July 1986.

53. *Iran Press Digest*, 30 July 1985.

54. For a thorough discussion of the *Hujjatiyeh*'s doctrine see *Iran Press Digest*, 12 October 1982, and *Sobh-e Azadegan* (27 Bahman 1361/16 February 1982).

55. *Keyhan* (10 Khordad 1362/31 May 1983), p. 1.

56. For a detailed discussion of *Fadaiyan*-e Islam's early activities, see Adele Kazemi Ferdows, *Religion and Nationalism in Iran: The Study of Fadayan-i Islam*, PhD Dissertation, Indiana University, 1967.

57. Hiro, *Iran Under the Ayatollahs*, p. 243.

58. *Iran Press Digest*, 12 April 1983, p. 18.

59. Ibid.

60. Ibid.

61. Ibid.

62. Ibid.

63. Shaul Bakhash, *The Reign of the Ayatollahs: Iran and the Islamic Revolution* (London: I.B. Tauris, 1985), p. 213. Ayatollah Golpayegani was, along

with Khomeini, Montazeri, and Khoi, one of the Grand Ayatollahs (*Ayatollah uzma*) alive at the time.

64. Speech on Iranian radio on 8 March 1987 as quoted by *FBIS-SA*, 9 March 1987.

65. *Keyhan* (31 Shahrivar 1363/22 September 1984), p. 2

66. Speech on Iranian radio as quoted by *Joint Publications Research Service Near East and Asia (JPRS-NEA)*, 22 July 1985.

67. Speech on Iranian radio on 16 February 1983 as quoted by *JPRS-NEA*, 15 March 1983.

68. *Ittela'at* (30 Azar 1362/21 December 1983), p. 2

69. Ibid.

70. *Kayhan* (3 Bahman 1364/23 January 1985), p. 26.

71. IRNA, 11 April 1987, as quoted by *FBIS-SA*. 12 April 1987.

72. Speech on Iranian radio on 26 June 1987 as quoted by *FBIS-NESA*, 29 June 1987.

73. Quoted in *Los Angeles Times* (16 July 1987), p. 14.

74. See, for example, the government's "new strategies and policies" in *Keyhan* (20 Mehr 1364/27 October 1985), pp. 17-18.

5

Iranian Political Culture

As previous chapters demonstrated, Iran's modern political history has been heavily shaped by recurring instances of political autocracy, foreign intervention, and revolutionary crises. It was argued that these features have played a pivotal role in Iranian history because of Iran's external and internal geopolitical attributes, evolving international circumstances, and skewed political development and muted institutionalization. These are fundamentally *political* developments which have continuously shaped and influenced the format of Iranian politics and history. This chapter explores other, nonpolitical elements present in Iran's political culture which have also contributed to the shaping of its political history. Such characteristics, it will be argued, have historically reinforced the stated triumvirate. They include tribalism, feudalism, religion, cult of personality, illiteracy, lack of political acculturation, and the existence of gross inequalities among the different social and ethnic strata.

Each of these features has distinctively contributed to the shaping of Iran's political history. Because of inter-tribal cleavages and rivalries, tribalism has helped facilitate the intervention of foreign powers into Iranian affairs and has also accentuated the autocracy of the central government. Feudalism, religion, and personality cult have on the one hand contributed to the despotism of the political establishment and have, on the other hand, brought about its eventual collapse. Both feudalism and religion have been conservative forces that have historically strengthened the powers of the political establishment. However, in instances when the political machinery has been unable effectively to control religion, that very conservative force has served to undermine the powers of the government. Feudalism was a main contributor to political autocracy while it lasted, but its removal unleashed forces with which the Iranian monarchy could not cope. Personality cult, meanwhile, has turned charisma into a potent force in Iranian politics. It has facilitated the appearance of personal dictatorships and revolutionary movements, depending on whether the charismatic figure is a political leader or a revolutionary activist. Finally, both illiteracy and inequality have made it relatively easy to mobilize the Iranian masses in various directions, be it in support of a demagogic revolutionary or that of an absolutist monarch.

TRIBALISM

Tribalism has always been one of the central features of Iranian political history. Its lingering political consequences have, in fact, been one of the main preoccupations of not only the Qajar and the Pahlavi dynasties but that of the Islamic Republic as well. Iranian tribes have been makers and breakers of dynasties, and establishing government control over them has been central to the success or the failure of Iran's dynasties and regimes. Despite this political centrality, with the notable exception of the Bakhtiaris and their contribution to the Constitutional Revolution, Iranian tribes have in recent times been conspicuously absent from the scene of national politics and have confined their rebellions and armed insurgencies to the periphery of their geographic boundaries. This lack of a consistent pattern of political participation by the different tribes has resulted from a persistent and often ruthless policy of "detribalization" pursued by all Iranian governments since the mid-nineteenth century. Furthermore, the exploitation of tribal differences by both the central government and by outside powers has also minimised the political efficacy of Iranian tribes. As a result of such adversities, Iranian tribes are often fragmented within themselves, resent and hold animosity toward other nearby tribes, and have steadily declined in size and strength.

In studying tribalism in Iran, it is necessary to examine Iranian tribes internally, in relation to one another, and in relationship to the society at large. These internal as well as the external features of Iran's numerous tribes have influenced the country's political process and its social life. Internally, Iranian tribes vary greatly in structure and organization, religion, language, and strength. In relation to the society at large, they are deliberately insular and introverted, deeply resentful of urban culture, be it traditionally oriented (i.e., religious) or modern (i.e., Western).[1] Both of these characteristics serve to highlight the political ramifications of tribalism and its impact on Iran's political history.

Division Among Tribes

Among themselves, Iranian tribes are divided into three broad groups. The most common are pastoral nomads who engage in seasonal migration. Although these tribes are not settled in any one area for more than a season, their migration takes place within loosely defined geographic regions. Such tribal confederacies include the Bakhtiaris and the Qashqais, residing in western and south-central parts of the country respectively, and the Baluchs, who are concentrated in the southeast. A second group of tribes spend part of the year migrating as nomads and part of the year in settled huts and clay houses, although they are not villagers and are also distinct form the peasantry. The Shahseven, in northeastern Azarbayjan, engage in both migration and in settled nomadism. Lastly, there are some tribal confederacies that have been forced by the government to settle in a particular area. The Kurds', whose persistent demands for autonomy been the most troublesome for the central government, have historically been most intensely subject to detribalization policies and are as a result mostly settled in the mountainous regions of western Iran.[2]

Tribal formations also differ in their internal power structure and organization. The tribes located south of the Zagros mountain range in western Iran, the Bakhtiaris and the Qashqais, tend to be more centralized and state-like, while those in the northwest, such as the Shahsavan and some Kurdish tribes, are fragmented and made-up of ephemeral confederacies. The Turkmen and Baluch tribes, found in the east and the south-east respectively, are also more diffuse and decentralized.[3] Although the extension of government authority over the tribes has greatly reduced the powers of tribal leaders and has disrupted the tribes' internal power structure, basic structural differences between decentralized and the more centralized tribes remain.[4]

Furthermore, the importance and the influence of the different tribes, at least in relation to the central government, differ in accordance to their geographic location. During the Qajar era, tribal chiefs had far more influence over their confederacies than they did under Reza Shah. As a general rule, the internal power structure of the tribes was highly centralized and tribal leaders often wielded considerable autocratic powers over their followers.[5] Reza Shah's efforts to minimize the powers of the various tribes and to bring them under state control significantly reduced the powers of the chiefs and the *khans*. Tribal leaders saw their powers decrease steadily after the 1940s, when, afforded greater opportunities, the government focused more of its attention on tribal affairs. Added to this was the government's efforts to expand the country's roads and to make existing

ones safe for passage and commerce. It was common for armed tribal
bands to raid the caravans and busses that passed through their
territory. During their seasonal migration, the Qashqais also
frequently damaged and looted crops belonging to peasants settled along
their migratory route.[6] The government's eventual success in
eliminating the frequency of such events further reduced the political
powers of the tribal chiefs, both within the tribal confederacy and in
relation to the government. As a result, tribal leaders came to
increasingly symbolize and represent the identity of their tribal
followers instead of exercising actual political power over them.

Nevertheless, a general pattern of power structure did emerge
among most of Iran's tribal confederacies. Tribes near important cities
and regions have generally been more influential and powerful. The
proximity of the Bakhtiaris to Isfahan and the Qashqais to Shiraz has
led to an increase in their economic powers through trade and political
significance.[7] Other tribes located in the more remote areas, such as the
Shahsavan, the Turkmen, and the Baluch, have never gained the
political importance that the Qashqais and the Bakhtiaris have but
have, nevertheless, managed to cause trouble for the central government
on occasion by sporadically attacking passing caravans and traders.[8]

Apart from structural differences, Iranian tribes are divided
among themselves by language and dialect, religion, and by the degree
of their affinity or resentment toward the central government. While
Farsi is most commonly understood in Iran, Turkish is the predominant
language of most Iranian tribes and is spoken by the Qashqais, the
Shahsavan, the Afshar, and the Turkmen. Kurdish tribes speak the
Kurdish language, Arab tribes in the southwest speak Arabic, and the
Baluch speak the Baluchi dialect. Added to linguistic differences are
religious ones, with tribal groups scattered along the country's borders
being mostly Sunni and the rest Shi'ite. The Kurds and the Arabs along
the western frontier, the Turkmen near the Soviet border in the
northeast, and the Baluch in the Baluchistan region all form the small
minority of Iranian Sunnis. There are, at the same time, differences in
the degree of religiosity among the remaining Shi'ite tribes
themselves. To begin with, Shi'ite tribesmen generally tend to be far
less observant of religious guidelines than their peasant or urban
counterparts.[9] They especially question religious orthodoxy, often hold
a pragmatic approach toward aesthetic matters, and are relatively
ignorant about specific religious doctrines and rites. Within the tribes,
the Shahsavan tend to be unusually religious although they still frown
at the comparative religious zeal of peasants and city-dwellers.[10] In
contrast, most tribes within the Bakhtiari and the Qashqai
confederacies are, and in fact consider themselves to be, only nominally
religious.[11]

Another divisive factor differentiating Iran's various tribes from one another is the nature of their relationship with the central government. While historically all tribes have fought with the government over the imposition of central rule and the policy of detribalization, in recent times open clashes in the state-tribe relationships have occurred almost exclusively between the central government and those tribes located along the country's borders, notably the Kurds, the Arabs, and the Baluch. The uneasy relationship between these tribes and the central government has been particularly tense and frequently violent since the establishment of the Islamic Republic, when a new dimension, that of religious ideology, entered into the relationship between the Sunni tribes and the avowedly Shi'ite state.

Yet the intensification of state-tribal conflicts are based more on political factors than on strictly religious ones. When the still-fragile revolutionary regime of the Islamic Republic was first established, the Arabs began renewing their old demands for secession, while the Kurds and Turkmen launched armed rebellions in pursuit of gaining regional autonomy.[12] All were ruthlessly subdued, but for some time to come the more belligerent Kurds continued their protracted guerrilla attacks against government forces in the mountainous region of Kurdistan.[13] However, the Islamic Republic's treatment of Shi'ite tribes has not been radically different from that meted out to Sunni tribes. When the leader of the Qashqais returned to Iran in 1979 after a long exile abroad, he was quickly imprisoned and then executed by the regime. The government also dispatched Revolutionary Guards to potentially volatile tribal areas, and the first post-revolutionary governor of Khuzestan province, where Arab tribes are concentrated, declared that any Arab inciting agitation against the regime would be charged with treason and thrown into the Persian Gulf. By about the same time as most of its internal enemies had been eliminated, around 1982, the potential for widespread tribal uprisings against the Islamic Republic had also largely disappeared.

The Tribes and the Rest of Iran

The tribes' relationship with other segments of Iranian society is marked by mutual resentment and dislike, separation from one another whenever possible, and a reluctance on the part of the tribes to become assimilated into the urban mainstream and to abandon their tribal identity. The same mechanisms that divide the tribes from one another--language, religion, and internal power structure--not only separate the tribes from the peasants and the urbanites but also cause them to resent one another. While most tribes except those in the southeast speak Turkish, Turkish is only spoken widely in a few

northwestern cities and is often ridiculed and made the subject of jokes
in the popular urban culture.

Religious differences between the tribes and the non-tribal
population are even more glaring and divisive. Some ninety percent of
all Iranians are Shi'ite, nearly six percent Sunni, and the rest adhere to
religions other than Islam. Yet almost all of Iran's Sunni population are
divided among the Arab, the Kurdish, the Turkmen, and the Baluchi
tribes. Thus, in Iran, the Sunni-Shi'ite divide is not only a matter of
differences in religious ideology but one of ethnic diversity as well,
with the Sunnis being predominantly tribal and the Shi'ites non-tribal.
As mentioned before, there are differences and disagreements even
between Shi'ite tribesmen and non-tribal groups, with the latter
accusing the former of being only nominally religious.

The internal power structures of both the tribal and the non-tribal
groups also serve to keep them apart and isolated from one another. The
continued practice of nomadism by most Iranian tribes is as much a result
of political and cultural opposition to the state and to urban culture as i t
is due to ecological and economic adaptation.[14] The widespread
practice of endogamy among Iranian tribes is another tool with which
tribal identity and heritage are kept intact and are protected against
outside infiltration.[15] Among the Qashqais, tribal leaders, called
Khans, have historically used culture to perpetuate the longevity of
tribal loyalties and ties. The divisive consequences of such efforts at
social and cultural segregation are readily apparent, with most
Qashqais viewing themselves as morally and ethically superior to
their non-tribal compatriots.[16]

A series of political and cultural factors concerning the urban
environment also hinder the ability of those tribesmen who want to
assimilate into the urban mainstream from doing so. The rigidity of
tribal values and norms and their alienation from the urban culture, the
absence of meaningful educational resources in most tribal areas and
even in many villages, and the numerous obstacles encountered by rural
immigrants in finding jobs in the cities have all substantially slowed
the pace of detribalization and subsequent urbanization. Despite these
factors, Iran's tribal population has steadily decreased since the
mid-nineteenth century, starting at about the time when the Qajars
became a national dynasty. Before then, Iran's tribal population was
estimated to be about thirty-nine percent of the country's total
population. This percentage decreased to about twenty-five percent
after the mid-nineteenth century, and down to about fourteen percent
after the 1950s.[17] The forcefulness of the government's detribalization
policy, added to the intense social change underway in Iran in the 1960s
and the 1970s, proved too overwhelming for even tribal loyalties to
halt a reduction in their size and strength.

In several important ways, tribalism has contributed to the persistent occurrence of political autocracy and foreign intervention in Iran's political history. Because of their deep-rooted differences, the tribes have historically been unable and in fact unwilling to form a unified and strong coalition, or at least to lessen the heterogeneity of Iran's ethnic mosaic. Not being united, the tribes could easily be defeated and dismantled as a political force. This gave political leaders the opportunity to consolidate their hold on power without having to worry about being overthrown by tribal leaders. Furthermore, in order to pacify the tribes, political leaders often tried to win the loyalty of their leaders through concessions such as land grants and provincial governorships.[18] Apart from political apathy, many tribes have gone so far as to directly support the central government and have helped reinforce its political autocracy. The Shahsavans are a classic example. As their name indicates, they originated as "lovers of the Shah" during the reign of Ismail Safavi, who established the Safavid dynasty and made Shi'ism Iran's state religion in the sixteenth century.[19] Later on, the Qajar tribe itself became a dynasty and its tribesmen for some time formed the backbone of the new regime's military might. In more recent times, leaders of the Qashqai tribe have opted for working through the existing system in order to maximize their tribal interests rather than directly confronting the state.[20] This has, albeit indirectly, in turn led to a strengthening of the central government and has facilitated the development of political autocracy.

The fragmentation of Iranian tribes and their conflictual relationship toward both the state and among one another has also eased the penetration of the country by foreign powers. Up until World War II, tribalism was in fact so effectively exploited by foreign powers, especially during the Qajar era, that it was difficult not to identify a tribal confederacy with an outside power. The policy of lending military and political support to different tribes was pursued by Germany and Great Britain in particular, with the British helping the Bakhtiari confederacy and the Germans aiding the Qashqais. These alliances became particularly strong during the two World Wars, when both European powers sought to strengthen their respective positions in Iran's strategic regions. Through their support for the Qashqais, the Germans were able to pose a serious threat to British interests in the oil-rich region of Khuseztan. The British in turn countered the German influence by continuing to support the Bakhtiaris, even after they had created the South Persia Rifles during World War I.

FEUDALISM

Despite the desired political and economic goals of the Land Reform program and other policies pursued by both the Qajars and the Pahlavis (i.e., peasant support for the regime, removal of feudalism, etc.), and the unplanned consequences of such policies, among them increased domestic immigration, rural Iran continued to remain detached and isolated from the cities. In the Qajar era, the central government's control over the provinces was tenuous at best and apart from control of a few important cities such as Tabriz, Isfahan, and Shiraz, it was unable to fully exert its authority over most rural areas. Even in the cities, the earlier Qajar Shahs often had to contend with rebellious provincial governors. As the Bakhtiari confederacies' contribution to the Constitutional Revolution demonstrated, the Qajars had been unable to establish their full authority over most rural areas even as late as 1905. The extent of the government's interaction with the more remote rural areas was mostly limited to the collection of taxes and at times the conscription of soldiers.[21] Villages were otherwise left on their own and the peasants were at the complete mercy of feudal lords. There was considerable concentration of land at the hands of proprietors, especially in areas furthest from the cities, and thus the peasants relied extensively on landlords for their economic security and well being.[22] As one observer writing on the conditions of peasants at the end of the Qajar era has noted, "The picture of Iranian villages . . . was one of utter poverty, misery, injustice, and complete domination of the peasants by landed proprietors and government notables."[23]

The establishment of a new dynasty in 1925 did not significantly alter the life of rural Iran, with feudalism continuing to serve as the overwhelming sociopolitical and economic force. Due largely to the centralizing efforts of Reza Shah, the feudal lords gradually changed from being titular princes in their domain into becoming ordinary landlords. There was also a general reduction in the size of the land that they owned.[24] They did, nevertheless, continue to exercise paramount and all too often tyrannical control over the peasantry. As in Qajar times, village residents continued to be divided into a dichotomy of landed proprietors on the one hand and miserable peasant masses on the other. The landlords could own up to several villages and were often absentee, residing mostly in the capital of the province where their lands were located. The peasants working for the landlord resided on his estate, paying rent with a share of the crop or in cash, or, as was often the case, by a combination of both. The share of the produce given to the landlord varied from region to region, but was usually as much as one half and even up to two-thirds of the total.[25]

Most landlords apportioned land to the peasants permanently, although some did so only on an annual basis. In most instances, the peasants had no security of land tenure and the landlord could easily throw them out at his whim.[26]

Early in the Pahlavi era, the conditions of the peasantry changed little from what they had been under the Qajars. Landlords were concerned mostly with the quantity of their landholdings rather than the quality of land or the life of the people living on it.[27] Often the more prosperous landlords leased their land to other absentees, who were even more tyrannical toward peasants than were the landlords.[28] Most peasants lived in extreme poverty, were often heavily in debt, and in addition to rent paid a variety of dues to landlords. Ann Lambton, a pioneer in the study of rural Iran, describes the condition of Iranian peasantry in the following manner:

> The landowner regards the peasant virtually as a drudge, whose sole function is to provide him with his profits and who will, if treated with anything but severity, cheat him of his due. . . Education, better hygiene, and improved housing for the peasants are regarded as unnecessary, except by a minority of the more enlightened landowners.[29]

The 1962-63 Land Reform ostensibly changed the peasant-feudal relations that existed in the countryside, though it did not automatically result in a betterment of the peasants' conditions. The Pahlavi regime's initiation of the Land Reform program was a highly significant occurrence in Iranian history, more significant than most Iranians realize or like to admit. Since the real force behind launching the Land Reform program was the Kennedy administration, most Iranian intellectuals and political activists, both past and present, dismiss it as further evidence of the shah's servitude to the United States and often belittle the program's social and economic importance. Admittedly, the Land Reform soon became part of a broader political gimmick dubbed the White Revolution and lost much of its potential as a force for rural social and economic development. Nevertheless, it did result in considerable economic and demographic changes in the life and the social composition of Iranian villages.

Land Reform and the Decline of Feudalism

The program's principal economic goal was to improve agricultural output by rearranging existing lots into largescale mechanized farming projects and turning agricultural goods into cash crops.[30] Pursuant to such goals, the Land Reform resulted in the eventual disappearance of feudalism and of feudal relations, bringing about instead a tenuous form of rural capitalism.[31] With the feudal classes removed, the class structure of rural Iran changed. Prior to the Land Reform, those residing in villages were divided into the four categories of landlords, peasants owning small parcels of land, landless peasants who worked as farm laborers, and another group of landless rural residents called the *khoshneshinan*.[32] Because of the Land Reform, the feudal classes were removed and four new classes of landed peasants emerged. They include a minority of rich and affluent peasants with relatively large land holdings, a sizeable group of peasants owning medium-sized lots, a vast majority with small land parcels but with little alternative financial resources such as livestock, and landless peasants often living in abject poverty.[33] Currently, approximately thirteen percent of peasants are considered as wealthy and affluent. They own some forty-six percent of all arable land and often control the prestigious Village Councils that supervise the distribution of irrigation water.[34] At the opposite end of the scale are the *khoshneshinan*, comprising about twenty percent of the village population, whose landless and often jobless status prompts them to engage in all types of economic activity in order to earn a livelihood, from money-lending to shopkeeping and farm labor.[35] The remaining peasants own land, either in medium sizes that suffice as means of economic production for a single household, or in small sizes that do not. The peasants whose land yields cannot be a sufficient source of income often either serve as farm laborers for the more affluent peasants or, along with the *khoshneshinan*, migrate to the cities.

Alongside such economic changes, the Land Reform had a number of significant social and demographic ramifications. The most dramatic development of this kind was the unprecedented growth of rural-urban immigration, undertaken primarily by landless peasants and the *khoshneshinan*.[36] Iran's rural population has consistently decreased as a result, from sixty-nine percent in 1956 to about fifty percent in 1986.[37] At the same time, while the country's urban work force grew at a rate of fifty-nine percent from 1956 to 1976, the rural work force increased by only twenty-nine percent during the same period.[38] Such a massive increase in domestic migration was largely due to the government's inability to realize the economic goals of Land Reform. The distribution among the peasantry of lands previously owned by feudal lords did not include the *khoshneshinan*. Many peasants who did receive land initially were later forced to sell it to the government in return for stocks in government-owned agricultural companies, thus becoming landless once again.[39] What resulted was the continuous landlessness of the *khoshneshinan* and the emergence of a new group of peasants who neither had land nor their previous jobs as farm laborers.

Furthermore, consistent with its policy of encouraging agricultural mechanization, the government supported the few newly-established big agricultural concerns at the expense of the more numerous smaller farms that were not mechanised.[40] With the 1973 "oil boom," agriculture became less and less of a priority for the regime, and the farming sector's slow growth kept its wages far below those of the manufacturing and the construction industries, both of which were centered almost exclusively in urban areas. While in 1964-65 the average annual income in the cities was twice as much as that in the villages, in 1975-76 it was four times as much.[41] Immigration to the cities was thus intensified as a result of both the perils of the village and the lures of city life.

The Land Reform succeeded in some of its goals but failed in most. It led to the permanent removal of feudal relations and to a more equitable distribution of land among the peasantry than had been the case before the 1960s. It also succeeded in turning most peasants into supporters of the regime, a support that was more passive rather than active. However, in the end the program failed to improve the state of Iranian agriculture. The mechanization of the agricultural sector, one of the main premises of the original Land Reform program, took place in only a few selected farming projects and never gained much of a hold in most of the country's rural areas. With the feudal classes removed, the peasants who had not received any land or who had sold their land to the government were left without the basic protection that they had previously had, even if under highly uncertain terms, like the provision of a home or a wage-earning job. Accentuating this failure was a general neglect of rural areas by the government and its ambitious pursuit of industrial and infrastructural growth in urban centers instead. Thus followed the massive flood of rural immigrants into the cities and its unforeseen consequences.

Feudalism, which lasted up until the 1960s, and the consequences of its abolition thereafter, contributed directly to the appearance of both political autocracy and revolutionary crises. Autocracy was strengthened by the predominance of feudal relations in the countryside, especially under the Qajars, when feudal lords practically ran their own fiefdoms. There was, and continues to be, a strong sense of conservatism among the feudal classes.[42] This resistance to change and the inclination to maintain the status quo by large landed proprietors made them a natural ally of the Qajar shahs, who for the most part wished only to augment their wealth and power. As long as the Crown did not initiate moves that jeapordized the landowners' socio-economic position, there were no reasons for the feudal lords to oppose or in fact not to support, the political establishment. Thus an implicit understanding existed between the Crown and the landed classes that kept them mutually supportive of one another.

The relationship between the Crown and the feudal classes changed only slightly under Reza Shah and in the first half of his son's reign. In this period, both monarchs largely ignored the conditions that prevailed in the countryside, although Reza Shah did zealously pursue a policy of detribalization. There were also some efforts by Reza Shah toward launching some form of land reform, although they were not followed through with any measure of continuity. Rural areas were also largely ignored by Mohammad Reza Shah, until their backward conditions and potential for trouble were brought to his attention in the early 1960s by the Kennedy administration. However, even after the celebrated Land Reform scheme, the Crown-feudal relationship continued to be one of beneficial co-existence. Prior to the 1960s, landed proprietors and the government had for the most part refrained from intervening in one another's affairs. After the reforms, former absentee landlords continued to maintain considerable powers in the countryside and had great social prestige and influence in the provincial cities where they lived, becoming part of the provinces' social and economic elites. These prominent families maintained their elite status by re-investing their wealth into industrial ventures and by cultivating close ties with the political establishment and even directly with the Crown. The most renowned members of the family often held an influential government position, usually a Majles seat or other high-ranking official positions.[43] In Shiraz, for example, the powerful Qavami family was even tied to the royal family by marriage.[44]

Landlessness and the Revolution

While the existence of feudalism and of feudal relations contributed to the strengthening of autocracy in Iran, their abrogation resulted directly in the occurrence of the 1978-79 revolution. Besides the removal of feudalism, the most significant effect of the Land Reform was an unprecedented increase in rural-urban immigration. To a large extent, the abrogation of feudalism provided the contextual background within which the 1978-79 revolution occurred. More directly, feudalism's fall released massive armies of footsoldiers without whom the revolution would have certainly had a different character. The rural immigrants, frustrated because of their inability to meet their economic expectations and to blend into the urban mainstream, were a highly volatile group which could be mobilized into political opposition against the regime with relative ease.[45] The proclivity of this group to engage in revolutionary activities was further accentuated in 1975, when many lost their jobs as construction laborers due to budget cuts and the imposition of an economic austerity program by the government. The political unrest of the late 1970s would certainly not have had the massive scale that they did had it not been for the participation of disillusioned, easily mobiliseable rural immigrants.

RELIGION

Of all features of Iran's political culture, religion has by far contributed most directly to the development of both political autocracy and revolutionary movements. This seemingly contradictory role has been played by religion in Iran because of its special relationship to Iran's political institutions. Throughout Iranian history, religion has either been an integral part of political establishment, or, if otherwise, it has been one if not *the* main source of opposition to the state. Religion has thus served either as a main cause of political absolutism or as a potent vehicle for political opposition. In order to explore the causes of this dual role of religion in Iranian political history, it is necessary to briefly sketch the historical development of Iran's religion, Shi'ism, and to examine its relationship with the state.

Shi'ism was declared as Iran's state religion in 1501 by the founder of the Safavid dynasty, Shah Ismail. There is some conjecture as to whether Shah Ismail's establishment of Shi'ism in Iran, which up to then was a predominantly Sunni country, was out of sincere religious devotion or a matter of political prudence, especially given the fact that the new ruler used Shi'ism as a justification for eliminating other potential contenders to power, most of whom happened to believe in Sunnism.[46] What is certain is that Shi'ite doctrine embodied in itself an amalgam of highly absolutist and millenarian tendencies. Shi'ite absolutism grew out of the enormous powers that it granted to the very few who it deemed qualified to rightfully govern the Islamic community. At the same time, its belief in the ultimate return of the Hidden Imam and the establishment of peace and justice thereafter enriched it with decidedly millenarian tendencies.

This emphasis on millenarianism was conditioned to a great extent by the circumstances in which Shi'ite theorists found themselves, especially during the reigns of the Umayyads and the Abbasids. Maintaining that only members of the Prophet's household and his direct descendants could succeed him as imams, Shi'ite theorists readily rejected majority opinion and consensus. The imams, they maintained, were infallible and only their rule was just, while all other rulers were usurpers.[47] Political activity and opposition to the (Sunni) state was thus viewed as irrelevant and impractical, since only with the return of the Hidden Imam Mehdi would justice and equity be achieved. In the meanwhile, the rule of the sultan, regardless of how usurper and unjust, was to be obeyed since any despotic authority was better than no authority.[48] Implicit in all this was a "rationalised defense of an embattled minority," one that had adopted a quietist posture for the sake of survival amidst a hostile majority.[49]

The establishment of the Safavid dynasty at the beginning of the sixteenth century and its zealous adherence to Shi'ism confronted Shi'ite theorists and *ulama* with a dilemma. On the one hand, for the first time ever they were able to rely on the strength and the support of a political patron and to freely practice and in fact successfully propagate their beliefs. On the other hand, the Safavids were temporal rulers, and although they claimed to be descendants of the Prophet, their claim to divine rule was cause for much doctrinal and theological discomfort and debate. Yet the Safavids relied almost solely on Shi'ism, both doctrinally as well as practically, as a source of legitimizing their rule and claimed to be divine reincarnations of the Hidden Imam. As a measure of compromise with the temporal Shah Ismail, Shi'ite theorists adopted a concept that had existed in pre-Islamic Iran: the shah was designated as the Shadow of God (*zill ul-llah*). His legitimacy, underwritten by the Shi'ite ulama and by his position as the Shadow of God, was in turn reinforced in the provinces by clerical *Qazis* and *Sheykh al-islams*, both of whom were appointed by the Court.[50] Thus began the marriage of state and religion in Shi'ite Iran, a phenomena first developed under the country's Zoroastrian kings.

The Shi'ite *ulama* were almost completely dependent on the state in the early phases of Safavid rule, both financially as well as politically. This dependence was gradually lessened as the Safavid state lost its military character and became administratively more and more differentiated. This trend continued in the seventeenth century and was accentuated by the growing decline of Safavid power, with an increasing number of Shi'ite *ulama* claiming to be better fit to rule.[51] Nevertheless, even by the time the Safavid state was near collapse, the *ulama* were far from having political autonomy. Even after the Safavids, the *ulama* continued to grant the title of "Shadow of God" to the Afshar, the Zand, and even to Qajar monarchs, although they increasingly assumed the "vicegerency" of the Hidden Imam themselves.[52] Nevertheless, the collapse of the Safavids brought with it an end to the thorough amalgamation of "church" and state that Shah Ismail had instituted. For sometime thereafter, the *ulama's* powers were significantly though temporarily curbed by Nadir Shah Afshar, who demoted Shi'ism to the same status as Sunnism.[53]

Under the Qajars, the *ulama* once again regained much of the powers that they had once had under the Safavids and, in fact, found more independence than at any time in the past. This growth in strength was due to several factors. An important reason for the *ulama's* increasing independence was the fact that the more influential figures within them resided in the holy Shi'ite cities that were located outside of Iran, notably Najaf and Karbala.[54] Also important was the fact that the *ulama* became financially independent from the state through the collection of religious taxes and tithes, called the *zakat* and the *khoms* respectively, and through their alliance with the *Bazaari* merchants.[55]

Two intertwined doctrinal developments further reinforced the growth in the autonomy and the strength of the *ulama*. In the eighteenth century, two schools of thought known as the *Akhbaris* and the *Usulis*, developed within Shi'ism. The *Akhbaris* refuted the need for a separate class of religious professionals such as the *ulama*, since, they claimed, the directives and the *hadiths* left by the Prophet were sufficient to guide the Islamic community until the Hidden Imam's return. The *Usulis*, on the other hand, emphasized the necessity of granting extensive powers to a living cleric who was equipped and qualified to interpret the necessary laws and doctrines until Mehdi's return. The position of the *Usuli* school had two important results. First, by emphasising the role of logic as practiced by contemporary mujtahids, the *Usuli* school embodied a sense of progressive dynamism which the *Akhbari* school did not have. Secondly, and a more immediate problem for the political establishment, was the natural increase in the *ulama's* influence under *Usuli* tenets.[56] The influence of the *Akhbaris*, which had increased under the Safavid for obvious political reasons, collapsed along with the Safavids in 1722 and the *Usulis*, who sought greater powers for the *ulama*, dominated Shi'ite thinking during the Qajar era. Later on under the Qajars, out of the *Usuli* tradition grew the concept of *marj'a taqlid* (source of imitation), according to which all religious authority and power was to be concentrated within a single living *mujtahid*.[57] It is perhaps no accident that this concept was developed and practiced in the second half of the nineteenth century, at a time when there was a marked increase in the clergy-state conflict over Nasir al-Din Shah's reforms.

Shi'ism and Revolution

Once it was divorced from the state, the same Shi'ism that contributed to political absolutism had the potential to cause revolutions. Contemporary scholars generally agree that there was and continues to be a direct link between Iran's Shi'ite tradition and its revolutionary experiences. However, they seldom agree over the exact dynamics which have resulted in the Shi'ism-revolutionism nexus. A dominant trend of thought holds that those political movements in

which Shi'ism and Islam in general play a pivotal role are "fully
religious movements which are inevitably politically conditioned."[58]
"Despite their differences," the argument goes,

> all the contemporary Islamic movements can be considered
> revitalization movements, propelled by rapid social change
> and in response to Western cultural influences which are
> perceived as gravely menacing and are virulently rejected.[59]

Along similar lines, others argue that

> The enforced and sudden modernization of Iranian society,
> with its unequal distribution of wealth, brought a backlash
> against and restiveness toward change and created a climate
> of conservatism and return to the traditional values espoused
> in Shi'ite Islam.[60]

Other scholars dispute the claim that there is an "endemic propensity"
toward traditionalism in Islam and especially in Shi'ism. Hamid
Algar, a noted scholar on the Qajar era, argues that the *ulama's*
participation in events such as the Tobacco Protests and the
Constitutional Revolution "was no more than a repetition of (their)
traditional role of leading opposition to the state."[61] Others maintain
that while self-interest did influence the *ulama's* political activities,
many religiously-voiced grievances against the state (especially under
the Qajars) were in fact expressed by progressive reformers who used
religion in order to give wider appeal to their beliefs and arguments.[62]
     The drive by the Qajars and far more intensely by the Pahlavis to
secularize Iran did infringe on many of the *ulama's* privileges and
prompted many to oppose the state in order to protect their own
interests. Yet not all of the *ulama's* efforts in opposing the political
establishment can be considered as reaction to secularization. Sheykh
Fazlullah Nuri opposed the Constitutional Revolution because he
feared a loss of influence in a constitutional system. But this could not
possibly have been the concern of all other notable clerics who
supported the Constitution. In the same vein, self-interest was hardly
the motivating factor for the *ulama's* participation in the
nationalization movement of the early 1950s. While it is true that
Ayatollah Kashani later broke off with Mussadiq and supported the
shah, his break with the prime minister was not over infringements on
the *ulama's* interests but rather over the *manner* in which Mussadiq
pursued his policies.[63] Similarly, a careful survey of the events of the
late 1970s reveals that the *ulama* were not only one of the many groups
who sought to overthrow the shah, but were, in fact, relative

latecomers into the revolutionary movement.64 Furthermore, they repeatedly vowed to establish a progressive and non-theological system in the post-Pahlavi era, hardly a self-serving proposition at the time. The success of the *ulama* in dominating the post-revolutionary regime was not due to their inherent conservatism but rather a result of the political incompetence of their former revolutionary colleagues.

Contrary to numerous scholarly assertions that have gained much currency in recent years, Shi'ism embodies tendencies that are neither inherently "revolutionary" nor "reactionary."65 Shi'ism has demonstrated the ability to adapt and to change in order to survive in different social and political climates.66 It has at times been as reactionary a force as it has been revolutionary in other times. This adaptability is derived from the doctrinal concepts that Shi'ism has historically come to embody. The concepts of the futility of political action until Mehdi's return, that of the temporal ruler as being the Shadow of God, and frequent opposition to secularization and reforms have at times caused Shi'ism to be the main protector of the status quo. Yet at the same time, the millenarian and messianic feature of Shi'ism, its rationalized defense of an embattled minority, and its promise of social justice for the downtrodden have often turned it into a potent force for social and political change. This vicissitude depends on the particular strands of Shi'ite doctrine that happens to be in the foreground in any one historical era. To a large extent, the doctrinal slant of Shi'ism, conservative or revolutionary, depends on 1) the character and the intentions of the *ulama* and the other religious interpreters of the time, and 2) on the nature and the policies of existing political institutions. Based on these variables, Shi'ism oscillates as either a politically disruptive force or as the main protector of the political establishment.

A glance at Iran's recent history illustrates this point most clearly. In the early 1900s, an overwhelming majority of the *ulama* supported the Constitutional Revolution because they were "freedom-seeking" (*Azadi-khahan*), both in name and in spirit.67 At the same time, Shi'ism became "quietist" after the 1953 coup primarily because the eminent cleric of the time, Hussein Burujerdi, did not advocate opposition to the state.68 This quietism was reversed once again in the early 1960s and in the late 1970s by the radicalism of yet another cleric, Rouhollah Khomeini.

The *ulama*'s political activism is also largely conditioned by the character of the prevailing political system. In the Safavid era, the *ulama* had no alternative but to support the status quo, for it was the Safavids who had brought Shi'ism into Iran and on whom the *ulama* were politically and financially dependent. The opposition of the *ulama* during the Qajar era was made possible by the decentralized nature of Qajar rule and by the*ulama*'s growing political and financial independence.[69] Similarly, under the Pahlavi dynasty the*ulama* embarked on political activity only when the absolutist rule of the state had somehow been weakened, as it was during the Mussadiq era, in the early 1960s, and again in the late 1970s. The Islamic Republic represents the first time in Iran's political history when the religious establishment is itself the state, or, rather, an overwhelming part of it. Shi'ism has once again become one of the main supporting pillars of the status quo, and the thrust of its doctrines have reverted into one of political quietism.

The role played by Shi'ism in Iran's political history can be summarized as one of either overwhelming support for the regime or intense opposition to it. Rarely has the state-religion relationship not been one of the two extremes. The efforts of the two Pahlavi shahs to secularize the political process as much as possible were successful only in the short run. What ultimately succeeded the Pahlavi dynasty was a thoroughly theocratic system, in which powers more extensive than those the monarchs had were granted to a supreme cleric entitled the *velayat-e faqih.*

INEQUALITY

Vast differences in social and economic privileges have consistently characterized practically all strata of Iranian society. Gross inequality has existed not only among the various economic classes but also among the different ethnic groups, between the sexes, and even among the various social classes. On the one hand, the continued existence of such inequalities has facilitated the preservation of the status quo and, through ensuring the domination of the powerful over the more subservient classes, it has strengthened political autocracy and despotism. At the same time, awareness of such inequalities and an unwillingness to be restricted by them has often served as one of the central demands and as a main locus for social and political change, and revolution.

Persian Cultural Dominance

The origins of social, economic, and ethnic inequalities in contemporary Iranian society are numerous and varied. Historically, ethnic Persians have been able to maintain a monopoly over political power and to ensure their dominance over the other groups. Nevertheless, several Turkic tribes were in certain historical instances able to defeat Persian dynasties and to acquire power. The Saljuqs and the Qajars were two noted examples of Turkic tribes that rose to dynastic glory in Iran. In all instances, however, they were unable to "de-Persianize" Iran, and themselves became integrated into the Persian-dominated society. This inability arose partly from the fact that the seat of power has historically been in areas with large concentration of Persians. Persians are scattered mostly in Iran's central plateau, an area that all rulers needed to firmly control if they were to secure their reign. Thus, dynastic capitals were mostly located in Persian areas. Shiraz, Isfahan, and Tehran have been Iran's most important capital cities, while Tabriz, whose population is predominantly Turkish, was briefly the seat of power only once.

Another factor that might have resulted in the continued domination of Persians throughout history has to do with their culture. Persian culture, it is often asserted, has the unique ability to absorb other values and cultural traits within itself and to Persianize them.[70] This argument can only be substantiated by a tautological reference to the historical resilience of Persian culture. It is true, nevertheless, that few alien cultural traits have left permanent marks on Persian culture. From the Greek conquest to the Mongul and the Arab invasions, from the country's more subtle "Westoxication" under the Pahlavis to its often brutal "Islamization" by Khomeini, a continuous thread of values and norms have remained that are generally perceived to be distinctively Persian and are readily observed by most Iranians. Persian culture, amorphous and intangible as it may be, has changed and varied through the ages. But the perseverance of its unique characteristics have endowed it with a dynamic vitality that has absorbed and converted (with political might behind it, of course) other, less resilient cultural forms.

Added to the historical causes of ethnic inequality are modern economic and political policies. In contemporary Iran, ethnic inequality has been sharply accentuated due to the development policies followed by the Pahlavi regime.[71] Not unlike other Third World leaders bent on the rapid modernization of their societies, both Pahlavi monarchs vigorously implemented policies that had a decidedly "urban bias."[72] Besides the obvious increase in rural-urban immigration, the Pahlavis's development and industrialization policies accentuated the inequalities that had historically existed between the predominantly urban Persians and other ethnic, mostly rural groups such as the Baluchis, the Kurds, and the Turks. Specifically, the shift from an agrarian to an industrially-based economy, the concentration of industrial centres in predominantly urban, Persian areas, and the slow growth of modern facilities in regions where non-Persians are concentrated has widened the gap between the Persians and the ethnic minorities. Most industrial complexes were built near major cities such as Tehran and Isfahan, while cities further from the center and with large ethnic populations were mostly ignored. Universities were almost the only complexes that were established in the Baluchi-dominated Zahedan and the mostly Kurdish city of Kermanshah. Tabriz, with its overwhelmingly Turkish population, was an exception and included two large industrial plants. It was, however, never included among a growing number of large cities in which members of the royal family took personal interest. Whereas the shah visited Shiraz and Isfahan several times a year, for example, he visited Tabriz only once during his thirty-five year reign.

In 1976, near the end of the Pahlavi era, approximately eighty percent of Persians living in the central plateau lived in urban areas. But this ratio was less than twenty-five percent for the Kurds and the Baluchis.[73] The preponderance of rural life style in the non-Persian areas in turn meant less access to better education and jobs, primitive standards of hygiene and health, and far fewer opportunities for social and economic mobility. Both Pahlavi monarchs further sought to gain legitimacy by evoking memories of Iran's pre-Islamic past, when the Persian empire encompassed most of the present Middle East. In the popular eye, therefore, there was a certain esteem and virtue attached to Persianhood, and anti-Persian prejudices were socially sanctioned and commonplace. This society-wide prejudice against ethnic minorities was reflected most poignantly through the popular idiom of jokes. The jokes most popular before the 1978 revolution revolved around themes stupifying Iranian Turks and portraying Arabs as backward. Adversely, few jokes ever portrayed ethnic Persians in a negative light.

Social and economic differences were equally important in leading to inequality among the various ethnic groups. The official emphasis on industrial growth and neglect of agriculture resulted in a massive influx of mostly uneducated and unskilled laborers into cities. A marginalised labor force was created, existing on the fringes of urban society and eking out a meager existence. Unable to reap the fruits of the oil boom, the burgeoning proletariat found themselves increasingly on the lower end of the economic scale. These economic differences were further polarized during the late 1970s and after the 1978 revolution, when the number of jobs that provided the most employment for these underclasses were substantially (though temporarily) reduced. Massive reconstruction efforts following the end of the Iran-Iraq war will offer some temporary relief for the rural immigrants by once again making them part of the employed labor force. It will not, however, solve the larger problem of massive wealth differentials between members of the urban society and the unending mass of villagers who try ceaselessly to join it.

The Modern vs. the Traditional

The sharp dichotomy of Iranian society into "modern" and "traditional" camps has already been alluded to. The Pahlavi regime's policies aimed at aggressively promoting social change and cultural modernity sharply exacerbated the country's social and cultural duality in the 1960s and the 1970s. Ironically, the zealous crusade of the Islamic Republic's leaders to eliminate all Western influences from Iranian culture and society has only served to accentuate Iran's cultural heterogeneity. The fanaticism of the state's ideology and its resort to Islam in order to gain legitimacy has produced as many silent nonconformists as devout followers. This division has generally taken place along the lines of cultural orientation laid down during the Pahlavi era. Those who were only nominally religious before the revolution and who valued Islam as a religion but observed few of its tenets have become even less devout under the Islamic Republic. These groups largely disapprove of the regime's excesses and have become scornful of Islam as an ideology and as a way of life. On the other hand, those who were observant of strict religious principles and who as a result were subject to much ridicule and harassment under the former regime form the bulk of the Islamic Republic's supporters. Susceptible to the regime's propaganda and its ideological manipulations, most of these groups have become even more orthodox in their religious beliefs and social outlook.

It is still too early to determine whether the increased polarization of Iranian culture under the Islamic Republic is a lasting or a temporary phenomenon. With the end of the war with Iraq and the coming to fore of less doctrinaire and more pragmatic leaders, the regime has eased its harsh conformist policies and has become less restrictive in its social programs, thus reducing the level of resentment against Islam in some quarters of society. Yet there is no denying that by manipulating Islam as a tool for political power Khomeini did in ten years what the two Pahlavi dictators could not achieve in half a century. Unlike a mere decade ago, very few Iranians still believe that Islam can be a viable tool for social and political progress.

Perhaps the most readily apparent form of inequality in Iranian society is that between the sexes. Under the Islamic Republic inequality between men and women is sanctioned through official and quasi-official policies that discriminate against women and ensure their subservient position in society both socially and legally.[74] Yet discrimination against women in Iran, as in elsewhere, is not merely a matter of official policy. It is embedded in social and cultural values that permeate Iranian life and are willingly adopted even by Iranian women themselves. Numerous policies were enacted by the two Pahlavi shahs aimed at elevating the social position of women and removing the barriers that have traditionally blocked their mobility and have prevented them from being considered equal to men.

In the end, however, the inferior status of women was not fundamentally changed. A number of factors underlied this continued pattern of inequality, chief among them chronic economic dependence, large-scale illiteracy and lack of adequate access to educational resources, highly patriarchal political systems, and the unabated persistence of masculine social attitudes.[75] The modernizing policies of the Pahlavi regime were half-hearted and allowed women freedom of activity only within the official limitations set by the government. For all his supposed modernity, even Mohammad Reza Shah was a notorious chauvinist, granting his wife only the title of Empress (*Shahbanu*) instead of the more grandiose Queen (*Malekeh*). In an interview with a female journalist, he said of women:

> Women are important in a man's life only if they are beautiful and charming and keep their femininity. . . . You've never produced a Michelangelo or a Bach. You've never even produced a great chef. . . . You've produced nothing great, nothing. . . . You're schemers, you're evil. All of you.[76]

ILLITERACY

The influence of education on Iranian political culture must be examined on two levels. First, there is illiteracy, which is highest among the more deprived social classes such as tribal masses, peasants, and rural immigrants living in the cities. Less easily detectable but as equally pervasive is the under-education of those who were supposed to be most learned in the social sciences. The large-scale and concurrent existence of these two developments has contributed to the shaping of Iran's modern political culture by facilitating the growth of mass-based revolutionary movements as well as dictatorial, populist regimes.

The Pahlavi regime had developed several plans aimed at combatting illiteracy, the most celebrated of which was the creation of the Literacy Corps under the auspices of the White Revolution. Although significant headway was made toward reducing the illiteracy rate, by 1976 only forty-seven percent of all Iranians knew how to read and write. At the same time, while the bulk of rural residents and the proletariat grappled with illiteracy, the educated elite had to deal with ignorance. The Pahlavis forcefully pursued a two-pronged educational policy: they wanted Iranians to become literate but not socially and politically educated. People were encouraged to learn to read and write the alphabet, but reading and trying to understand books that were suspected of being threatening to the state was punishable by long prison sentences. Works by communist thinkers and the publications of several Iranian*ulama,* and even a number of novels and litarary essays, were classified as subversive literature and were banned, while the shah's own book, *Enghelab-e Sefid* (White Revolution), was part of the assigned reading in schools and universities. The shah always believed that Iranian universities were the main centers of agitation and esspionage against his regime. Writing after his fall from power, he confirmed his critics's assertion that he deliberately kept the number of Iranian university students down in order to reduce their potential threat. "I have come to realize," he wrote,

> ... that I moved too rapidly in opening the doors of the universities, without imposing a more severe preliminary selection. The entrance examinations were too easy.[77]

In order to ensure the ideological purity of its university student population, the Islamic Republic has gone even further than the Pahlavi regime. It has initiated several measures designed to control both the doctrinal beliefs of students and the academic curriculum which they are taught. All universities were closed down from 1979 to 1981 under the pretext of a Cultural Revolution, according to which curriculums were re-written, disloyal faculty and students were purged, and new standards and exams for admitting students and hiring faculty were set.

Strict government control over the content of secondary and higher education has severely retarded the quality and the intellectual horizon of Iran's educated elite, especially insofar as their understanding of the social sciences is concerned. As a result, Iranian intellectuals suffer from an incurable ignorance of ways and means to understand and analyze their own society, and, despite what most think of themselves, often do not possess even a scant understanding of the social sciences. There is little freedom and opportunity to freely read the writings of social scientists and political theorists, most of whom are considered to be subversives and political misfits. Lack of sufficient exposure to and detailed knowledge of different political doctrines and ideologies often turns the mere examination of theoretical works into an act of political opposition rather than an exercise in intellectual investigation. Within such a context, doctrines and theories are understood only superficially and form part of one's political activities rather than civic or academic education. Iranian intellectuals thus invariably equate their dogma with what they consider to be a "scientific" understanding of society. Demagoguery breeds where opinions prevail but knowledge lacks. Iran is a nation full of demagogues but few intellectuals.

Illiteracy, Ignorance, and Politics

The existence of large-scale illiteracy, coupled with the under-education of Iran's educated elite, has facilitated the development of both political autocracy and revolutionary movements. At the most fundamental level, these two developments have substantially simplified the concept and the practice of politics for most Iranians. Most notably, mass mobilization, both in support of and opposition to a political system, has been greatly facilitated as a result. When dictatorships have been intact and in full command, they have manipulated their subjects with relative ease by cultivating the support of the "blank masses."[78] When their monopoly on power has been weakened, however, those same masses have been manipulated by revolutionary elites and turned into potent revolutionary forces. Perhaps unknowingly, Iranian revolutionaries have also historically resorted to demagoguery instead of cohesive ideologies in order to gain public support. Demagogues can be understood much easier by the mostly illiterate and under-educated masses than can theoriticians and ideologues.

Throughout Iranian history, few political figures have ever had concrete plans for achieving their promised dreams, while most sum up their ideals in slogans and catchy phrases. It is true that all such terms are supposed to represent deeper ideological connotations. But, regardless of whether the political activists have known it or not, it is to their demogogic slogans rather than their ideological doctrines that the masses have paid the most attention. Mussadiq coined the term "negative equilibrium"; the shah liked to encapsulate his policies and his reign in such catchy phrases as "positive nationalism," "Great Civilization," the "White Revolution," and a host of others; and Khomeini popularised the slogan "neither Eastern nor Western, the Islamic Republic". Throughout Iranian history, the rhetorical pronouncements of political actors have competed each other just as intensely, if not more, than their underlying beliefs and principles.

PERSONALITY CULT

Not unrelated to demagoguery is the phenomenon of personality cult, whereby individuals are popularly endowed with almost superhuman qualities and are mythicized if not necessarily worshipped. The tendency to breed and to nurture such cults of personality has been a strikingly persistent feature of Iranain political history. Just as rhetoric has replaced logic in Iranian political culture, personalities have replaced principles. Iranian history has essentially been a history of personalities, authoritarian to the core, and consists mainly of accounts of what they did and of what happened to them.[79] Even in modern times, individuals have in one way or another come to personify historical events and developments. Reforms in the Qajar court are known almost exclusively by way of Amir Kabir's efforts. The Constitutional Revolution is best remembered by *'Adl-e Mozafar* (Mozafar's Justice), a title bestowed on Muzafar al-Din Shah after he signed the Constitutional decree in the last days of his life. Reza Shah, entitled "The Great" by the Majles, single-handedly dominated what has come to be known as the Reza Shah era, and the oil nationalisation movement's political and economic significance often take a back seat to the efforts and the personality of its principal proponent, Dr. Mussadiq. Finally, although the 1978-79 revolution has yet to be called Khomeini's Movement, the ayatollah became the nation's "Imam" and then appointed other "Imams" to succeed him.

The pervasiveness of personality cult in Iran's political history is due in large part to its strong influence in Iranian values, ideology, and historic tradition, and also as a product of the country's various political experiences. Specifically, personality cult has thrived in Iran due to the pervasive nature of patrimonial social and political practices. Family structures and kinship ties have been most conducive to the development of cult-like devotion to individual personalities, reinforced by dominant Shi'ite norms and practices. Lack of political institutionalization and prevelant patriarchical practices have only strengthened the dominance of political personalities and eased the growth of cults around them.

The family is the most basic social unit in which Iranians experience and in turn create cults of personality. Submission to a strong patrimonial authority is a virtue instilled in children from their earliest days.[80] The father's decrees and intents are beyond the reproach of his children, and at times even beyond those of the mother. Respect and unquestioning obedience to one's father, and to all other elders for that matter, is a central part of children's education in the family as well as in school. The adversity of breaking with patrimonial familial bonds is dramatized in Ferdowsi's historic epic, *Shahnameh*. Two of the main heroes of the book, Rostam and Sohrab, father and son respectively, battle one another, unaware of the true identity of their opponent. After a long and dramatic struggle, Rostam fatally wounds Sohrab and realizes his mistake too late to save his dying son.

Shi'ite doctrines and institutions have been another cause for the unabated appearance of personality cult in Iran. It is worth repeating here that Shi'ism owed its very origin to a dispute over *who* could ascend to the legitimate leadership of the Islamic community. Shi'ite doctrine is thus enriched with elitism, esoterism, and particularism.[81] The fact that Shi'ism looks forward so intensely to the second coming of the Mehdi, a prophet endowed with supernatural qualities, also strengthens the central role of personalities in popular culture and religion. Much personal appeal and attraction can be generated by living charismatic individuals who, intentionally or not, come close to the popular image that people have of the Mehdi. Eager for the return of their Messiah, Shi'ites have historically not hesitated to attribute messianic traits similar to those of the Mehdi to their national heroes. This image was perpetuated as recently as the 1978-79 revolution, when a nationwide rumor was circulating that "Imam" Khomeini's picture could be seen on the face of the moon.

This claim to supernatural divinity was used by Iranian rulers even before the country's conquest by invading Arab Moslems. Sassanid shahs went so far as to call themselves Gods, and imitated them in attire and appearance.82 All Iranian kings thereafter, except the Pahlavis, called themselves Shadow of God, thus using religious doctrine and symbolism to perpetuate their charisma and aggrandize their powers. Reza Shah was an exception to the norm, as he did not seek to use religion as a means to legitimize his rule. This he consciously avoided since his aim was to curb the *ulama*'s powers and to replace religious ideology with nationalism as the primary social force to bind the country together. His son also tried to do away with religion as much as possible, but similar to his father he found the task insurmountable. Yet he did try to forge for himself a position similar to the Shadow of God by coining the slogan "God, Shah, the Motherland" (*Khoda, Shah, Meehan*), thus placing himself only one step below God and superior to the country.

Personality cult has in more recent years been institutionalized under the auspices of Shi'ism with the development of the concept of *marj'a taqlid*, out of which later grew the even more powerful position of *velayat-e faqih*. The *marj'a taqlid*, who is in effect a replacement for Mehdi until he returns, is the ultimate source of all authority--religious, judicial, executive, and military. Admittedly, the Islamic Republic represents only the first time in Iranian history when the clerical establishment has directly held political power. Yet the development of the concept of *marj'a taqlid* did much to accentuate the personalism that permeated pre-revolutionary regimes: it placed one personality, the "vicegerent of the Imam," in a position parallel if not equal to another, the "Shadow of God." A cult was created around one (religious) personality in order to balance out the powers of a different cult revolving around another (temporal) personality.83

Lastly, personality cult has been paramount in Iranian history because of the way that Iranian political systems have operated. Iran has had a rich tradition of charismatic rule, historically by kings and more recently by the *ulama*.84 The whole system has in fact often been made up of a chain of personalities in the form of a bond between the ruler down to his lieutenants. Prior to the Pahlavis, patrimonial rule existed alongside decentralized political institutions, which by themselves were not strong enough to secure the king's rule over the entire territory. The monarch thus delegated much power to local governors, appointees whose very position was based on their personal relationship with the shah. The personal nature of politics was changed in form but not in substance under the Pahlavis and the Islamic Republic. Devotion to the person of the ruler and to any superior official, not merit, was and continues to be the main criteria for political advancement and even social mobility. Power politics have been summed up in inter-personal politics. As one observer has noted, throughout Iranian history, "power has not flowed from institution to institution but rather from individual to individual."[85]

The effects of personality cult on Iranian political history are rather obvious. Socially, personality cult has fostered an intense sense of individualism, while politically it has led to dictatorships based on the personal traits of the ruler. These two developments, social individualism and political authoritarianism, are not unrelated. Since political institutions revolve around the ruler and those he appoints, loyalty has been directed toward individuals rather than toward institutions. Thus the stability of political institutions has depended on the longevity of individual leaders. This has resulted in the instability of political administrations and has fostered individualism among the masses, with almost everyone trying to secure his own position in society, feeling little or no sense of responsibility to the larger community or to high ideals.[86] It is more than coincidental that Iranians excel in individual competitions far more frequently than they do in team sports. Polo, developed in Iran, soon died out and is hardly played in Iran any more today, while individually competitive sports such as wrestling and weight-lifting continue to produce impressive athletes.[87]

The political ramifications of personality cult are even more readily apparent. By giving primacy to individuals rather than institutions or principles, personality cult has resulted in a simplification of the political process. The nature and character of political systems can be best understood through the personality of their leaders instead of their supporting institutions or ideologies. Personality cult has muted the evolution of Iranian politics and has left political institutions at the mercy of the character and the wishes of whoever happens to hold power. The system has invariably reflected the personality of the ruler: zealous and militant under the Safavids, lax and corrupt under the Qajars, regimented and brutal during Reza Shah's reign, "modern" under Mohammad Reza Shah, and austere and militant under Khomeini. Personality cult even permeates the basis of Iran's revolutionary movements. Revolutions and political movements are seen first and foremost as the crusade of one personality against another. Just as Imam Hussein "heroically" battled the "infidel" Yazid in Karbala some 1,400 years ago, a drama whose memory is kept alive every year through huge processions and passion plays, so did Mussadiq fight against the shah and the British, and Khomeini battled the Shah and later Saddam Hussein. Even those claiming to spearhead a second revolution against the Islamic Republic have gotten entangled in a personality cult that revolves around their leader. Two of the *Mujahedeen's* most telling slogans are "Death to Khomeini, Long live Rajavi" and "Rajavi, Iran; Iran, Rajavi," hardly propositions attesting to the superiority of their ideology over Khomeini's.

CONCLUSION

In Iran, the practice of politics has historically been a decidedly urban affair. The fact that major Iranian dynasties ruled from cities such as Persepolis, Shush, Isfahan, Tabriz, Shiraz, and Tehran is more than historical coincidence. It reflects the overwhelmingly urban character of Iranian politics. With few exceptions, in all historical eras the powerholders's main base of support as well as that of their opponents were located in the urban centers. In pre-Islamic times, the powerful Zoroastrian clergy, centred in the cities, formed the dominant support-base of the Acheamanids and later the Sassanids. A similar relationship was forged between the Safavids and the Shi'ite *ulama*, turning into a changeable nexus of alliances and opposition under the Qajars and the Pahlavis. This did not mean, however, that the conditions that prevailed in the countryside did not influence the overall character of the political process. Tribalism and feudalism profoundly affected Iran's political history. Tribalism resulted in the fragmentation of the periphery and the centralization of the center. It also eased the penetration of the country by foreign powers. Feudalism, meanwhile, strengthened political autocracy and reinforced conservatism. For its part, religion provided much of the fuel for both autocracy *and* revolutions. Its special appeal was strengthened by low levels of education throughout society and by the prevalence of dogmatism as an intellectual tool for supporting or refuting religious beliefs. Finally, all Iranian political systems and revolutionary movements alike, both ancient and recent, have been based on a cult-like devotion to a single individual. This cult of personality has in turn facilitated the appearance of both autocracy and revolutionary movements.

There has not been a regular and consistent pattern of political participation in Iran. The public's input into the political process has either manifested itself in the form of massive and sudden revolutionary outbursts or has been perfunctory and cosmetic. So far, the Islamic Republic has proven to be somewhat of an exception, cultivating a sort of inclusionary pluralism rarely practiced in Iran before. This pluralism is, nevertheless, a severely restricted one and encourages political participation by only those whose ideology and beliefs meet the regime's narrow requirements. Throughout Iranian history, a nexus between prevailing political attitudes and existing political institutions has been conspicuously non-existent. As one observer has noted, "Authority has a tenuous base in Iranian political culture; while accepting political authority, the polity has a general mistrust of it."[88] Ingrained characteristics such as personality cult, religion, vastly unequal privileges, under-education, and tribal and feudal relations have made Iranians feel a necessity for a strong central figure. At the same time, these same characteristics have fostered the frequent appearance of revolutionary movements and the intrusion of foreign powers.

Notes

1. For a discussion and critique of the division of Iranian culture into "modern" and "traditional" see Jalal Al-Ahmad's provocative book, *Gharbzadege* (Westoxication) (Tehran: Ravvaq, 1341/1962).

2. T. Feerouzan, "Darbare-ye Tarkib va Sazman-e Eelat va Ashayer-e Iran" (Concerning the Composition and Structure of Tribes and Clans in Iran), Agah Institute, *Eelat va Ashayer* (Tribes and Clans) (Tehran: Agah, 1362/1983), pp. 7-9.

3. Richard Tapper, "Introduction," Richard Tapper, ed. *The Conflict of Tribe and State in Iran and Afghanistan* (London: Croom Helm, 1983), p. 45.

4. Gene Garthwaite, "Tribal Confederations and States: An Historical Overview of the Bakhtiaris in Iran," Tapper, ed., *The Conflict of Tribe and State in Iran and Afghanistan*, p. 328.

5. Ann Lambton, *Landlords and Peasants in Persia* (Oxford: Oxford University Press, 1953), p. 158.

6. Ibid, p. 157.

7. Lois Beck, "Iran and the Qashqai Tribal Confederacy," Tapper, ed., *The Conflict of Tribe and State in Iran and Afghanistan*, p. 239.

8. Tapper. "Introduction," Tapper, ed. *The Conflict of Tribe and State in Iran and Afghanistan*, p. 58.

9. Richard Tapper, "Holier than Thou: Islam in Three Tribal Societies," Akbar Ahmad and David Hart, eds., *Islam in Tribal Societies: From the Atlas to the Indus* (London: Routledge & Kegan Paul, 1984), p. 249.

10. Ibid, p. 254.

11. Ibid, pp. 256-257.

12. See Lois Beck, "Revolutionary Iran and its Tribal Peoples," *Merip Reports no.* 87(May 1980), pp. 14-20.

13. See an interview with the leader of the Kurdish Democratic Party, Abdolrahman Qasemlu, in "The Clergy Have Confiscated the Revolution,"

Merip Reports no. 98 (July-August 1981), pp. 17-19.

14. Tapper, "Introduction," Tapper, ed., *The Conflict of Tribe and State in Iran and Afghanistan*, p. 45.

15. T. Feerouzi, "Darbare-ye Tarkib va Sazman-e Eelat va Ashayer-e Iran," Agah Institute, *Eelat va Ashayer*, pp. 53-4.

16. Beck, "Iran and the Qashqai Tribal Confederacy," Tapper, ed., *The Conflict of Tribe and State in Iran and Afghanistan*, p. 291.

17. Feerouzi, "Darbare-ye Tarkib va Sazman-e Eelat va Ashayer-e Iran," Agah Institute, *Eelat va Ashayer*, pp. 14, 17.

18. Lambton, *Landlords and Peasants in Persia*, p. 157.

19. Tapper, "Holier than Thou: Islam in Three Tribal Societies," Ahmad and Hart, eds. *Islam in Tribal Societies*, p. 254.

20. Beck, "Iran and the Qashqai Tribal Confederacy," Tapper, ed., *The Conflict of Tribe and State in Iran and Afghanistan*," p. 293.

21. Lambton, *Landlords and Peasants in Persia*, p. 175.

22. Ibid, p. 176.

23. Agah Institute, *Masa'el-e Arzi va Dehghani* (Land and Peasant Issues) (Tehran: Agah, 1361/1982), p. 244.

24. Lambton, *Landlords and Peasants in Persia*, p. 260.

25. Ibid, pp. 172-173.

26. Ibid, p. 171.

27. Ibid, p. 262.

28. Ibid, p. 272.

29. Ibid, p. 263.

30. Babak Ghahreman, "Dou Yaddasht Darbare-ye Keshavarzi-ye Tejari dar Iran" (Two Observations About Commercial Agriculture in Iran), Agah Institute, *Masa'el-e Arzi va Dehghani*, p. 135.

31. Ahmad Ashraf, "Dehghanan, Zamin, va Enghelab" (Peasants, Land, and Revolution), Agah Institute, *Masa'el-e Arzi va Dehghani*, p. 11.

32. Ibid. *Khoshneshinan* literally means the "well-sitters," or those who sit idlely around not doing anything.

33. Ibid, p. 18.

34. Khosrow Khosravi, *Jame'e-ye Dehghani dar Iran* (Peasant Society in Iran) (Tehran: Payam, 1358/1979), p. 83.

35. Ibid, p. 80.

36. F. Hesamian, et al. *Shahrneshini dar Iran* (Urbanization in Iran) (Tehran: Agah, 1363/1984), p. 110.

37. Agah Institute, "Amarha-ye Roustaii va Keshavarzi-e Iran" (Iran's Rural and Agricultural Statistics), *Masa'el-e Arzi va Dehghani*, p. 157.

38. Ibid, p. 158.

39. Ann Lambton, "Land Reform and Rural Cooperative Societies." Ehsan Yarshater, ed. *Iran Faces the Seventies* (New York: Praeger, 1971), p. 41.

40. Saeed V. Fallah, "Mashini Shudan-e Keshavarzi dar Iran" (Mechanisation of Agriculture in Iran), Agah Institute, *Masa'el-e Arzi va Dehghani*, p. 99.

41. Khosravi, *Jame'e-ye Dehghani dar Iran*, p. 139.

42. Lambton, *Landlords and Peasants in Persia*, p. 394.

43. William Royce, "The Shirazi Provincial Elite: Status Maintenance and

Change," M. Bonine and N. Keddie, eds., *Continuity and Change in Modern Iran* (Albany, NY: SUNY Press, 1981), p. 259. See also M. Delvecchio Good,"The Changing Status and Composition of an Iranian Provincial Elite," pp. 229-248, in the same book.

44. Ibid, p. 253.

45. See Mehran Kamrava, *Revolution in Iran: Roots of Turmoil* (London: Routledge, 1990), Chapter 5.

46. Said Amir Arjomand, *The Shadow of God and the Hidden Imam* (Chicago: University of Chicago Press, 1984), p. 109.

47. Hamid Enayat, *Modern Islamic Political Thought* (London: Macmillan, 1982), pp. 24-25.

48. Lambton, *Theory and Practice in Medieval Persian Government* (London: Variorum Reprints, 1980), pp. I: 415-416.

49. Enayat, *Modern Islamic Political Thought*, p. 19.

50. Arjomand, *The Shadow of God and the Hidden Imam*, p. 124. The *Sheykh al-Islam* was a city's chief religious dignitary and the *Qazi* was its religious judge.

51. Nikki Keddie, "The Roots of the *Ulama*'s Power in Modern Iran," Nikki Keddie, ed., *Scholars, Saints, and Sufis: Moslem Religious Institutions in the Middle East since 1500* (Berkeley, CA: University of California Press, 1972), p. 221.

52. Lambton, *Theory and Practice in Medieval Persian Government*, pp. III: 142-143.

53. Azar Tabari, "The Role of the Clergy in Modern Iranian Politics." Nikki Keddie, ed., *Religion and Politics in Iran: Shi'ism from Quietism to Revolution* (New Haven, CT: Yale University Press, 1983), p. 48.

54. Lambton, *Theory and Practice in Medeival Persian Government*, p. III: 145.

55. Keddie, "The Roots of the *Ulama*'s Power in Modern Iran," Keddie, ed., *Scholars, Saints, and Sufis*, p. 225.

56. Enayat, *Modern Islamic Political Thought*, pp. 167-168.

57. Juan R. Cole, "Imami Jurisprudence and the Role of the *Ulama*: Morteza Ansari on Emulating the Supreme Exempler," Nikki Keddie, ed., *Religion and Politics in Iran: Shi'ism from Quietism to Revolution.*, p. 40.

58. Said Amir Arjomand, "Introduction: Social Movements in the Contemporary Near and Middle East," S.A. Arjomand, ed., *From Nationalism to Revolutionary Islam* (Albany, NY: SUNY Press, 1984), p. 13.

59. Ibid, p. 19.

60. M. Reza Behnam, *Cultural Foundations of Iranian Politics* (Salt Lake City, UT: University of Utah Press, 1986), p. 86.

61. Hamid Algar, "The Oppositional Role of the *Ulama* in Twentieth-Century Iran." Keddie, ed. *Scholars, Saints, and Sufis*, p. 254.

62. Lambton, *Theory and Practice in Medieval Persian Government*, p. VII: 29.

63. Yann Richard, "Ayatollah Kashani: Precursor of the Islamic Republic?" Keddie, ed., *Religion and Politics in Iran: Shi'ism from Quietism to Revolution*, p. 104.

64. See Kamrava, *Revolution in Iran: Roots of Turmoil*, Chapter 3.

65. While Arjomand claims that Shi'ism is an inherently conservative

social force, there are others, even less successful than him, who claim that Shi'ism is inherently revolutionary. See, for example, Soroush Irfani, *Revolutionary Islam in Iran* (London: Zed Books, 1983).

66. Enayat, *Modern Islamic Political Thought*, p. 160.

67. Ibid, p. 164.

68. Shahrough Akhavi, *Religion and Politics in Contemporary Iran* (Albany, NY: SUNY Press, 1980), p. 102.

69. Keddie, "The Roots of the Ulama's Power in Modern Iran," Keddie, ed., *Scholars, Saints, and Sufis*, p. 213.

70. Peter Avery. "Iran: A Culture Challenged," *Contemporary Review*, vol. 223, no. 1355 (December 1978), p. 303.

71. Akbar Aghajanian, "Ethnic Inequality in Iran: An Overview," *International Journal of Middle East Studies* 15 (1983), p. 222. Due to a paucity of existing industrial infrastructures in the more remote areas, the Islamic Republic has so far been unable to radically alter the heavily urban-oriented development policies that its predecessor followed. Nevertheless, sporadic efforts to divert greater resources to a larger number of peripheral areas have taken place under the auspices of the post- revolutionary regime's development programs.

72. For an examination of the concept of "urban bias," see, Michlael Lipton, "Why Poor People Stay Poor: Urban Bias in World Development," Joseph Guglar, ed., *The Urbanization of the Third World* (Oxford: Oxford University Press, 1980), pp. 40-51.

73. Aghajanian, "Ethnic Inequality in Iran: An Overview," p. 215.

74. Guity Neshat, "Women in the Ideology of the Islamic Republic'" Guity Neshat, ed., *Women and Revolution in Iran* (Boulder, CO: Westview Press, 1983), p. 195.

75. Shahla Haeri, "Women, Law, and Social Change in Iran," Jane Smith, ed., *Women in Contemporary Moslem Societies* (London: Associated University Press, 1980), pp. 229-230.

76. Oriana Fallaci, *Interview With History* (New York: Liveright, 1976), pp. 271-272

77. Mohammad Reza Pahlavi, *Answer to History* (New York: Stein and Day, 1980), p. 116.

78. Mao referred to the peasantry as the "blank masses,"arguing that they had the most potential for revolutionary mobilization since they had not been "corrupted" by bourgeois ideas. See Stuart Schram, *The Political Thoughts of Mao Tse Tung* (New York: Praeger, 1969), pp. 241-246.

79. Behnam, *Cultural Foundations of Iranian Politics*, p. 17.

80. Ibid, p. 96.

81. Hamid Enayat, *Modern Islamic Political Thought*, p. 30.

82. Arjomand, *The Shadow of God and the Hidden Imam*, p. 93.

83. This been the case with the Mujahedden Organization as well, though they protray Khomeini as Yazid and their leader, "Brother" Masoud Rajavi, as an almost unearthly figure.

84. For a discussion of charismatic kingship in Iran see Arjomand, *The Shadow of God and the Hidden Imam*, pp. 90-94.

85. James Bill, "The Plasticity of Informal Politics: The Case of Iran," *Middle East Journal* vol. 27, no. 2 (1973), p. 135.

86. Behnam, *Cultural Foundations of Iranian Politics*, p. 99.

87. For more on the individualism of Iranians see Richard Gable, "Culture and Administration in Iran," *Middle East Journal* vol. 13, no. 4 (1959), pp. 407-421.

88. Behnam, *Cultural Foundations of Iranian Politics*, p. 12.

6

Conclusion

The preceding chapters have chronicled the tumultuous evolution of Iranian political history. In three centuries, the country has evolved from a tribal kingdom into a post-revolutionary populist state built on the legitimacy of Islam and the support of mobilized masses. In the process, the dramatic changes that have engulfed Iran's political history have also altered its diplomatic role and significance in the international arena, its perception of itself, and its culture and social values. A new Iran has evolved into being, vastly different from the one ruled over by either the Qajars or the Pahlavis. Today's Islamic Republic is a result and a living progenitor of Iran's multidimensional metamorphosis throughout history.

In modern times, Iran has had to come into terms with its new self. It is no longer the center of its self-created universe, its constellation of stars having been smashed at the hands of greed, diplomacy, and economic realities. It has had to search for itself new purchases of identity both domestically and internationally. In the international arena, Iran has progressively found itself no longer the centrestage but rather a diplomatic footnote, no longer the magnificently powerful kingdom to which all other kings paid homage but only another victim of the ravages of diplomacy and strings pulled by much more powerful players. The King of Kings was reduced to accepting the superpowers' lists of parliamentary deputies, his once mighty empire a playground for blatant occupation and international intrigue. Once the proud bastion of *Shi'ism*, boastfully brandishing its radical religion to its more humble neighbors, the country has speedily found itself on the defensive, having to cry out protestations of foul play to the likes of Salman Rushdie in its own embattled defense in the international community. No more the global, nay regional, centerstage, Iran has had to uneasily come into terms with its new image as a co-equal among neighbors and indeed in some instances as an inferior partner. The "Persian Gulf" might have retained its name (and even that precariously), but the Persians are surely no longer the trump-wielding diplomatic highrollers that they once were. The tides of the regional and international poker games have dramatically altered, with Iran having in recent decades to rely more and more on hollow bluffs in order to merely stay in the game.

Even the hollow propaganda of the last shah failed to achieve a whole lot, instead merely raising hopes to a high pitch and instilling a misplaced sense of false pride, which, curiously enough, existed side by side with a national inferiority complex. What was billed as "the Japan of the Middle East," "the Gendarme of the Persian Gulf," proved to be anything but. What industrial development there was, and there indeed was a lot of it, remained inherently superfluous, never penetrating the thinly-veiled facade of bourgeois urban life. The country remained at best only minimally developed, the less glittery aspects of industrial evolution often being completely ignored in favor of the more opulent. Even the most educated policy-makers could not abandon their flair for the flashier side of development. Cadillacs and Chevrolets were assembled in Tehran; donkey carts lined the dirt roads of not-too-distant villages. Elegant boulevards adorned larger and smaller cities alike; only to be paralleled by open gutters into which ran the most unsanitary garbage. Full-scale industrial development was declared to be within reach in a few years; but the people could not be fed without importing almost all of the needed food. Even the much prized military, propped up by the most sophisticated American hardware, proved to be an empty shell when put to test. The commanders of the Gendarme of the Gulf were unable to command when it came time to save their own selves, failing miserably to flex their supposedly mighty muscle in their first and only real challenge. Unarmed revolutionaries overran the regime as if it were a house of cards.

This is not to downplay the internationally tantalizing effects of Iran's 1978-79 revolution. "The little bearded man from Qom," as the Western media often mocked the revolution's leader, did indeed change the geopolitical face of the region more profoundly than perhaps even he himself fully realized. Attributing the revolution solely to Qom's bearded sage is simplistic and incorrect. But so is the belittlement of the international ramifications of the revolution. It would not be an exaggeration to claim that the Iranian revolution forever altered the diplomatic make-up and geopolitical alignment of the Persian Gulf, the Middle East, and indeed beyond. Iran's belligerent pursuit of a bloody and costly war with Iraq despite seemingly insurmountable obstacles proved more than just the resolve of a stubborn revolutionary nation. It proved to the rest of the nations of the Middle East, none too fond of the new governing zealots in Tehran, that Iran's turbaned warriors were not only for real but were in fact deadly serious in their pursuit of a new international order. They thus hurriedly rushed to the aid of the one Arab country that stood up to Iran's challenge, Iraq, pumping it with artillery and with petrodollars for eight years in a thinly-veiled multinational effort to contain Iran's revolution within its own borders.

Effective as their efforts were in preventing the establishment of other Islamic Republics, they none the less could not stop Iran from further exploiting the Lebanese quagmire. The Party of Allah became one of Tehran's most profitable ventures, a kind of a third party through which human hostages were bartered for weapons, spare parts, and oil sales. The Iranians had earlier gained invaluable experience in what at some point became the fashionable practice of hostage-taking. For 440 days, they imprisoned fifty-two Americans in their embassy in Tehran. The fate of those held captive in "the Nest of Spies," as the occupiers dubbed their new loot, became the focus of great international attention. For Iranians, the affair was yet another act of revolutionary valor. In all of the Third World, they were the ones who had finally stood up to the "Great Satan." To those in the West it was a barbaric act of savagery defying all norms of diplomatic and human conduct. To those on the inside in both opposing camps, however, the lingering fiasco looked progressively like a carefully worked out deal by some in Tehran and in Washington. The world nervously watched the drama drag on week after week and month after month. At stake were the freedom of fifty-two people, millions of dollars in frozen Iranian assets and purchased military hardware, and the American presidential elections. Despite accusations by credible Iranian and American insiders of a deal between Tehran and officials of the Reagan campaign team, no conclusive evidence of a conspiracy to time the release of the hostages in favor of Reagan's campaign has yet been furnished.[1] But there is enough suspicion to lead one to wonder if the preacher from Qom did indeed lend a helping hand to the cowboy from California. *If* he did, the effects of his revolution have resonated to heights never possibly imaginable before.

In a broader perspective, Iran's political history is even more inextricably entwined with the bigger drama of Middle Eastern history, its guiding dynamics part of larger forces which rarely confine themselves to national boundaries and borders. The very essence which for so long and with such intensity has summed up Iran's nationhood as opposed to those of its neighbors, *Shi'ism*, is itself part of a historic schism involving multitudes of distinctive nationalities and political identities. Iran is but a player, albeit a prominent one, in a historic process encompassing nations as distant as Indonesia to the east to Morocco and Mauritania to the west. And Islam is only one such nationally transcendental phenomena which has affected the shaping of Iran as we have come to know it today. Patrimonial practices both in politics and in social relations, feudalism, tribalism, personality cults, and other similar characteristics have long marked not just Iran but the entire Middle East region and beyond. These and other attributes have influenced peoples socially and politically since well before current political borders were drawn. Only in recent decades, when regional governments have begun jealously guarding against the flow of influences from across their modern borders, have such developments assumed somewhat of a "national" character.

Domestically, Iran's history has been marked by ceaseless efforts aimed at rediscovering and coming into terms with itself. The country's endless search for its own identity has long produced a mixture of sporadic intellectual brilliance coupled with onslaughts of mass violence by disillusioned souls longing to rediscover themselves by rallying behind demagogues and idealists. From the geniuses of Amir Kabir and Malkum Khan under the Qajars, to Ali Shariati's often overlooked gift for literature in recent years, Iran's history is inundated with brief examples of brilliant intellectuals swiftly stifled under the weights of political despotism and sociocultural solitaire. What has resulted is a disjointed body of intellectual knowledge, a muted and unevolved heritage of modern scholarship whose sharper edges have been softened in order to salvage survival. What has instead thrived is an endless thread of popular disillusionment, a tormenting inability to self-analyze and to understand the seemingly uncontrollable realities of everyday life. In desperation, mass refuge has been sought in the convenient, the understandable, the familiar. Again and again, Islam has served as just such a median, around which are wrapped the causes of the wretched and the disinherited, championed and spearheaded by charismatic demagogues.

The 1978-79 revolution is but the latest manifestation of Iran's desperate search to come into terms with its own self. Its causes were as much psychological and cultural as they were political and economic. Its clerical leaders were as much the unwitting products of lackluster secular intellectual development as they were tactful strategists and tacticians. Contrary to frequent assertions, the revolution did not occur because "the Pahlavis went too fast," nor was its draconian nature in the heydays of Khomeini's reign of terror a violent backlash to the country's "Westoxication." It was, instead, a result of the nation's discovery in the late 1970s that it was not only lost but was for the first time able to openly voice its uneasy sense of being lost. With the growing political exigencies of the Pahlavi regime, the nation found space to express its feelings of collective disillusionment. The people poured into streets, not knowing exactly what they wanted but being certain that there was something sufficiently wrong which warranted demonstration. They thus rebelled against the most readily apparent symbol of the status quo, the political system. The regime, meanwhile, had not helped its own cause by its history of corruption and dictatorship, and by its flaunting refusal to reverse its unpopular course. The missing ingredients for revolution soon fell into place: a political language of protest was soon found in the form of Islam, and leaders with mass following emerged from among a group of politically-minded clerics. What was a largely spontaneous search for self-identity soon turned into a historic revolution.

Like so many others before it, the revolution did not take long to betray itself, devour its own children, and to destroy any and everything in its path by claiming to uphold higher moral principles. In its march toward victory, the revolution had given birth to a colorful array of personalities, each having entrusted themselves with an assortment of historic missions and in the process having gathered bands of faithful followers. There was the sagacious-looking Mehdi Bazargan, long an opponent of the shah and later the highest-ranking politician of the post- revolutionary government. There was also the brash and blunt Ayatollah Mahmoud Taleghani, revered by most for his well-chronicled torture by SAVAK and outspoken independence. A host of new faces also peppered the post-revolutionary scene, most having been former students who had for years planned for their moment in the political spotlight in the dormitories of French and American universities. Abolhassan Banisadr, the French-educated philosopher-activist, and Sadeq Qotbzadeh, the linguist known for his acid tongue and sharp one-liners, were two of the more celebrated of such figures.

And then there was the dean of the revolutionary activists, the grandfather of them all, the Ayatollah Khomeini. To sum up the revolution and its outcome as the effects of Khomeini's actions and deeds is unforgivably reductionist. But one cannot help but to take note of the Ayatollah's personal march, not too subtle and by no means gentlemanly, to the apex of political power in the post-revolutionary order at the expense of all others. Within months, the dean was disenchanted with his pupils and dispensed with them one after another. Bazargan was forced out of office and ridiculed on grounds of incompetence and mismanagement. Taleghani died under questionable circumstances. Foreign Minister Qotbzadeh, who had at one point referred to inquisitive foreign reporters as "those damned sons of bitches," was accused of treason and executed. President Banisadr was impeached and forced into hiding. And scores of lesser-known names found their way into Amnesty International's list of missing or executed Iranians. Through it all, Khomeini looked on, consolidated his own position, and held on to every ounce of political power with unremitting zeal. In the end, having outlived the revolution's many famous as well as nameless children, he died of natural causes in 1988.

FROM DYNASTY TO STATE
TO NATIONAL SELF-EXAMINATION

In retrospect, the political history of modern Iran can be divided into three distinct phases, each corresponding with the country's evolutionary maturation as a nation-state. From the beginning of the Qajar era in the eighteenth century up until its end in the early 1900s, the country as a whole and the political establishment in specific strove to achieve greater degrees of cohesion, unity, and centralization. It was toward these ends that political initiatives and reforms were directed. During this period, the *state* within the nation-state was still struggling to emerge out of its embryonic formation and to wrest control of the prevailing social and political forces that floated throughout the territories that it ostensibly controlled. Thus the national political agenda preoccupying both politicians and independent intellectuals, if there ever was one, was the attainment of centralization and political unison. Centralized national rule became synonymous with political autocracy and despotism, reinforced in turn by emerging international dynamics and superpower rivalry.

A second phase was inaugurates with the ascension to power of Reza Pahlavi, the founder of the dynasty that bore his name. In this period, national unity was achieved and a functioning, comparatively modern state was established. With this fundamental task achieved, *modernization* became the new goal toward which all efforts--political, economic, intellectual, and social--were directed. This new objective was at first pursued through sheer force and naked brutality, seen as necessary by Reza Shah in order to instill the virtues of modernization and modernity among his uncooperative subjects. Gradually, the extensive reliance on coercion as a political tool was tempered by the growing sophistication of the political machinery, especially under Reza Shah's successor, Mohammad Reza, though systemic coercion and brutality were never really completely abandoned by either of the Pahlavis up until the very end.

The combined effects of the earlier periods of Iran's political history, phases in which political centralization and modernization formed the national agendas, helped launch the third phase of the country's political history. In this third phase, which stretches from the mid-1970s up until the present, Iran as a nation has undergone a period of collective self-evaluation, a grand and national soul-search in which the priorities set previously are being questioned and replaced by newly formulated ones. This, unlike the other two, has been a reflective period, dealing most fundamentally with intangibiles. It is the intangible aspects of Iranian life that the current phase is most concerned with: not political centralization but culture, not economic modernization but the aesthetics of human life. It is, indeed, in these intangible, politically peripheral domains where the 1978-79 revolution has made its most enduring contributions. True, political structures have changed, political values replaced, and leaders and their aspirations are different. But the dynamics and forces which underlie the political system and shape and determine its ultimate character are hardly different today from what they were before the revolution. The Iranian political system still is an essentially dictatorial one, much the same as it was before the revolution for which some 60,000 people died. What is different in today's Iran is the emphasis on what human life is all about. The national agenda has been switched, no longer striving for national unity or modernization but now seeking to redefine the basic premises of Iranian life and culture.

It is here where the elusive fruits of the 1978-79 revolution lie, in redefining the national agenda and in launching a new phase in Iran's political history. What these new cultural priorities are is still unclear and in fact rather confusing. Clearly, the value of human life is cherished no more now than it was in the past, as made unashamedly clear by the massacres committed by the post-revolutionary regime. New national priorities such as self-sufficiency and economic nationalism are intensely propagated, as are personal values like piety and moderation. The endurance of these values and the success of the revolution's intended and unintended outcomes is a matter that history has yet to answer. What is clear for now is the inauguration of a new and distinctive phase in Iran's political history.

Note

1. See printed transcripts for "The Election Held Hostage," *Frontline* (Show no. 916, Air date: April 16, 1991). See also Abolhasan Bani-Sadr, *My Turn to Speak: Iran, the Revolution and Secret Deals with the U.S.* (New York: Brassey's, 1991).

Bibliography

Abbot, John. *The Iranians: How They Live and Work*. London: David & Charles, 1977.

Abrahamian, Ervand. *Iran Between Two Revolutions*. Princeton, NJ: Princeton University Press, 1982.

_____. "The Causes of the Constitutional Revolution in Iran," *International Journal of Middle East Studies* 10 (August 1979): 318-414.

Adamiyat, Fereidoun. *Amir Kabir va Iran*. (Amir Kabir and Iran.) Tehran: Pirouz, 1334/1955.

_____. *Ideolozhi-ye Nehzat-e Mashrute'h Iran*. (Ideology of Iran's Constitutional Movement.) Tehran: Payam, 1355/1976.

Adibi, Hosein. *Tabagheh-ye Motevaset-e Jadid dar Iran*. (The New Middle Class in Iran.) Tehran: Jame'eh, 1358/1979.

Afkhami, Gholam R. *The Iranian Revolution: Thanatos on National Scale*. Washington, D.C.: The Middle East Institute, 1985.

Afrachteh, Kambiz. "The Predominance and Dilemmas of Theocratic Populism in Iran." *Iranian Studies* vol. XIV, no. 3-4 (Summer-Autumn 1981): 189-213.

Afshar, Haleh. ed. *Iran: A Revolution in Turmoil*. London: Macmillan, 1985.

Afshari, Mohammad Reza. "The Pishivaran and Merchants in Precapitalist Iranian Society: An Essay on the Background and the Causes of the Constitutional Revolution." *International Journal of Middle East Studies* 15 (1983): 135-55.

Agah Institute. *Eelat va Ashayer*. (Tribes and Clans.) Tehran: Agah, 1363/1984.

_____. *Masa'el-e Arzi va Dehghani*. (Land and Peasant Issues.) Tehran: Agah, 1361/1982.

_____. *Masa'el-e Iran va Khaveremianeh*. Vol. 1. (Problems of Iran and the Middle East.) Vol. 1. Tehran: Agah, 1360/1981.

_____. *Majmueh Maghalat darbare-ye Iran va Khavarmianeh*. Vol. II.

Tehran: Agah, 1362/1983.

Aghajanian, Akbar. "Ethnic Inequality in Iran: An Overview." *International Journal of Middle East Studies* 15 (1983): 211-224.

Ahmad, Akbar S. and David Hart, eds. *Islam in Tribal Societies: From the Atlas to the Indus.* London: Routledge & Kegan Paul, 1984.

Ahmad, Ishtiaq. *Anglo-Iranian Relations, 1905-1919.* Bombay: Asia Publishing House, 1975.

Akhavi, Shahrough. *Religion and Politics in Contemporary Iran.* Albany, NY: SUNY Press, 1980.

_____. "Elite Factionalism in the Islamic Republic of Iran." *The Middle East Journal* vol. 41, no. 2 (Spring 1987): 181-201.

Alaolmolki, Nozar. "The New Iranian Left." *The Middle East Journal* vol. 41, no. 2 (Spring 1987): 218-33.

Albert, David, ed. *Tell the American People: Perspectives on the Iranian Revolution.* Philadelphia: Movement for a New Society, 1980.

Al-Ahmad, Jalal. *Gharbzadegi* (Westoxication). Tehran: Ravvaq, 1341/1962.

Algar, Hamid. *Religion and State in Iran, 1785-1906.* Berkeley, CA: University of California Press, 1969.

_____. *Mirza Malkum Khan.* Berkeley, CA: University of California Press, 1973.

Amanallahi, Sekandar. *Kooch-neshini dar Iran.* (Pastoral Nomadism in Iran). Tehran: BTNK, 1360/1981.

Arjomand, Said Amir. "The Ulama's Traditionalist Opposition to Parliamentarianism: 1907-1909." *Middle Eastern Studies* Vol. 17, no. 2 (April 1981): 174-190.

_____. *The Shadow of God and the Hidden Imam.* Chicago: University of Chicago Press, 1984.

_____, ed. *From Nationalism to Revolutionary Islam.* Albany, NY: SUNY Press, 1984.

Avery, Peter. *Modern Iran.* London: Ernest Benn, 1965.

_____. "Iran: A Culture Challenged." *Contemporary Review* vol. 223, no. 1355 (December 1978): 298-303.

Azzud al-Dowleh, Ahmad Mirza. *Tarikh Azzudi.* (Azzudi History.) Tehran: n.p., 1327/1948.

Bakhash, Shaul. *The Reign of the Ayatollahs: Iran and the Islamic Revolution.* London: I.B. Tauris, 1985.

_____. *Iran: Monarchy, Bureaucracy and Reform under the Qajars: 1858-1896.* London: Ithaca Press, 1978.

Bakhtiar, Shapour. *Mabani-ye Andishe-haye Siyasi va Barname-haye Ejraii.* (Principles of Political Thoughts and Executive Programs.) Paris: n.p., 1983.

Bakhtoortash, Nosratollah. *Tarikh-e Parcham-e Iran.* (History of

Iran's Flag.) Koln, FGR: Mehr, 1986.

Banani, Amin. *The Modernization of Iran 1921-1941.* Stanford, CA: Stanford University Press, 1961.

Bani-Sadar, Abolhassan. *Khianat beh Omid.* (Betreyal of Faith). Paris: n.p., n.d.

_____. *My Turn to Speak: Iran, the Revolution and the Secret Deals with the U.S..* New York: Brassey's, 1991.

Bashiriyeh, Hossein. *State and Revolution in Iran.* London: Croom Helm, 1984.

Bayani, Khan Baba. *Siyasat-e Napelon dar Iran dar Zaman-e Fath Ali Shah.* (Napoleon's Policy in Iran During Fath Ali Shah's Reign.) Tehran: Chapp-e Ketab, 1318/1939.

Beck, Lois. *The Qashqa'i of Iran.* New Haven, CT.: Yale University Press, 1986.

_____. "Revolutionary Iran and Its Tribal Peoples." *Merip Reports* no. 87 (May 1980): 14-20.

Behnam, M. Reza. *Cultural Foundations of Iranian Politics.* Salt Lake City, UT: University of Utah Press, 1986.

Bill, James. *The Eagle and the Lion: The Tragedy of American-Iranian Relations.* New Haven, CT: Yale University Press, 1988.

_____. "The Social and Economic Foundations of Power in Contemporary Iran." *The Middle East Journal* 17 (1963): 400-18.

_____. "The Plasticity of Informal Politics: The Case of Iran." *The Middle East Journal* vol 27, no. 2 (1973): 131-151.

_____. "Power and Religion in Revolutionary Iran." *Middle East Journal* vol. 36, no. 1 (Winter 1982). pp. 22-47.

Bonine, Michael and Nikki Keddie, eds. *Continuity and Change in Modern Iran* Albany, NY: SUNY Press, 1981.

Bosworth, Edmund and Carole Hellenbrand, eds. *Qajar Iran: Political, Social, and Cultural Change 1800-1925.* Edinburgh: Edinburgh University Press, 1983.

Browne, Edward. *The Persian Revolution of 1905-1909.* Cambridge: Cambridge University Press, 1910.

Carter, Jimmy. *Keeping Faith.* London: Collins, 1982.

Chubin, Shahram and Sepehr Zabih. *The Foreign Relations of Iran: A Developing State in a Zone of Great-Power Conflict.* Berkeley, CA: University of California Press, 1974.

Cole, Juan and Nikki Keddie, eds. *Shi'ism and Social Protest.* New Haven, CT.: Yale University Press, 1986.

Cottam, Richard. *Nationalism in Iran.* Pittsburg: University of Pittsburgh Press, 1979.

Davani, Ali. *Nehzat-e Rouhaniyun-e Iran* (The Struggle of the Iranian Clergy.) Vols. 1-10 Tehran: n.p., n.d.

Ebrahim, Mohammad. *Siyasat va Eghtesad-e Asr-e Safavi.* (Politics and Economy in the Safavid Era.) Tehran: Seyfalishah, 1348/1969.

Enayat, Hamid. *Modern Islamic Political Thought.* London: Macmillan, 1982.

Esfandiary, Soraya. *The Autobiography of H.I.H. Princess Soraya.* C. Fitzgibbon, trans. London: Arthur Barker, 1963.

Eshraghi, F. "The Immediate Aftermath of the Anglo-Soviet Occupation of Iran in August 1941." *Middle Eastern Studies* vol. 20, no. 3 (July 1984): 324-351.

Esposito, John. *Islam and Politics.* Syracuse, NY: Syracuse University Press, 1984.

Fallaci, Oriana. *Interview With History.* New York: Liveright, 1976.

Fatemi, Faramarz. *The U.S.S.R. in Iran.* London: Thomas Yoseloff, 1980.

Fatemi, Khosrow. "Leadership by Distrust: The Shah's Modus Operandi". *Middle East Journal* vol. 36, no. 1 (Winter 1982): pp. 48-61.

Fatemi, Nasrollah Saifpour. *Diplomatic History of Persia, 1917-1923.* New York: Russell F. Moore Co., 1952.

Feerouzan, T. "Darbare-ye Tarkib va Sazman-e Eelat va Ashayer-e Iran" (Concerning the Composition and Structure of Tribes and Clans in Iran) Aghah Institute *Eelat va Ashayer* (Tribes and Clans) Tehran: Agah, 1362/1983, pp. 7-62.

Ferdows, Adele Kazemi. *Religion and Nationalism in Iran: The Study of Fadaiyan-i Islam.* PhD Dissertation, Indiana University, 1967.

Fischer, Michael. *Iran: From Religious Dispute to Revolution.* Cambridge, MA: Harvard University Press, 1980.

Floor, Willem. *Industrialization in Iran 1900-1941.* Durham: University of Durham, 1984.

_____. "Hotz versus Muhammad Shafi: A Case Study in Commercial Litigation in Qajar Iran, 1888-1894." *International Journal of Middle East Studies* 15 (1983): 185-209.

_____. "Change and Development in the Judicial Sysytem of Qajar Iran (1800-1925)," Edmund Bosworth and Carole Hillenbrand, eds, *Qajar Iran: Political, Social, and Cultural Change 1800-1925,* Edinburgh: Edinburgh University Press, 1883, pp. 113-147.

Gable, Richard W. "Culture and Administration in Iran." *Middle East Journal* vol. 13, no. 4 (1959): 407-21.

Garthwaite, Gene R. "The Bakhtiari Ilkhani: An Illusion of Unity." *International Journal of Middle East Studies* 8 (1977): 145-60.

_____. *Khans and the Shahs: A Documentary Analysis of the Bakhtiari in Iran.* Cambridge: Cambridge University Press, 1983.

Golabian, Hossein. *An Analysis of the Underdeveloped Rural and Nomadic Areas of Iran.* Stockholm: The Royal Institute of Technology, 1977.

Graham, Robert. *Iran: The Illusion of Power.* New York: St. Martin's Press, 1980.

Guglar, Josef, ed. *The Urbanization of the Third World.* Oxford: Oxford University Press, 1980.

Hairi, Abdul-Hadi. "Shaykh Fazl Allah Nuri's Refutation of the Idea of Constitutionalism."*Middle Eastern Studies* vol. 13, no. 3 (October 1977): 327-39.

Halliday, Fred. *Iran: Dictatorship and Development.* New York: Penguin, 1979.

Hanel, Alfred and Julius Otto Muller. *On the Evolution of Rural Cooperatives with Reference to Governmental Development Policies - Case Study Iran.* Marburg, FGR: Institute for Cooperation in Developing Countries, 1976.

Hanson, Brad. "The 'Westoxication' of Iran: Depictions and Reactions of Behrangi, Al-e Ahmad, and Shariati." *International Journal of Middle East Studies* 15 (1983): 1-23.

Hesamian, F. Etamadi, and M.R. Haeri.*Shahrneshini dar Iran.* (Urbanisation in Iran.)Tehran: Agah: 1363/1984.

Hiro, Dilip. *Iran Under the Ayatollahs.* London: Routledge & Kagan Paul, 1985.

Irfani, Soroush. *Revolutionary Islam in Iran.* London: Zed Books, 1983.

Jacobs, Norman. *The Sociology of Development: Iran as an Asian Case Study.* New York: Praeger, 1966.

Johnson, Gail Cook. *High Level Man Power in Iran: From Hidden Conflict to Crisis.* New York: Praeger, 1980.

Kamrava, Mehran. *Revolution in Iran: Roots of Turmoil.* London: Routledge, 1990.

Kasravi, Ahmad. *Tarikh-e Mashruteh-e Iran.* (History of Iran's Constitutionalism.) Tehran: n.p., n.d.

_____. *Shi'e-gari.* (Shi'ism.) Tehran: n.p., 1335/1956.

_____. *Bahai-gari.* (Bahaism.) Tehran: n.p., n.d.

Katouzian, Homa. *The Political Economy of Modern Iran 1926-1979.* New York: New York University Press, 1981.

_____. "The Aridisolatic Society: A Model of Long-Term Social and Economic Development in Iran." *International Journal of Middle East Studies* 15 (1983): 259-81.

Kazemzadeh, Firouz. *Russia and Britain in Persia, 1864-1914.* New Haven, CT.: Yale University Press, 1968.

Keddie, Nikki. *Iran: Religion, Politics, and Society.* London: Frank Cass, 1980.

_____. *Roots of Revolution.* New Haven, CT.: Yale University Press, 1981.

_____. ed. *Religion and Politics in Iran: Shi'ism from Quietism to Revolution.* New Haven, CT.: Yale University Press, 1983.

_____. ed. *Scholars, Saints, and Sufis: Moslem Religious Institutions in the Middle East Since 1500*. Berkeley, CA: University of California Press, 1972.

Khomeini, Rouhollah. *Velayat Faqih*. (Governance of the Religiously Learned.) Qom: n.p., 1350/1971.

Khosravi, Khosrow. *Pazhuheshi dar Jame'e-ye Roustai-ye Iran*. (A Research on Iran's Rural Society.) Tehran: Payam, 2535/1976.

_____. *Jame'e-ye Dehghani dar Iran*. (Peasant Society in Iran.) Tehran: Payam, 1358/1979.

Kianouri, Noureddin. "For Unity Among Patriotic Forces." *World Marxist Review* (July 1981): 15-9.

Kramer, Martin. ed. *Shi'ism, Resistance, and Revolution*. Boulder, CO: Westview, 1987.

Lambton, Ann. *The Persian Land Reform 1962-1966*. Oxford: Clarendon Press, 1969.

_____. *Theory and Practice in Medieval Persian Government*. London: Variorum Reprints, 1980.

_____. *Qajar Persia: Eleven Studies*. London: I.B. Tauris, 1987.

_____. *Landlords and Peasants in Persia*. Oxford: Oxford University Press, 1953.

Laing, Margaret. *The Shah*. London: Sidgwick & Jackson, 1977.

Ledeen, Michael and William Lewis, *Debacle: The American Failure in Iran*. New York: Alfred Knopf, 1981.

Lenczowski, George, ed. *Iran Under the Pahlavis*. Stanford, CA: The Hoover Institution Press, 1978.

Litwak, Robert. *Detente and the Nixon Doctrine: American Foreign Policy and the Pursuit of Stability*. Cambridge: Cambridge University Press, 1984.

Looney, Robert. "Origins of Pre-Revolutionary Iran's Development Strategy." *Middle Eastern Studies* vol. 22, no. 1 (January 1986): 104-19.

Lorentz, John. *Modernization and Political Change in Nineteenth-Century Iran: The Role of Amir Kabir*. PhD Dissertation, Princeton University, 1974.

Mahdavi, Shireen. "Women and the Shii Ulama in Iran." *Middle Eastern Studies* vol. 19, no. 1 (January 1983): 17- 27.

Mahid, Mohammad A. *Pazhuheshi dar Tarikh-e Diplomacy Iran*. (A Research in Iran's Diplomatic History.) Tehran: Mitra, 1361/1982.

Mahmoudi, Hassan Gol. *Divan-e Nasis al-Din Shah*. (Nasir al-Din Shah's Poems.) Tehran: Pasand, 1363/1984.

Martin, V.A. "The Anti-Constitutionalist Arguments of Shaikh Fazlallah Nuri." *Middle Eastern Studies* vol. 22, no. 2 (April 1986): 181-96.

Meredith, Colin. *The Qajar Response to Russia's Military Challenge,*

1804-28. PhD Dissertation, Princeton University, 1973.

Millspaugh, Arthur C. *Americans in Persia.* New York: Da Capo Press, 1976.

Mirashinkoff, L. *Iran dar Jang Avval Jahani.* (Iran in the First World War.) A. Dokhaniati, trans. Tehran: Farzaneh, 1357/ 978.

Mohammady, Hasan Gol. *Divan-e Naser al-Din Shah.* (Naser al-Din Shah's Poems). Tehran: Pasand, 1366/1984.

Momayezi, Nasser. "Economic Correlates of Political Violence: The Case of Iran." *The Middle East Journal* vol. 40, no. 1 (Winter 1986): 68-81.

Momen, Moojan. "The Social Basis of the Babi Upheavals in Iran (1848-53): A Preliminary Analysis." *International Journal of Middle East Studies* 15 (1983): 157-83.

Mortimer, Edward. *Faith and Power: The Politics of Islam.* New York: Random House, 1982.

Mostoufi, Abdollah. *Tarikh-e Edari va Ejtemai-ye Qajar Ya Sharh-e Zendegani-ye Man* (Social and Administrative History of the Qajars or My Autobiography) Vol. I. Tehran: Zavvar, n.d.

Mottahedeh, Roy. *The Mantle of the Prophet: Religion and Politics in Iran.* New York: Pantheon Books, 1985.

Mujahedeen. *Majmueh E'lamiye-ha va Mouze-giriha-ye Siyasi-ye Mujahedeen-e Khalq-e Iran.* (Collected Communiques and Political Positions of the People's Mujahedeen Organisation of Iran) Vols. I-II. Tehran: Mujahedeen, 1358/1980.

Najmabadi, Afsaneh. "Iran's Turn to Islam: From Modernism to a Moral Order." *The Middle East Journal* vol. 41, no. 2 (Spring 1987): 201-17.

Neshat, Guity. *The Origins of Modern Reform in Iran.* New York: Praeger, 1984.

_____. ed. *Women and Revolution in Iran.* Boulder, CO: Westview Press, 1983.

Pahlavi, Mohammad Reza. *Mission for My Country.* London: Hutchinson, 1961.

_____. *Answer to History.* New York: Stein and Day, 1980.

_____. *Enghelab-e Sefeed.* (The White Revolution.) Tehran: n.p., n.d.

Pakravan, Amineh. *Agha Mohammad Ghadjar.* J. Afkaari, trans. Tehran: de l'Institut France-Iranien, 1953.

Parsons, Anthony. *The Pride and the Fall, Iran 1974-1979.* London: Jonathan Cape, 1984.

Pesaran, M.H. "The System of Dependent Capitalism in Pre- and Post-Revolutionary Iran." *International Journal of Middle East Studies* 14 (1982): 501-22.

Petrushevsky, I.P. *Islam in Iran.* Hubert Evans, trans. London: Athlone Press, 1985.

Prigmore, Charles. *Social Work in Iran Since the White Revolution.* University, Alabama: University of Alabama Press, 1976.

Qasemlu, Abdolrahman. "The Clergy Have Confiscated the Revolution." *Merip Reports* no. 98 (July-August 1981): 17-9.

Raeen, Ismail. *Anjoman-haye Serri dar Enqilab-e Mashruteh Iran.* (Secret Societies in Iran's Constitutional Revolution.) Tehran: Javidan, 2535/1976.

_____. *Faramoushkhaneh va Feramasonery dar Iran.* (Faramoushkhaneh and Freemasonry in Iran.) Tehran: Amir Kabir, 1357/1978.

Rafiqzadeh, Mansour. *Witness: From the Shah to the Secret Arms Deal.* New York: Morrow & Co., 1987.

Ramazani, Rouhollah. *The Foreign Policy of Iran: 1500-1941.* Charlottesville, VA: University Press of Virginia, 1966.

Reid, James J. *Tribalism and Society in Islamic Iran, 1500-1629.* Malibu, CA: Udena Publications, 1983.

Sami'ee, Ahmad. *See-o Haft Sal.* (Thirty Seven Years.) Tehran: Shabaviz, 1365/1986.

Sanasarian, Eliz. *The Women's Rights Movement in Iran.* New York: Praeger, 1982.

Schahgaldian, Nikola. *The Clerical Establishment in Iran.* Santa Monica, CA: The Rand Corporation, 1989.

Shoaee, Rokhsareh S. "The Mujahid Women of Iran: Reconciling 'Culture' and 'Gender'." *The Middle East Journal* vol. 41, no. 4 (Autumn 1987): 519-37.

Sick, Gary. *All Fall Down: America's Tragic Encounter with Iran.* New York: Random House, 1985.

Smith, Jane. ed. *Women in Contemporary Moslem Societies.* London: Associated University Press, 1980.

Sykes, Percy. *A History of Persia,* Vol. II. London: Macmillan & Co., 1930.

Taheri, Amir. *The Spirit of Allah: Khomeini and the Islamic Revolution.* London: Hutchinson, 1985.

Tapper, Richard. ed. *The Conflict of Tribe and State in Iran and Afghanistan.* London: Croom Helm, 1983.

Volodarsky, Mikhail. "Persia and the Great Powers, 1856-1869." *Middle Eastern Studies* vol. 19, no. 1 (January 1983): 75-92.

Watson, Robert Grant. *A History of Persia.* London: Smith, Elder, 1866.

Weber, Max. *The Theory of Social and Economic Organization.* New York: Free Press, 1947.

Wilbur, Donald. *Riza Shah Pahlavi: The Resurrection and Reconstruction of Iran 1878-1944.* Hicksville, NY: Exposition Press, 1975.

_____. *Iran, Past and Present.* Princeton, NJ: Princeton University Press, 1967.

Yarshater, Ehsan. ed. *Iran Faces the Seventies.* New York: Praeger, 1971.

Yektaii, Majid. *Tarikh-e Edari Iran.* (Administrative History of Iran.) Tehran: Pirouz, 1340/1961.

Zabih, Sepehr. *Iran Since the Revolution.* London: Croom Helm, 1982.

_____. *The Mussadegh Era.* Chicago: Lake View Press, 1982.

Zonis, Marvin. *The Political Elite of Iran.* Princeton, NJ: Princeton University Press, 1971.

Index

About the Author

MEHRAN KAMRAVA holds a Ph.D. in Social and Political Sciences from King's College, Cambridge University and is currently assistant professor of international studies at Rhodes College. He is the author of *Revolution in Iran: The Roots of Turmoil, Politics and Society in the Third World,* and *Revolutionary Politics* (Praeger, 1992).